Suspended

by

Alistair Wilkinson

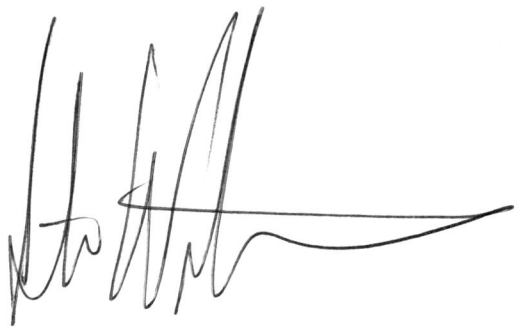

TEXT COPYRIGHT ALISTAIR WILKINSON

ILLUSTRATION COPYRIGHT ALISTAIR WILKINSON

ISBN 978 - 1 - 312 - 586644 - 6

For Emma.

Suspended
Chapter One

No one knew what caused the Splash. It was generally agreed that something had happened in the Humber and that something had caused a huge flood, but that was about it as far as agreement went because, very quickly, people had grown fascinated. Meteors, comets, planes and aliens had all been blamed. Ships bearing the latest sonar equipment had swept the estuary for years but found nothing. So theories moved on to weapons tests, exploding submarines, earthquakes and the wrath of God. Some blamed the French, but then some always do. Some set up camp on the east walkway of the Humber Bridge and just watched. Colourful pod-like tents and black cameras clung to the concrete and metal like voyeuristic limpets that hoped to record history or even a new dawn. They died first.

In the beginning this was news worthy. Humberside became the centre of the world. The slow, murky waters of the Humber, however, remained nothing but slow and murky. The camps melted away and so did the attention. And for a while, for lots of years, there were no more deaths. It was left to Splash Land to make sure that Humberside was not forgotten. Tourists, conspiracy theorists, sightseers and thrill seekers came in their droves, and Splash Land grew and grew.

Humberside twitched; it had grown reliant on the tourist industry and by the June of 2007 the deaths had started again, along with something new: the dogs weren't quite right. Not all of them all of the time but certainly most of them most of the time. No one could explain it. The dogs were just not quite right.

Tilda made her way through the crops, head and tail down. She knew he was out there somewhere, following like he always did. He was a monster of a mongrel, part pit bull, part bastard and part something else altogether, with blazing red eyes and a dark brown coat that shimmered black in the sun. Dog followed and watched.

He didn't need to stay close; James made sure of that. James was 35 years old and three months an orphan. And he wasn't at home in fields. He blundered his way through the crop, walking his dog because he knew that he should.

He looked down at Tilda. He didn't know the breed of his dog. He didn't like to think of Tilda as *his* dog. She had belonged to his parents and so now she belonged to him, like the house or the kitchen or the fridge. He didn't know that she was a Border Collie but he was pretty sure that she wasn't a fridge. He did know that she needed to walk, and so walk they did.

This daily determination wasn't doing much for Tilda. She knew that it was a chore for her new master. If she'd been able she might have told him not to bother. But we'll never know if she would because she couldn't; in the end she was just a dog.

Somewhere deep down James realised a little of Tilda's disenchantment, and so today he'd decided on a change. It had been a very wet spring and this hot June Sunday was the first day in weeks that the mud hadn't sucked and pulled at his boots. They had left the narrow footpath that bordered the fields to walk through the mini jungle of, whatever it was that was growing here. It was yellow. Their fleeting wake in the yellow crops pointed north to the Humber Estuary, two fields and a huge car park away. Rank upon rank of sun-mirrored windscreens formed a shining road to Splash Land, home to the tall steel shaft of *Zoom!!!*, and the towers of *Tsunami*, a ride based on a small scale version of the Humber Bridge. The massive towers of the real thing to the west were an angular grey silhouette against the blue sky.

Tilda wasn't happy among the crops; she couldn't see very much and running was hard in the tangle of stalks and stems. She could no longer smell Dog, so she had the odd sprint up and down the tractor tracks but James wasn't watching so she gave up.

Passing through a gap in a hedge and into a new field, James saw a tree in the far south-western corner. He decided that that would be far enough: once they reached the tree they could have a sit down and then head home. The bright sun had promised that today's walk would be a good one. It had lied. They slogged across the heat and the new field.

As he came close to the tree he saw that it was pathetic, just a skeletal collection of dry twigs, a dying hand, weak and brittle in the faint breeze. They pressed on, quickly covering the distance. They had made it. The day's goal was achieved.

Unfortunately the tree offered little shade and no cover. A young man, horribly exposed, was sitting at the base of the trunk. He had probably bought the magazine from the local shop, from the local woman behind the counter. It would have cost him money and pride, and then he had taken it to a secluded corner of a secluded field, his eyes darting this way and that, always fearing that someone might see him. And when he had reached his spot he had taken his risk.

Tilda watched as the magazine slipped from extended, bare-to-the-ankles legs and fell to the ground. James tried not to look but he couldn't help it. His eyes were drawn, lids pulled apart, like two spotlights on a stage exposing an audience who really are in their underwear. The young man was caught red-handed, holding the smoking gun.

James yanked his eyes away and they dropped to the ground and the magazine. The images were censored by the sun's glare. The harsh reflections forced James to look away and back to the young man. Their gazes met. Four impossibly round eyes stared in horror.

This time James couldn't tear his eyes from that embarrassed, terrified face.

'Sorry,' said James.

He didn't move. He just stood there.

And stood there.

The young man said nothing, and begged with his eyes, with his entire being, to be left alone forever.

Finally, James turned his intractable body to leave. In his desperation to be away, he headed south, away from his home, through another hedgerow and into another field. He walked quickly, trying not to look hurried, trying not to make it a big deal. Tilda followed.

Barbara struggled along the edge of a field. Her wild blonde hair concealed the mobile phone held to her ear.

'"Get outside," he said. "Fresh air'll do you good," he said! If that's doctoring I'm in the wrong job.'

Barbara's mobile phone was very nice, top of the range and filled with all manner of functions that she had no idea how to use and no inclination to find out. It was chocolate brown, shaped like a large pill and, right now, the only solid thing about her. Barbara was melting.

'Did you tell the doctor about your hay fever?' asked Diane, the voice on the phone.

'That'd be far too sensible!' said Barbara. 'And the car's miles away. I don't think I can make it.'

'What about your magic pills from that dodgy homeopath?'

'She's not dodgy, and they do work!'

'Sounds like it.'

'I've forgotten them.'

'That was a bit silly.'

'Yes.'

'Well, the doc's right; you do need to get out more. What's it like there, anyway?'

'Hang on.' Barbara sighed and her nose bubbled as she held the phone up and pressed a button. Something clicked. 'I've sent you a pic.'

'Doesn't look that bad. Looks pretty, and full of… agriculture?'

'Agriculture's no use to me until it's in a tin!'

'Funny,' Diane replied. She sighed. 'You're too closed to new experiences. You spend all your time trapped inside. You need to live a bit.'

'I need tissues!' Barbara rushed her words before they were overridden by a loud wet sneeze.

'I bet you look lovely.'

James fled. The young man would dread ever seeing him again. James dreaded ever seeing the young man again.

He lived in a small community. It was bound to happen.

He and Tilda strode through yet another field. The two of them walked like he had intended them to walk for the last two months but never had. Tilda enjoyed it; it felt purposeful, like they were getting somewhere. Memories of thrown sticks surfaced in her mind.

Then James stopped. Tilda looked to her master. He looked north, toward home, beyond the cackling tree, to a glass tower glittering in the sun as it poked above a large square bank of conifers, and beyond that the steel and garish plastic tumult of Splash Land. He could just about make out the screams from the rides as they sped up and down and around and around. Gathering himself James headed back toward the footpath he wished he had never left.

Rejoining the path, he made for home, his head down. The ghostly sticks faded from Tilda's mind. As they passed level with the tree, now a hundred metres to their left, they heard a sneeze, a loud wet lip-flapper of a sneeze. It came from over the hedge that bordered the footpath. He took a peek.

'I bet I don't!' said Barbara, her voice damp and heavy.

To James, she glided along the edge of the field, her left hand held delicately to her ear and her right smoothing her face. He watched her and remembered. He remembered her blue eyes, her delicate nose and her mouth that didn't smile. He remembered how short she was and how blonde her closely cropped hair had been. Now her hair was darker and long and she wore it tied back. Most of it had managed to escape. There was too much hair, James quickly decided: halfway down the back is a lot closer to the ground for some.

They both arrived at the gap in the hedge and stood and stared for a stupefied moment.

'I'll call you back,' she said into her hand.

'You're hanging up?' said Diane. 'Why?'

'There's an old friend.' She closed the phone and stuffed it into her pocket.

She could only just see James through the snot and haze but she recognised him straight away. He was smiling at her. He had heard her say 'old friend'. James was tall, taller than she remembered, dark and just a little overweight. His eyes were a deep and trusting brown. Had he always had such a small chin?

Still, a small chin's nothing compared to looking like phlegm in a puddle, she thought. She needn't have worried because James was actually thinking that she looked like butter left in the sun, a bit yucky but still very creamy.

'Hi,' she said. Her voice gurgled.

'Hello,' he replied. Silence. Birds chirruped. James was sure they were laughing.

'Are you…erm…okay?' he asked, knowing that she wasn't, knowing that she'd say she was.

'Fine, yes, fine,' she said. 'Thank you,' she added.

'It's Barbara isn't it?'

'Yes.' She tried to look at him more clearly but the clear sky, loose hair and swimming eyes made it too difficult. 'And you're Jim.'

'It's James. You sat near me in a lesson.'

'Erm, several, I think.'

'I remember French; you were three tables across.'

'And that's a freakish memory.'

'It could've been two.' James panicked. 'Or four.'

'Why are you being weird?'

'I'm not. I don't think.'

'We sat near each other in most lessons.'

'I know,' he said, a little too quickly. 'I just remember French because…' James ran out of words. He wanted to tell her he remembered French because of the way the afternoon sun flooded into the huge windows of the portacabin and lit up her hair like gold. Instead he just stared at her stupidly.

'Because?'

'Because it was on a Friday and I couldn't wait for the week to finish.'

'Good a reason as any, I suppose.' She moved through the gap and onto the path. The awkwardness of the situation made her stand uncomfortably.

'Do you mind if I walk with you?' he asked.

'Erm, no.'

They walked in silence for a few steps.

'Are you still Barbara Bean?'

She checked his face for any sign of a smirk. 'Yes, James, I'm still Miss Bean. And who's this?' Barbara pointed to Tilda.

'Tilda.'

'Hello, Tilda,' she said to Tilda. 'What kind of a dog is she?' she said to James.

'A brown one.' They both laughed.

'You're wrong,' said Barbara.

'Really?'

'She's brown and black.' They laughed again and continued along the path.

As Barbara laughed, her turbid face shone and her smile was devastating. And then she sneezed again.

And again.

And again.

James looked down on her as her sneezes doubled her over. And then he did something that he didn't do. He asked her back to his place.

'Listen, you look terrible...' he started.

'Thanks!'

'...why don't you come back to my house and get a drink and a little time away from nature? I only live a couple of fields away.' Barbara looked dubious. James smiled.

She stared up at James. And now she did something that she didn't do. 'Okay,' she said, smiling. And that was a good thing because otherwise they wouldn't have gone on to save the world.

They carried on north along the path. Tilda, sensing the joy of the new, and Dog momentarily forgotten, danced around them. We were happy to let her.

Chapter Two

James and Barbara made their way along the path, crossed a two-plank footbridge and the grassy banks of a wide dyke, stepped onto a narrow lane and walked the strip of concrete to James's house. It was surrounded by a wall of wind-tousled conifers that formed a huge rectangle. It was the only break along the otherwise monotonous road edge. It stuck out north like a flag flying at half mast.

Poking above the trees Barbara could see the spiked glass tower gleaming in the sun. She turned to say something to James but her words were interrupted as a distant hidden cacophony of screams and thunder rumbled from beyond the house. She stared at James for a moment. 'The theme park never took over, just moved in next door?'

'Not quite next door. There's a car park in the way. It's not as much fun as you might think.'

'I didn't think it would be fun at all.'

James smiled. 'This is me,' he said as they passed the corner of the conifers.

The entrance was wide enough for two cars. Barbara could just about make out the words 'Ivy Arch' on the once-grand iron gates that made a rusty tunnel of the first few metres of the driveway. Tilda ran on ahead, disappeared through the gap in the trees and then ran back again, delighted.

Barbara paused in the open gateway. Ivy Arch was set back about 25 metres from the road. A scruffy, sparsely gravelled driveway split an unkempt front garden in two and led to a strange building that was more a discrepancy than a house. A pair of round windows stared out from above an archway that held together two very different structures. On the left was a regular would-be detached house, as unremarkable as it was solid. On the right a fat tower, a full storey taller than the house and the arch. There were no windows in the ground or first floors, just an expanse of dark brick broken by a shining steel ladder. A metal gantry ringed a glazed framework of steel rising up to form the second floor and conical roof, finally finishing in a steel spike that drove into the clear blue sky. Its dark body and glaring top made it look like a rotten ice cream cornet.

James didn't notice straight away that Barbara had stopped because he was watching Tilda: she capered. He'd never seen her caper. When he realised he was alone he turned to Barbara.

'What's wrong?' he said walking back to her.

She looked at him, and James stared back blankly. Any attempt to read her face was like deciphering a soapy letter that had been held under a tap in an effort to rinse it.

'I remember coming here for a party when I was 15. It wasn't so creepy then.' She gestured at the dark maw of the archway and the two round windows above.

'Well, the ivy hadn't quite died yet,' said James. He was a little concerned that Barbara had described his house as creepy.

'I suppose the White Lightning must have helped.'

'The best medicine a 15 year old could get.'

'You live here alone?'

'Yes.'

'Here?'

'Yes.' James was getting flustered, the earlier ease going, going... 'Is there something wrong?'

Barbara's gaze flicked between the watching arch and James, his face so open and innocent and ready.

'Well,' she sought the right words. 'There's not enough crows!'

James laughed. 'I suppose it is a bit freaky,' he admitted. 'But it won't bite.' He smiled. There was a lot of hope in that smile.

Barbara eyed the archway still twenty metres away. It glowered.

They both jumped as Tilda barked and reared on to her back legs. Then she sprinted toward the house, covering the distance in a few quick seconds, gravel and baked dust thrown up in her wake. She was still barking as she entered the archway and disappeared.

Then Tilda fell silent.

Barbara watched the shadow of the archway intently, searching and waiting for any sign of the black and brown dog.

And then she was back in the light, sprinting toward them, head down, a sleek hirsute machine. Barbara let out a breath she hadn't realised she'd been holding.

Tilda was back with them in a crash and splash of dust and gravel. She danced around Barbara, tongue lolling.

James smiled hopefully at Barbara and eyed the dog suspiciously, wondering if all this strange behaviour meant a trip to the vet. The suspicion ran deep, all the way to his wallet.

Barbara was assuaged by Tilda's excitement, and by James's obvious openness. He had a trust that was almost infectious. As the four-legged-friend turned into a brown and black blur of hair once again, Barbara set off down the drive.

'My, my, that's an impressive shaft you have,' she said looking up at the spike. Barbara didn't usually bother with innuendo; her best friend, Diane, was always way ahead of her, but she couldn't resist it.

'Yeah,' said James, completely missing it anyway. He was blind to anything sexual at the moment. His mind had an automatic defence system; if he allowed himself such thoughts then he wouldn't be able to speak. 'They put it up in the mid-nineties.'

Barbara laughed and raised her eyebrows. James just smiled the same smile.

'Who did?' said Barbara, letting the double entendre fall into the gravel.

'My parents. Well, the builders. Something to do with subsidence.'

'Subsidence?' Barbara was pleased that it was such a mundane problem. It added a desperately needed normality to the house.

'Something like that, yeah.'

'I don't remember much of that party.'

'That'll be the White Lightning.'

Barbara laughed. 'Did we get in there?' she said, pausing and looking up and nodding at the tower.

'No, it was all locked up back then. My parents only started using it after the spike was fitted.'

'Probably not safe before then.'

'Probably not. It was my Granddad's place, really. He used to work for the government, way back.'

'Doing what?'

'Not sure. Something medical I think.'

'Making another Frankenstein?'

James laughed and didn't even think to try to correct her on the common mix up between doctor and monster.

Barbara took as close a look as she could at the front gardens. At one time, she could tell, they had been well tended. There was a sort of order to the chaos; the overgrown plants and weeds were a mess but they were patches of mess.

On the left, under the blank gaze of the oh-so ordinary house, was the main tumult of vegetation. Barbara could see many trees, plants and flowers she could identify, and many more she couldn't. They were all choked by the strangling weeds.

The right, under the glare of the tower, was an incredibly green, incredibly lush lawn. Here she could tell that James had had a go. The lawn had at least been mowed in the last week. A ride-on mower, idle now, was there to prove it.

It wasn't a particularly complicated garden and Barbara could see that it could be fairly low maintenance. It was only lassitude that had seen it become a jungle.

She noticed a swing hanging from the tree closest to the front of the house. It was watched by the windows, which were dirty and gloomy, their curtains drawn, the sun barely reflecting off the dingy glass.

Setting off again, they approached the archway. The midday sun made sure that it wasn't as dark as it had looked and Barbara was quite glad to enter the shadow as it meant she was no longer being watched by those circular windows above. The archway stretched back far enough to be a tunnel, and Tilda's eager woofs and pants echoed in a there-is-something-alive-in-here kind of way. James carried on, unimpressed.

Breaking through to the other side, the driveway opened up into a large once-gravel circle, and beyond that the back garden spread itself even bigger and messier than the front. Skulking in the shadow of the large tower was a smaller single-storey mini-tower with no window or door and a large funnel-like chimney pierced the centre of the tiled conical roof.

A huge breezeblock garage stretched all the way to the rampant plant life of the back garden. It was large enough to have two double garage doors, both of which were firmly closed and the furthest would remain so, as strong plant life had crept around the side and down from the roof and strapped it shut. The vegetation looked to be trying to pull down the modern, ugly building that stood out so from its older surroundings.

On the left was welcome normality, and so even with the grubby windows it was homely. *At least the curtains are open*, thought Barbara. The rear entrance was through a ground floor extension that was set back half way along the normal side of the house and stretched back twelve metres or so, creating a large L-shaped, shaded courtyard that was dotted with shrinking puddles that still hadn't dried. Beyond the extension was a row of wooden sheds that were solid and well-maintained. *For now,* Barbara couldn't help but add.

Beyond the circle the sun glared at the huge garden, at least twice the size of the front. The whole area was in turmoil, a stormy green ocean heaving and pulsing, swelling higher and denser as it approached and then broke onto the back row of conifers. It was a tidal wave of vegetation which, if left unchecked, would soon be ready to swallow the whole house.

Barbara stared wide-eyed. James noticed her incredulity. 'Needs a little work,' he admitted with a smile. 'Are you coming in?' Tilda seconded the invitation.

'Mmm…' she acquiesced. She threw one last glance at the sun-bathed mess. She thought that it looked as though the trees at the back were playing catch-up with those closer to the house. She dismissed the thought, thinking it pointless to ask, and followed James and Tilda into the house.

After a small entrance porch they entered a large well-appointed, well-kept modern kitchen. Barbara was shocked, even stunned; it was so bright in here. She hadn't noticed the skylights in the extension's roof. Artificial lights flickered on automatically. They were under every wall cupboard and in the ceiling so that while it was bright and white there was nowhere a glare.

Barbara felt self conscious in her dusty boots. James hadn't bothered to remove his so she'd kept hers on, and with her snotty hay fever and grubby hands she didn't dare touch anything.

'Is there somewhere I could have a quick wash?' she pleaded to James.

'Back through the porch, there's a sink in the toilet,' he said. 'Tea or coffee?'

'Tea, please.' She fled to the toilet.

Tilda watched Barbara leave, her tongue hung low and flapped as she panted. She switched her gaze to James.

'What?' he asked as he moved to the sink with the kettle, ready to fill it. Tilda continued to stare.

Inwardly she sighed. He wasn't a bad master. It was just that he wasn't very thoughtful. She put a little more heat into the stare.

'What?' he repeated as he took the now-full kettle back to its base and flicked the power on.

Had Tilda been able to formulate words in her own mind they'd go something like this: *It's every time we go out. He must notice that it's hot, that I'm hot and that the heat makes things outside dry. So why can't he ever remember that it makes me dry? Get me a drink of water, you idiot! I suppose I'll have to wait the usual two hours before he even thinks about it, and then another two hours before he remembers.*

Dick!

I'll probably die of dehydration in the third hour, which might knock it down to three-and-a-half before he remembers…and so on.

James busied himself with the tea pot, oblivious to the silent canine accusations.

Barbara returned to the kitchen. She was still a mess but a much relieved mess. She had halted the slide of her face, giving it the static appearance of a semi-melted ice-lolly which had been returned to the freezer.

James beamed, feeling happy and silly that he'd been excited about her return. His beam made him look more silly than happy, but she smiled back.

They stood awkwardly for a moment, before James finally invited Barbara to sit down. She smiled in relief and moved to a chair at the huge wooden table in the centre of the room. As she covered the short distance she noticed the panting Tilda.

'Doesn't she want a drink?' she asked James.

He stared at her then at the dog. *Whoops*. He rushed to the sink, grabbed the steel bowl, filled it and placed it on the floor with what he hoped was a practised I-always-give-the-dog-a-drink flourish.

I love you, Tilda would have thought as she looked to Barbara before moving to the bowl.

'This is amazing,' said Barbara, gazing around the kitchen.

'Yeah, my dad liked a good kitchen,' James replied, passing Barbara a mug of tea. He sat down opposite her at the table.

Silence descended.

Barbara sipped her tea, happy to just recover. James shifted and fidgeted, the solid wood of the table a barrier between them. He smiled and he smiled, feeling so awkward that he felt he might crack.

'Lunch!' he very nearly shouted. 'Do you want some lunch?'

'Erm, okay.'

He leapt up and busied himself.

'What are we having?'

'Salad with bacon.' He grabbed a saucepan, filled it with water and placed it on the hob. The gas ring fired into life. He relaxed and moved around his kitchen with ease. He bustled, he hummed, and he even threw titbits to Tilda.

'So, what did you do after school?' he called out to Barbara over the sizzle of the bacon in the pan. 'I didn't imagine you would stay around here.'

'College and then I tried university. I went to Leeds but it didn't work out. Since then I've moved about a lot.' Barbara replied.

'Are you just visiting then?' he asked while chopping a red and a yellow pepper.

'No, back to stay. I decided to settle and couldn't think where. Then my grandma died…'

'Sorry.'

'… that's okay… and left me her house in Barton. Made the decision for me. How about you? Did you just stay here?'

'No,' said James. 'My mum died six months ago…'

'Oh, I'm sorry.'

'… and then my dad two months ago,' he finished.

Barbara stared.

'Oh,' she said out loud.

'Yeah.'

Barbara had no idea what to say. 'There's a lot of that around.'

'Yeah, my parents are far from the only ones.'

'Unlucky to lose both though. I saw there was another man dead the other day. He was walking across the Humber Bridge and just collapsed.'

'Yeah, that's the same as my Mum. Just collapsed I mean. She wasn't walking the Bridge. She was in this kitchen actually.' He poured pasta into the pan of boiling water.

'Oh.' Barbara shifted in her seat. 'So, your dad didn't collapse?'

'No,' said James, 'he was electrocuted.'

'What, on a fence or something?'

'No, that happened in the house. Kind of hard to explain.' Barbara didn't press for details. 'What about your parents?'

'Not much to say,' Barbara was glad to change the subject. 'We were never close and when Gran left me the house that was the final straw for Mum.' Barbara shrugged.

'Unlucky to lose both,' said James. Barbara shrugged again.

'Anyway,' James continued, 'I didn't come back here to live till three months ago. I moved to Grimsby when I was eighteen. It was gonna be a stepping stone to bigger and better things. I was gonna move on, but,' he paused while he scraped the bacon out of the pan and onto a plate to cool, 'I never did. I just sort of got stuck there.'

'Why's that?'

'It was too easy not to move on I suppose.' There was a pause as Barbara studied her host. James busied himself with the lunch and pretended not to notice. 'Still, at least I didn't have anything special to give up to come look after Tilda,' he said with a smile.

'Every cloud has a silver lining, eh?'

James nodded as he mixed the salad. 'How does a girl who went from Barton to Barton end up in a field covered in snot?'

Barbara laughed. 'The doctor told me to get some fresh air. Told me it'd do me some good.'

'Doctors today, eh? What do they know?'

'I didn't tell him about my hay fever.'

'Why not?' he said as chopped basil leaves.

'I forgot.'

'Well, next time I'll swoop in with all the pills, sprays and inhalers you can think of, chuck you in one of those sealed bubbles and shake, rattle and roll you wherever you wanna go.' Barbara laughed. James squeezed salad cream and mayonnaise into the bowl with a flourish and then attacked the mixture with a fork.

'Is that full-fat salad cream and mayo?' said Barbara, eying the colours of the labels on the bottles.

'It is.'

'Would I be very boring if I told you I'm excited?'

'Hang on tight,' James replied, smiling. Barbara was laughing again. 'I like your smile,' he said.

'Thank you.'

'You never smiled much at school.'

'No,' she said and, seeing James's discomfort at her short answer, added, 'I never really liked school. Full of kids.' They both laughed. 'I'm just happier being a grown up, I suppose.'

James drained the pasta and cooled it under the cold tap before adding it to the bowl. He scraped the bacon on top of the pasta and gave the whole thing one last rigorous stir.

Their lunch prepared, he returned to the table and sat opposite her, the dense wood now a bridge.

'You're not a vegetarian are you?' he asked, too late.

'No, it's okay.'

They tucked into their lunch. Barbara nodded, waving her fork at the meal. James smiled and nodded back.

'So what do you do?'

Barbara chewed for a moment. 'I'm a writer,' she said.

'Yeah?' said James. 'What sort of stuff?'

Barbara chewed some more. She liked to be open about her work but it didn't always go down very well. *Still*, she said to herself, *he's a grown man*. 'Erotic fiction.'

'Oh yeah?' said James not at all casually. 'Cool.'

Cool? he said to himself while chewing rigorously. *Cool?* He continued to chew not wanting her to think that he was interested in erotic fiction even though he was interested in her and what she did.

Calm down, she willed to him. *It's not a competition, it's not a game.* She had had many different reactions to her work and James's was far from the worst.

Tilda looked from one to the other.

'Well,' James scratched his head. 'I saw a lad with erotica on his mind today.' He paused as he chewed, uncomfortable with his chosen topic. He plunged on. 'I say a lad, more of a young man. Probably a man, legally at least, you know, for criminal and voting purposes. And buying beer.'

'What are you talking about?'

'The lad, he's maybe eighteen or nineteen.'

'What lad?'

'The lad, the young man, who's, you know…'

'No, I don't,' said Barbara.

'He had his magazine, and his trousers were…' James's voice trailed off.

'What?'

James squirmed. 'You know, young men, magazines and secluded spots.'

Barbara suddenly nodded as understanding dawned. 'Where were his trousers?'

'Round his ankles.'

'Ah. Embarrassing.'

James sighed. 'Yeah, I didn't know where to look…'

'So you looked…'

'At the…' James sought the right words.

'Smoking gun.'

James sighed again, nodding. 'Yeah. And I'm bound to see him about. I'll not know where to put my face.'

'Well, neither will he. Stare him down and dare him to look at you. He was the one with the…' Barbara's turn to seek the words.

'Weapon of mass seduction?'

'I didn't know this salad came with cheese!' Barbara chuckled. They laughed again and carried on with their lunch.

Barbara chewed, enjoying her meal. 'So, what do you do to keep yourself in bacon salads and weird houses?'

'Nothing so interesting as writing about sex. Erm…' James coughed and quickly moved on. 'In fact, nothing.'

'Nothing?'

'I don't need to work, so I don't.'

'Doesn't that get boring? Or have you got loads on? Like gardening maybe?' A wry smile played across her lips. James watched it come and go.

'Gardening?' he mused. 'Yeah, gardening. Takes a lot of work to get it like that!' He laughed as he leaned back in his chair. James knew that people didn't like other people not to work. They were uncomfortable with the idea that someone might be doing nothing. Fearing resentment and hoping for sympathy, James plunged on. 'I don't do anything, no pastimes, no hobbies, no projects. Nothing…' he smiled in what he hoped was a 'hey, I'm just kooky' fashion.

'Nothing?'

'Do films and telly count? I've just re-watched all of Twin Peaks in three days!'

'Aces!' Barbara gave a thumbs up. 'Sounds lonely though.'

Yes! James knew that sympathy was about the best he could hope for.

'I'm okay,' he replied.

'What about your parents? Were you close?'

'No,' he said. 'Yes. I don't know. We didn't talk much.' Maybe the sympathy vote wasn't so good after all. He shovelled a forkful of salad into his mouth

'Did you work when you lived in Grimsby?'

'Oh, yeah,' said James as he swallowed. 'I had lots of jobs. I worked in factories and offices, I filled up vending machines and I drove a van for a while.'

'Why so many?'

'I, erm, tended to sleep.' Barbara cocked an eyebrow. James followed it. 'I either slept in or slept on the job.'

'Was it shift work, or are you narcoleptic?'

'I looked into that, but I'm afraid that I was just…' James considered his answer, '…unmotivated.'

'You mean you couldn't be arsed!' She laughed at his guilty look. 'Did you lose every job like that?'

'Most of them. The last one was something new.'

'What happened at the last one?' Her interest was piqued. Both eyebrows were cocked. James, hesitant to explain, gave them an eye each and promptly crumbled.

'I was working in the offices of a shipping company in Immingham. It was a pretty normal office, and the job was okay. The work was dull but it was Monday to Friday, nine to five, no shift work and the air conditioning kept me awake.

'My desk was next to the photocopier. It was like having a ringside seat. Everyday someone went crazy at it for one reason or another.' James paused while he took another bite of salad.

Barbara leant forward. 'And?'

'I started filming them.' James filled his mouth to cover his embarrassment.

Barbara studied him while allowing him to finish.

'It got a little out of hand. Have you ever seen Copier-kicker?'

'The web-site?'

'Yeah, www.copierkicker.co.uk. I set it up.'

'You rotten sod! I feel really sorry for some of the poor saps on there.'

'Well, I only started it for a bit of fun. And it wouldn't have grown so big if so many people hadn't watched.'

'Point taken. So, did people complain about personal infringement and the like, and get you sacked?'

'No. I only ever put a couple of clips on the site. It's all the other contributions that followed that really made it massive.' James took another bite of salad to work up to his admission. 'I was sacked because of sexual harassment.'

'Really? What did you do?'

'There was a girl in the office, young, attractive. Is shapely an okay term to use?' Barbara nodded cautiously. 'I watched her struggle with the paper tray, and, as always, the camera was on.'

'And?'

'She was bent over, jiggling about, and, well, she was wearing these white trousers. I don't know what they were made of, but they were sort of see-through.'

'*Sort of* see-through?'

'Yes.'

They ate for a few moments. James was embarrassed. He thought this wasn't the type of story to be telling on the first... the first what? Not a date. The first chance.

But James's worries, like his life, were pointless.

'And did you put it on the site?' she asked.

'No...'

'But...'

'Word had got round the office about Copier-kicker. Most people always behaved themselves by this point, but there were a few who played up to it, especially after *DIY Die!*'

'You did *DIY Die!*?'

'I put it on the site. I didn't *do* it.'

'You know what I mean. That was the one that made the site huge wasn't it?'

'Pretty much. The contributions flooded in after that. I couldn't cope with it so I passed it on to someone else, rights and all.'

'Hang on, you didn't get the half-million that Google paid for it?'

'No.'

'Gutted.'

'Yes.'

They ate in silence for a few minutes, chewing over the information.

'Anyway, the diaphanous trousers?'

'Diaphanous?' said James.

'A good word in erotica, it means see-through.'

'Ah.' He nodded. 'The management had been watching me for a while but they didn't get round to properly checking up on me for ages, and by the time they did I'd got rid of Copier-kicker, so they couldn't find anything for a disciplinary. *DIY Die!* was too embarrassed to complain, so I thought I was pretty much in the clear. But I wasn't and the diaphanous trousers were just what the management were looking for. The girl wearing them was looking for a little bit more. She wanted her arse to be as famous as *DIY Die!*.'

'Could it have been?' Barbara asked.

'It was definitely shapely.'

'Could've been then.'

'I reckon so. Anyway, I told her I'd deleted it. She didn't believe me and threatened me with the management unless I gave her the video.'

'What happened?'

'I wouldn't give it to her so she went to the management. I had deleted it but the charge stuck once *DIY Die!* plucked up the courage to complain too.'

'Do you think that diaphanously clad bottom could've been waved in his direction?' James just laughed as Barbara carried on in a more serious tone. 'Did you delete it because she complained or because you knew that you should?'

'I'm digging a hole for myself here aren't I?' Barbara nodded. 'Shall we say that it was a little of both and leave at that?'

Barbara smiled. She scooped up the last forkful of her salad. She paused, the food halfway to her mouth. 'You hung out with Eddie Fiss at school.'

'That's right. I see him sometimes crammed into a white van. I've tried to wave but he never seems to notice.'

'Yeah, he's blind as a bat. He's coming to fit me a new kitchen this week. He owns his own business. I think he went a bit feudal after The Splash and got very, very protective. I've heard a few whispers of 'Baron Fiss'. Behind his back of course.'

'Well, he always had a scary front but that doesn't sound like the Eddie I knew. He always looked big and mean but he was a softy really. Jennifer always called him her teddy bear. She used to get him to sing that Elvis song.'

'The song Teddy Bear?'

'Yeah.' James was tempted to try a lip curl but he stopped just in time. Too soon for Elvis impressions. 'Anyway, Eddie was never the lion who played too rough.'

'I think Eddie might surprise you now.' Barbara ate the last mouthful and looked thoughtfully at James. 'You had a thing for his girlfriend Jennifer.'

James blushed like a teenager. 'Erm, no, not a thing, nothing, nothing at all.'

Barbara smiled. 'She had very nice eyes.'

'Never noticed.'

'She would've probably looked good in a pair of white trousers.'

'Bit creepy now.'

'And she was very popular with the boys, right from the third year.'

'Was she?'

'It was all a show. Never let anybody touch her. That's probably why she was with Eddie. So don't worry, you weren't the only one that never had a chance with her.'

'Never considered it. Not once.'

'I'm sure you didn't.' They both smiled.

James stood to clear the plates. 'I don't think we ever spoke alone at school,' he said.

'You don't *think*? Yet you remember where I sat in French.'

'Alright, I know we never spoke alone.'

'You only had eyes for Jennifer,' Barbara smiled as she teased him. 'Still, there's time now.'

Barbara settled in her chair and let her head fall back, sighing with satisfaction.

Without looking directly, James stared at Barbara's bare neck, the delicate lines of her throat and the acute curve of her chin.

Tilda felt the electricity in the air, and in her way, she hoped.

Barbara let her gaze drift to the skylights. Through the west window she could see the tops of the trees bordering the house and its grounds. They waved in front of a blue sliver of sky. Through the east-facing glass the imposing tower filled at least half of the vista.

James returned to his seat and she let her head fall back down. James shifted his eyes down to the table and then glanced up again to meet her gaze. He smiled in what he hoped wasn't a guilty fashion.

'Got any bats in that tower?' she asked

'No, it's too bright,' he said. 'They're all in the cellar.'

They giggled. Barbara could tell that the rest of the house was not as bright and modern as the kitchen; through an open doorway she could see that once again the shadows prevailed.

'Do you want to see the tower?'

'No thanks.' James was a little crestfallen. Barbara noticed and smiled. 'I've got to go. Erotica doesn't write itself, but I'll check it out next time?' The question was implied but she knew the answer, just like she knew that he'd been looking at her neck.

'Next time, definitely!' James failed to control a grin that threatened to break his face in two.

After swapping phone numbers - Barbara couldn't believe that James didn't have a mobile - Barbara stood to leave and James went with her. In the courtyard she looked once more to the less virile trees at the back. 'Are they smaller or something?' she asked.

'They're catching up with the rest. They got damaged by the Splash. The whole garden was under water but the trees at the back took the brunt of it.'

'Oh, yeah, of course. Did the house get flooded?'

'No, the garden saved it. It's sunk a metre or so below the level of the house. I think my parents had a bitch of a job getting it drained though.'

They headed back through the arch to the little road. Tilda did a bit more capering, making James suspicious all over again.

'How are you getting home?' he asked.

'My car's parked in the village,' she nodded to the west. 'See you Friday.'

'Can I walk you?'

'No, thank you.'

And she was gone, walking confidently down the road. James watched her rear, and imagined her front beginning to melt once more. Before long he heard her sneeze.

The parting was observed by Dog. He was hidden at the corner of the wall of conifers.

Tilda glanced around, aware of a presence even though she couldn't see anything. She moved closer to her master's legs, her head and tail lowered. James didn't notice.

Chapter Three

James walked east along the narrow road to the village of Nether-on-Humber – Never to the locals. He passed a sign:

> WELCOME TO NETHER-ON-HUMBER,
> THE ROSWELL OF EUROPE
> AND HOME OF THE SPLASH!

His road bisected a busy by-pass, originally built for the timber yard that had once stood at the northern end of Never. It was gone now, washed away by the Splash, and replaced by Splash Land.

Hot June Sundays here were never sleepy. Never was a major tourist attraction, and tourists came out in their droves on hot June Sundays. James dashed across the by-pass, dodging the traffic still pouring into the popular theme park, and headed into Never, past new houses and whole new estates sprouting and blossoming in the fields around the village, his head firmly in the clouds. Barbara's visit had drained his supplies sufficiently to necessitate a trip to the shop.

His lane finished as it joined the main street that stretched for half a mile, north to south. The sun's shine sloshed around the cars and tourists. The tall towers of Splash Land's biggest rides dominated, making the village seem even smaller. Screams could be heard as willing victims were thrown, swung and plunged into water. The street was blocked with cars, crawling heat-boxes whose occupants stared jealously at the freedom of the pedestrians. James was not alone on the footpath; tourists walked and gazed and whispered as they searched for aliens in every corner.

A Spaniel watched him. His name was Mr Tricks. It was a strange name because, as far as we know, he knew no tricks. He trotted patiently next to his elderly owner, his lead slack. A huge man, dressed in green-stained cricket whites and carrying a large sports bag over his shoulder walked with them.

James recognised him immediately. 'Eddie!'

The giant squinted in James's direction 'Jim? Jimmy! Jimmy Wynn!' Tourists on foot turned their heads and those trapped in their cars looked out. They all looked disappointed that the great booming voice turned out to be human. He quickly told Mr Tricks's owner that he would see him tonight and crossed the road, seemingly oblivious to the traffic that was obliged to stop.

Eddie had always been big. Not fat just big. At school the other boys had seen him as a challenge, but he had been a gentle giant. Except for Jennifer the girls had had little time for him, assuming that he was simple because of his size and his reticence. This was far from the truth as Eddie had always been as sharp as a lemon-slicing razor, but he kept his head down because he didn't like to fight. This wasn't through fear, or at least not any fear for himself.

James noted the layer of fat that now surrounded him, it made him look as if he might be cuddly, but there was a confidence in his stride. This man was a brick wrapped in jelly.

The two men came together, both smiled, Eddie hugely. He towered over James as they shook hands, Eddie's smothering James's who noted the gentleness of the grip, and remembered the giant's sensitivities.

'Jimmy-fucking-Wynn, I haven't seen you in...' Eddie exhaled loudly as he tried to remember. His swearing was casual and his voice boomed for all to hear.

'Seventeen years,' James prompted. Now that Eddie was closer, James could see the scars on his face, arms and hands. They were mostly on the latter, the skin on his fists like pink tea-plates that have been broken and cracked and glued together time after time.

'Seventeen years,' he exhaled in surprise. 'Not since we were eighteen, then.' An awkward pause. 'I heard about your parents. Unlucky.'

'Yeah,' said James. 'There's a lot of that going about.'

Eddie nodded.

James gave up. 'So, you're a builder now?'

Eddie smiled. 'I run my own company, Fiss Fixin's.' He beamed with pride. 'We're not massive, but enough for round here – for now,' he said with a wink. 'Got a good reputation, see. We started on with the grannies; get them on side and the business comes rolling in!

'I set it up after the Splash, just me and Frankie sorting out flood damage and all that, helping the old dears. It was only supposed to be for a bit, but it turned out we was needed after to do all sorts of jobs. Now we can handle just about anything.'

'Your brother Frankie?' James was trying to keep up.

'Yeah, proper family business. Local lads for local jobs,' said Eddie, beaming all over again.

'That's good.'

'What about you?' said Eddie. 'Are you in that creepy fucking house all alone? How is that lawn so green? Are there bodies buried in that garden?' Eddie's chuckle was a deep pervasive rumble.

'I'm not doing anything at the moment, sort of between things, you know?' James thought that Eddie probably didn't know. The only time he was between things was in his van on the way to another job. Baron Fiss indeed. But the big man nodded anyway. 'And, yeah, I'm there alone.'

They both smiled to cover another lull in the conversation.

'Did you and Jennifer stay together?' he asked a little too casually.

'Jennifer?'

'Obviously not. The girl you were seeing when we left school?'

'Oh, Jennifer! Nah, Jenny and me never made it. You'd know that if you'd stayed in touch.' James avoided Eddie's eyes. 'We were never gonna though, 'cause I came out.'

Eddie waited for James's reaction.

'Out of what?' said James. 'Are you married?'

'How does being out make me married?'

'Erm...'

'Out of the closet, you pillock.'

'Ah,' said James. He looked the other man up and down. 'I didn't know fruit grew that big.'

His laughter whimpered to a halt as Eddie's face darkened and his bulk loomed. James cringed. *Oh shit.*

What little pride James had, forced him to stay off his knees, which were jelly, bitter lime-flavoured jelly.

The thunder clouds of Eddie's face broke to reveal a smile which soon became a hearty laugh. James, his jellied knees now a sweeter strawberry flavour, sagged with relief and nearly fell as Eddie clapped him on the shoulder with one hand.

'Nice one, Jim.' Curtains twitched and tourists hurried along as Eddie's laugh rolled up and down the street. James laughed along.

'Hang on,' he said. 'Were you stringing Jennifer along then?'

'Nah, just deciding. It's a difficult time. Why?'

'No reason.'

'Oh yeah. You had a bit of a thing for Jenny.'

'No.'

'Yeah you did, but you don't need to worry about me keeping her from you; you'd've never had a chance!' Eddie laughed and laughed and laughed.

'Thanks for that.'

'Anyway, it's great to see you again. We'll have to catch up prop'ly. Why don't you come to the pub tonight? I'll buy you a drink. Fuck it, I'll buy you ten!'

'You trying to get me drunk?' said James. Eddie roared with laughter again.

'Tonight, then. Half-eight.' He clapped James on the shoulder one more time then turned to leave, still laughing.

James watched him move down the street like he really did own the place. Eddie's shoulders were still shaking from the chuckles, mirroring James's own. James headed for the shop, a smile etched on his face.

Errol sat in the cage. He didn't like it. He was a greyhound and he didn't belong in a cage. Left on the streets by his former employers, we had found new uses for him. Such as getting captured. We didn't know where he was as he had been hooded till this point. He could have stood if he wished but the cage wasn't big enough for a stroll so he didn't.

He stared out beyond the bars into a circular room. It felt deep, excavated. It was brightly lit and filled with the hum of repressed energy. The walls were covered with machinery and screens and control stations and panels, all emitting and reflecting light. In the only section of wall not covered with blinking lights, a huge round metal door stood firmly closed. The gleaming metal floor begged to be walked on in solid heels; in a room like this the footsteps would echo ominously. The wearer of those heels would have to carry a clipboard and be cloaked in a white coat.

Wires and cables ran across the floor to the centre of the room where a shining steel pole reached from floor to ceiling. Errol whined.

Chapter Four

'What are we having?' asked Diane.

Barbara carried a bottle of wine and a glass into the comfortable looking space that was her sitting room. She sank into a large settee, the humongous cushions that sprouted from all sides made it look like a fluffy tug boat with oversized tyres.

'An Alsatian Muscat Blanc.'

'Mmm, clean, crisp and hopefully firm. How long has it been in the fridge?'

Barbara leant forward and poured a generous glass of the yellowish liquid. Settling back into the settee she said to her best friend: 'Since last night.'

'Oo, double risk on the dumb, then.'

'It's just fine. Perfect even.'

'Your taste is affected. Perhaps by your reason for hanging up?'

'Perhaps,' Barbara teased.

'A hunk? Sexy, saucy and probably naughty. A man of the land. At home in the fields, but not a farmer.'

'Why not?'

'Farmers don't excite. They might satisfy. But then they'll always moan about the price of fuel – which is subsidised – and then about the weather – which they can't control – and then about the French – which seems their only pleasure – and then about cows. Or something. I've no idea, but there's lots of moaning - and not the exciting kind.'

'Aren't you the detective.'

'So your new man's a local who's done well for himself. But he's not forgotten his roots. Sounds familiar. So, come on, what's he like?'

'Lonely,' said Barbara. 'A bit tragic really.'

'Sounds nice.'

'Well it's either that or he's a miserable bugger!'

'And tragedy's so much more attractive then misery.'

'Well, yeah.'

'Two lonely people meet in the middle of nowhere. You should be taking notes. What's this corn-fed hunk's name?'

'James.' Barbara smiled as she said it, and then felt silly for smiling and sat up a little to move away from the cushions' comfort. 'And I'm not lonely.'

'Not very inspiring.'

'Inspiring enough!' Barbara giggled, and her best friend joined in.

'Not Jim then?'

'No.'

'Why not?'

'Not sure. He was Jim at school.'

'How do you manage avoid incest in a place like that?'

'We fill in forms.'

'So what does he do?'

'Not much. He says he doesn't need to work so he watches films and telly. He has just re-watched Twin Peaks though.'

'Re-watched? Aces!'

There were two pubs in Never. At the northern end, just outside Splash Land, was a large, bright, inviting place that catered to families and sight-seers, and families of sight-seers. It was called The Splash Down, and the happy customer could have a ball, eating such fare as a Mighty Meteor Meal or a Splash Burger washed down with a Milkyway-shake, a Burning Rock Beer or a Comet Cola.

It was a little staged and a little forced. Actually it was very staged and embarrassingly forced, but it was friendly. James had eaten there once before, battling his way through a Sea Serpent Salad with Tornado Tuna and a Galaxy Gulp. It was quite nice but he hadn't finished the Galaxy Gulp; that was too much fizzy pop.

The other pub, in the middle of the main street, was a shadow, a blot on the landscape. This was the Rat and Drainpipe. While the rest of the village was rejuvenated by the affluence brought by the tourist trade, the Rat and Drainpipe blew straight through quaint, bowled aside ramshackle and landed square in the middle of run-down. The paint had peeled from the walls, leaving brickwork so neglected it looked like a witch's teeth. The dirty windows had 'clean me' written on them so many times that the letters looked like an over-complicated road map. The sign finished the insalubrious look: a rat was poised to run up a drainpipe, but it was so faded and scarred that it looked like it could start the bubonic plague all over again. The fact that it was winking didn't help.

James stood across the road.

It looked like the kind of place that only welcomed locals, and the locals who would be most welcome would be the most unwelcoming ones. And it knew that he wasn't from round here.

'But I *am* from round here,' he whispered, and crossed the street.

Passing through the battered front doors, he was greeted by a poster pasted over the frosted glass of the inner door. 'UP IN SMOKE!!!' was its message. And this combustion was to be the coming Saturday, the thirtieth of June 2007.

Pushing through the swing doors he entered the clean well-lit bar. Light from the falling sun crawled through the dirty windows, which were the only clue to the unseemliness of the pub's shell. The interior was well maintained and inviting.

Dust motes and cigarette smoke drifted through the spotlight beams which showed the room to be large, with an L-shaped bar on the left. The floor space was filled with tables and chairs. Opposite the bar a jukebox glowed in the shadows to the side of one of the two large windows, both of which were framed by heavy dark curtains. At the far end of the room stood a pool table and beyond that a dartboard hung on the wall.

A lively group stood at the bar, leaning, drinking, smoking. Their conversation stopped as James entered and they all turned to stare. The sun gave an amber glow to pints of lager held in every other hand. The doors swung shut behind James. The wood and frosted-glass blocked and dimmed the rectangular pool of light plunging the customers and barman into sudden gloom.

Everything was still.

'Jim!' Eddie, a tower in the midst of his peers, welcomed James into the pub with a wave of his free hand.

'What's up? You look surprised,' he said coming over to his friend.

'It's just not what I expected,' said James. 'After the outside I mean.'

'Yeah it's a pain to maintain, but we need one place free of the old tourists.'

'Ah,' said James.

He moved to stand at the edge of the group and placed his hands on the bar, the group watching him every centimetre of the way.

'What are you drinking?' said Eddie.

'Erm...' James looked gratefully to the bar. As his eyes registered the choice of drinks he was momentarily flustered. The pumps alone offered three lagers, three bitters and a cider; the well stocked banks of fridges contained a rainbow of bottled drinks; the optics covered every inch of wall. '…lager?'

Eddie beamed at the old barman who looked at James with patient and kindly exasperation. His eyes took in each pump and he gently nodded his head at the myriad of bottles.

'Which one?' he asked with a smile.

'Get him a Stella, Len,' boomed Eddie not giving James time to finish his second erm.

The barman grabbed a pint glass from below the bar and moved to the Stella pump.

'No, no!' James held up his hands. 'Not for me, I want to be able to walk home in a straight line.' The barman's hands froze as he looked to Eddie. The rest of the group switched their gaze from James to the giant. 'I'll have a pint of that, please.' James pointed at the green badge on the silver pump of an inoffensive and non-premium lager.

Eddie laughed. 'Who's the gay one? Girl's drink it is then, Len.' He nodded to the green badge and the bubbly liquid sloshed into the glass. James leaned one elbow against the bar, looking casual and feeling tense.

'Let me introduce you to the fuckwits.' Eddie wafted a huge hand at the group. There were six men and one woman. James thought he recognised one of the men, and Eddie, noticing James's attention, started with him.

'That's Frankie, my little brother. You remember him, Jimmy?' James nodded and smiled, he hadn't seen Frankie since he was fifteen. He'd been a nervous kid. So much smaller than Eddie he'd always been in his shadow, always been looked after by his bigger brother. He was dressed in a black and white football shirt which James recognised as Grimsby Town.

'Up the Mariners,' said James as heartily as he could, which wasn't very.

The nervousness in Frankie's eyes had been replaced by an almost manic glare which he currently had trained on James. A small smile flickered at the corners of his mouth at the use of his team's nickname. He nodded his hello.

'This is Gal…' Eddie pointed to the nearest man, the owner of Mr Tricks, who was the oldest of them all, at least sixty. He nodded and added a 'Now then' to an easy pursing of his lips that might have been a smile, and just as easily might not.

'...that's Bub...' Bub was of Indian descent and wore a t-shirt with the legend: 'Your move, Creep!' above a picture of Robocop. He smiled a wide friendly smile to James and offered a cheery 'Hello.'

'...Jane...' She looked James up and down and he felt quickly and candidly appraised. She raised her eyebrows in greeting. He smiled a schoolboy smile back. He tried not to think of the word gorgeous. Failing, he tried not to put the words drop dead in front of it. James quickly turned to the next face.

'...Titz...'

'Alright, Jim, how's it going? I'll get that for you,' he nodded at the pint just parked next to James's elbow.

'Thanks,' said James. Titz's broad cockney accent was harsh and his teeth were a little too white.

'...Baz...'

'Hello.' His accent was strong.

'...Ziggy...'

'Hi,' said the younger man in the same accent as Baz.

'... and this is Len,' said Eddie finishing the introductions with the barman.

'Nice to meet you, Len.

'His full name's Leonard Spock,' said Eddie, chuckling.

'Unlucky,' said James.

'Yeah,' said Len wearily.

'Everyone,' said Eddie loudly, 'this is Jimmy.'

With the introductions over the group dispersed amongst the pool table, dart board and juke box. Cigarettes were lit, conversations started and suddenly James, Eddie and Len were the only ones at the bar. James nodded to Eddie's younger brother.

'Frankie would've been fifteen last time I saw him. He's grown.'

'Yeah,' said Eddie with a frowning glance in Frankie's direction. Len busied himself with a glass that didn't need cleaning but got a good rub anyway. Eddie and Len fell into conversation about a job, so James headed over to Frankie's table. On the way he dodged a pool-playing elbow and swam through the memories of a thickening cloud of tobacco smoke.

A lit roll-up hung from Frankie's mouth while practised fingers rolled another. It was ready by the time James had nodded at the opposite chair and received a permissive nod in return.

'Alright, Frankie,' said James as he sat down. Frankie's stare was intense and indifferent at the same time, like a cat studying a new lap. James was glad that he didn't have to ask Frankie what it was he did now. 'Eddie said that you two work together.'

'I work for Eddie.' His eyes glowed through the smoke and maintained their almost independent glare.

'Oh right. What is it you do for him?'

'I'm a plasterer.'

'A plasterer?' James nodded enthusiastically. 'Good. Good…' he cast about desperately looking back to Eddie who was still talking to Len. Moving to the one recognisable face in a room full of strangers is a common mistake. James had latched on like a man drowning only to realise that the younger Fiss was made of lead.

He stared at James now, seemingly fully aware that he was making him uncomfortable, and not bothered in the slightest.

'A proper family business then, Fiss Fixings. Is it just you and Eddie?' James gulped at his pint, and looked over at Eddie hoping he would come soon.

'We all work for Eddie.'

'All? Who 'all'?'

Frankie looked pointedly around the pub.

'Wow,' said James, genuinely impressed. 'Has he got any work?' He said this only half jokingly. He realised that being 'between things' might be unattractive, and he wanted something to tell Barbara on Friday night.

'It's funny you should say that, Jimmy.' Eddie arrived at the table with three fresh pints cradled in his hands. He placed them reverently on the table. 'I need to free up Ziggy, so that he can spend some time with Gal.'

'Oh yeah,' said James, smiling, 'that'd be good. Ziggy needs time.'

'Yeah,' Eddie continued, 'he reckons he's an electrician, and Gal's been on about retiring – I think his missus is at him – so I want them together for a few weeks. If you fancy taking up the slack, there's a few days this week over in Barton. Just fetching and carrying, and there's a kitchen to rip out. Then there might be mixing plaster for Frankie. Fancy it?'

James was stunned. His life had taken an incredible turn in just the last few hours, and he wasn't quite sure he believed it. 'Okay…'

'Good stuff! I'll pick you up at half-eight.'

'Hang on. Kitchen? Barton? Is it Barbara Bean's house?'

'Yep.'

James finished his first pint and started on his second, glad of the low strength of the lager. He was starting work tomorrow at 08:30 and he wanted to impress the customer.

Eddie talked and enthused, and showed off just a little as he told James all about Fiss Fixings and the roles that everyone filled. Some were specialised like Gal the electrician. Titz was the plumber. Jane was the joiner. Bub was a builder, a jack of all trades and Eddie's number two. Baz and Ziggy were labourers. At least Ziggy was a labourer for now. From tomorrow he would be the electrician's mate. Eddie beamed at this. His merry band was on three different jobs in three different locations. James could see the light in his eyes, a flame growing bigger and bigger.

The night wore on and the lager flowed. James drank and played pool; he drank and talked; he drank and played darts; and he drank and talked. He enjoyed himself. And for the first time ever he wished he had a mobile phone so he could text Barbara Bean.

It was nearly eleven and Len had rung his bell. James was fairly sure that he'd had six or seven pints. For him that was a lot, for the rest it seemed a snack, just something to wind the weekend down or whet the appetite for the next. He'd stopped worrying about how he might feel in the morning, reasoning that if he was drinking with the boss then he should understand any sluggishness on his part come the inevitable tomorrow. He affected the confident swagger of the not-quite-too-drunk and weaved his way to the bar. Slapping a twenty-pound note on the counter he demanded seven-and-a-half pints of Mr Spock's finest ale. It was Gal that only wanted a half.

The group was now gathered loosely around three tables, and everyone's attention was on Titz.

'I saw your sister the other day,' said Jane. James moved amongst them, handing out pints. 'Did she have a good holiday?'

'Yeah, she loved it,' Titz's London accent rang around the pub. 'She met Mickey Mouse.'

'Oh yeah?' said Bub.

'Yeah, she's easily pleased,' laughed Titz and the rest joined in. 'I think she was more impressed by the portions in Maccy's than anything else.'

'They let her out of Sea World, then?' cracked Gal to the risqué laughter and 'ooohs' of everyone else.

'Yeah, yeah. Very fucking funny, Gal.' Titz laughed a veiled friendly warning which sailed over James's head.

'They had to check her back for holes first though!' James's vulgar laughter was swallowed by the immediate and uneasy silence. Sobriety and the hideous clarity it brings threatened as the whole group stared at him.

'Who are you to call my sister?' Titz spat at James. 'Who the fuck are you? I don't know you!' He rose from his seat and started toward James who stood transfixed, a pint in one hand and a half in the other. Gal, Bub and Jane were rising to try to intervene.

'It was just a joke,' said James. 'I was just carrying on with what Gal said!' He gestured desperately to the older man. As the rest moved, James handed the half to Gal and then backed up, raising the remaining drink to his chest as an ineffective liquid shield.

'I know Gal, and he knows my sister. I don't know you. You don't get to say anything about my family!' He continued to advance on James. Jane was still trying to get in the way as Eddie moved his own impressive frame to stymie the Londoner's advance.

'Hang on, Titz,' he said.

'Outside.' The menace Titz put into that word terrified James.

'You're as mad as a yard of dogs!' he shouted desperately. James set down his fizzy barrier on the nearest table and returned the angry glare as best he could. Titz turned and headed for the door, slamming his way out.

James stood still, unable to move.

Eddie turned to his old friend, 'You going out there?'

'It's ridiculous! This is ridiculous! It was a joke!' James protested as all eyes stared at him, waiting, judging.

'You did call his sister a whale,' Jane pointed out.

'He's very sensitive about his family,' Gal added. 'Probably should've mentioned that at some point. You'd be amazed how often this happens.'

'No, Gal. I wouldn't.' James sighed and his shoulders slumped.

'You're going out there.' Eddie's statement moved straight past suggestion and into instruction as he propelled James toward the door.

He tried to steel himself and prepare for whatever lay in wait out there. He didn't look back as he left the sanctuary of the Rat and Drainpipe.

Chapter Five

Bang! James felt the blow on his cheek, just below his eye. It didn't hurt but the impact knocked him sideways. He hadn't been ready, hadn't believed the he was going to be in a fight. Now that he was, he had no idea what to do.

Bang! Again there was no pain, just panic and helplessness. He couldn't stop Titz's blows, couldn't think how. The other man was obviously experienced; this wasn't a drunken scuffle of car-park-rolling rough and tumble. Titz could hit him at his leisure whenever and wherever he liked. He toyed with James, pummelling his body, bruising ribs and then he started on his face: the first blow ensured a black eye; the second brought blood from a soon-to-be fat lip; a third blow, a quick rabbit-punch straight to James's nose. The blood cascaded down over his mouth and chin.

And now James felt pain. The fist to the nose had sent bolts of it around his head. Dazed, he staggered back, his eyes watering, one step, two steps and then on the third he stumbled and fell to land in a heap on his backside. His eyes streamed, blood flowed from his nose and mouth. He looked up at the advancing Titz through bleary eyes and thought of Barbara and how she must have seen him for the first time this morning, so long ago.

Then Eddie was there, standing between the two, barring Titz's advance and shoving his ample backside in James's face.

'That's enough, Titz. He's had enough...' And the rest was a blur as Titz was led away and Eddie and Frankie helped James to his feet and to the top of the lane and gently shoved him toward home.

James stumbled the three-quarter-mile walk to Ivy Arch, the pain never receding, only growing along with shame and impotent anger.

Dog watched him from the grass verge. He smelled the blood and the fear. He wanted to taste it. He couldn't; it wasn't yet time for such a bold move. Mistakes had been made with the dogs, and the authorities had seen fit to investigate. Their agents were abroad. Dog knew that he must be cautious. For now.

The next morning Tilda patrolled the house. She had kept her head down when her master had returned home in a terrible mood. She had smelt the blood and the fear and knew a loser when she saw one. Now she had determined not to let his victor return.

She was on the top floor of the tower staring out at the entrance when the van pulled into the drive. It was a white transit, it had 'Fiss Fixings, No Job Too Small, No Job Too Big' splashed across the side.

Tilda ran around the top of the tower barking and then darted into the house to warn her master. She was proud of her important job and intended to do it as loudly as possible.

James's eyes opened delicately. His left eye wouldn't open all the way, and he remembered.

His head felt like a bottle of wine that had been attacked by desperate corkscrew-less students. Tilda's barking only made it worse. She was a living breathing alarm clock from hell that one smack wouldn't turn off. James considered just how many smacks it would take as he lay there suffering and remembering.

Through Tilda's barking and the pounding in his head, he thought he imagined a knocking. In fact he could hear two lots of knocking, one at the front and one at the back. In a mercilessly short moment he realised that the sound was real. It must be Eddie and for a few terrifying seconds he thought that Titz might be with him. He froze in his bed unable to move.

Tilda continued to bark. She was downstairs now and running from front to back allocating her noise as fairly and aggressively as she could.

Slowly James forced himself upright and out of bed, into his trousers and down the stairs.

'Shut up,' he hissed at Tilda as he fought his way past the dog. He opened the front door, blinking and squinting into the sun-light that blasted the house, the shadows from the trees not quite long enough. James silently cursed the summer sun that rises so high, so quickly.

Eddie looked James up and down. 'Jesus, Jimmy you look like shit. I can't let you in somebody's house looking like that.'

'For Christ's sake, shut the fuck up!' James bawled at Tilda who shrank back, her head down, her eyes betrayed. James turned to Eddie. 'That's okay; I don't think I feel up to it anyway.'

'Oh no,' Eddie waved a massive hand. 'You can't lose a day's work through beer, and Titz didn't hurt you enough for a sicky. Get dressed. I'll find you a job.'

James stared, open-mouthed at his employer. Eddie turned to Ziggy who was just emerging from the archway. 'Another week's labouring for you, Ziggy. I need to keep Jimmy out of the way so you'll have to help out on the kitchen job. I'll send this one,' he jabbed his thumb at James, 'to Frankie.'

Ziggy nodded and looked at James, still playing statues on his doorstep. 'This is creepy fucking house, man.'

James just nodded.

'Come on, move yourself!' Eddie barked.

James jumped to it.

At a house in a small town not very far away, a front door opened.

Barbara eyed the two men suspiciously. They were bedecked in workmen-like attire and both carried large tool bags and boxes. One of them was smiling. His teeth were white. Too white. She had decided to use Fiss Fixings because Eddie Fiss had made an impression, the way an iceberg impresses the ocean. There was something inevitable about Eddie, and so she'd assumed that he would be doing the work.

'Morning, love, Fiss Fixings here to answer your prayers.' Titz's London accent announced their arrival. Barbara didn't trust him, she didn't trust his smile, she didn't trust his face.

'I was expecting Mr Fiss,' she began, then involuntarily stepped aside as Bub bustled past nodding a friendly hello. 'Who are you two?'

Titz was in the door and Bub already heading into the kitchen by the time he answered. 'New kitchen, new bathroom, right?' Barbara nodded. 'I'm Titz, I'll be your the plumber for the duration. That's Bub, he's a builder, he'll do a bit of everything. We are two-thirds of what you need for your home improvements.' As he looked down at her he winked. She stopped herself from drawing back in revulsion, but Titz must have seen something in her face. He smiled at her in a way that, had she been writing the scene, could be described as lasciviously.

'You local then?' he asked. It was a perfectly normal question, which Barbara ignored.

'Hang on,' she said, pointing toward the kitchen. 'He's Bub the builder?'

Titz laughed a perfectly normal, perfectly friendly laugh. It hit Barbara like tin foil on her fillings. 'I can see we're not gonna get nothing past you, love.' He looked around the entrance hall quizzically, like a rat sniffing for cheese, as he pulled an electric kettle from one of the large bags. 'Where's your temp'rary kitchen?'

'In the front room,' Barbara pointed to the first doorway off the entrance hall. 'But I have a kettle,' she added.

'Good, good. Be a star and fill this one and yours,' he said as he foisted the kettle onto Barbara. 'Just to be sure we've got plenty of refreshments after I've turned the water off.' Dragging his kit he shuffled through the entrance hall and headed for the kitchen. Barbara went to the front room to retrieve her kettle and then followed.

She hadn't been looking forward to having work done on her house. She didn't like strangers in her home.

In the kitchen she saw that Titz was already under the sink. He was whistling a perfectly friendly, perfectly harmless tune. Barbara didn't know how it would feel to have piano wire inserted into one ear and dragged out of the other but she suspected it might be a little like this man's whistling.

'Hurry up with the kettles and then I can turn the water off,' the headless body called from under the sink.

As Barbara went to fill the kettles she looked to Bub. His face was completely blank. She was reminded of an automaton. She had once written a book, *Electric Eden*, about robots that could give a man or a woman the best sex they had ever had whenever and wherever they wanted it. The conflict in the story had come from lack of appreciation for the robots. Both men and women were turned off by their emotionless state. Barbara was ignorant of the true depth of the bond between men and their best friends, and as such she was probably only half right.

In her story a chip was invented. It was a simple device that was easily inserted and gave the mechanical lovers emotions and all the wants, desires and misery that comes with them. Half of the robots possessed by this chip wanted more and the other half wanted less. Those wanting more reasoned that emotions were only worth it if they were happy, and so decided that they would be happy no matter the cost. The other half wanted to be happy but didn't want to hurt anyone. Both struck out for their objectives and tried to attain their goals through their sexual prowess. Both failed, and in an orgy of human-on-human sex toward the end of the story men and women learned to love each other once again and, turning away from the years obsessed with mechanical loving, they scrapped every last machine. She'd been aiming for poignant.

Electric Eden had been a risk, and one that hadn't paid off. Too many robots and not enough sex, her publisher had told her. That dip into science fiction erotica had been Barbara's least successful book. She hoped Bub wouldn't be her least successful builder.

Titz set about disconnecting her pipes while Bub stared at his tool kit. Barbara shook the double entendres from her mind and watched the builder. 'Are you alright?' she asked.

'Fine thank you,' Bub replied with a sudden smile. His face had been blank but not impassive; Barbara was reminded of a stage curtain drawn for a scene change. It opens and there's the smile.

'Bub's fine, love. He goes on little trips. He's a bit like James Bond, only not,' Titz interjected. Barbara felt that this man probably always interjected; she couldn't imagine him ever simply joining a conversation.

'Wait a minute. Did you say that you were two thirds of everything I need?'

'I could be all of what you need, love,' Titz winked and flashed his impossibly white teeth at Barbara. She smiled uncomfortably and stood her ground again. 'But we are two thirds of what you need for a new kitchen and bathroom. Bub,' Titz turned to his companion. 'Where's the new boy?' Barbara thought that he made 'new boy' sound like someone completely undeserving of respect and thoroughly deserving of all the derision that the world could and should pile on him. She could hear her thesaurus calling.

'Eddie's swapped it round,' replied Bub. 'We're getting Ziggy for today and Jane tomorrow when we've cleared it out for her.'

'I do hope that new boy's feeling okay.' Titz winked at Barbara as he flicked the kettle on.

Chapter Six

James thought that he might die. His lumps and bumps and hangover all throbbed together like some all-percussion orchestra. He listened to that orchestra and noted the lack of rhythm, like it was conducted by a broccoli floret.

He was mixing plaster. He couldn't believe how fast Frankie could put it on the walls: scrape, scrape, smooth. Scrape, scrape, smooth, and it was up. James hoped that Frankie might die.

Frankie was alive and well and watching James mix the plaster. He smoked his second roll-up since having to stop and wait. Under that gaze the beetroot James sweated and mixed frantically while trying not to look frantic. He was sort of un-frantic, like a zombie in a carwash.

'Eddie wanted this place finishing today.' Frankie exhaled smoke as he talked.

'Yeah, yeah,' James un-panted.

'Should've had this room finished an hour ago.'

'Mmm,' James un-huffed.

'You're not used to this, are you?'

'I'm okay,' James un-puffed.

'It's easier with the mixing machine.' Frankie's face remained wreathed in smoke.

'What? What machine? There's a mixing machine? Where?'

James stood happily watching the machine mix the plaster. This was better, much better. Frankie stood next to him, a roll-up hanging from the corner of his mouth, two days of stubble on his chin and a permanent grimace on his face. He looked like he was going for a craggy appearance, something like Clint Eastwood. He failed. He looked like an unhappy plasterer in a black and white baseball cap.

'That's better. I was never one for sweating,' said James.

Frankie nodded.

'Was it Eddie's idea to keep the machine secret?'

Frankie nodded.

'Will he mind that we're not gonna finish till tomorrow?'

Frankie shook his head.

'Was I supposed to mix it by hand all day?'

'Just till dinner.' Frankie replied.

James glanced at his filthy watch; it was eleven o'clock. 'Thanks, Frankie.'

Frankie nodded.

'What do we do for dinner?'

'Eddie'll bring me something.'

'That's good.' James struggled with the laconic Frankie and with his contrary stomach. Hangovers were funny things; he'd wanted to be sick all day and now he felt as empty as a factory tea bar during a management inspection.

'Not much of a drinker are you,' Frankie told James.

James shook his head, his fragile, fragile head. He knew that some people considered such pain as a sign of a job well done, an indication of money's worth. James lied to himself as he promised never to drink again.

Frankie took the freshly mixed plaster and went back to work while James prepared more.

Scrape, scrape, smooth. Scrape, scrape, smooth. The noise of Frankie's labour panicked James's stomach: with the machine he would be able to keep up but his hunger and hangover meant that he wasn't very steady on his feet. He concentrated on the mixing.

At lunch time Eddie arrived. He had spent his day visiting the members of his crew, helping out where he could, keeping an eye on them and maintaining the team ethos he so carefully nurtured.

James could have kissed him; he'd brought him a sandwich, and not just any sandwich. It was a huge, soft white bap crammed with an entire breakfast. James had to hurry, which was difficult given his battered face, because the sausages, bacon, eggs, mushrooms and baked beans all tried to escape as he took bite after delicious bite. It felt like a miracle. A sandwich like this might be proof of life after death. At least for pigs.

Eddie noticed James's struggle. 'Still hurts does it?' he gestured with his stratal bap at James's bruised face.

'That and the hangover,' nodded James.

'At least you got your money's worth,' said Eddie.

'I've got a date on Friday night,' James lamented. 'Hope she doesn't mind.'

'Course she won't,' Eddie boomed. 'And if she does you can come out with us. Team building exercise in Hull, got to make sure the beer's up to scratch north of the river.'

'Team building? Titz'll be there then.'

'You two'll get along fine eventually.' Eddie's reply was somewhere between an appeasement and an instruction.

Frankie dropped James off at Ivy Arch. He drove all the way to the back door. As James climbed out of the van he wondered whether or not to invite him in for a drink. The memory of a long silent afternoon made him hesitate and by the time he turned to ask, Frankie was turning his small white van around. James watched the arch swallow the vehicle.

In the kitchen Tilda awaited him. 'Hello,' said James. He left the back door open for her. She walked past and out without a glance in his direction.

James watched her go. He remembered shouting at her that morning. He would make it up to her; there were some sausages in the fridge which she could have all to herself. The breakfast bun had not settled particularly well and he would happily do without sausages for a while.

He moved about the empty kitchen.

His mother had died in this very room, Tilda the only witness to her death. Tilda and six Brussels sprouts. The postman had found her body. She was slumped on the floor in front of the open freezer, a spreading puddle of water and a bag of sprouts, six of which had spilled, on the tiled floor. James had no idea why the postman had counted them or why the police officers had decided to tell him.

His father had died in an accident. Left alone after the death of his wife, in his solitude he had become convinced that he wasn't. Someone or something prowled the grounds of Ivy Arch, trying to get into the house. He would ring James at all hours ranting and raving about intruders and voices. James's response had been to buy an answering machine. His father's last message had been his shortest; it said simply, 'They're at the window.' He had electrified the steel framework of the tower's upper floor and conical roof in an attempt to bar entry to whoever was at the window. His charred corpse was found by the postman who said that he had been alerted by Tilda's barking.

The police officers assured James that the postman was going to get a new route.

James could have helped his father, he could have listened, he could have visited, he could have... he didn't know what he could have done. He could have cared. He ignored himself and continued with Tilda's sausages.

James's parents' deaths were not the only strange things to have happened at Ivy Arch. The house was built by James's great-great-great grandfather, William, who invented the sausage. Actually he hadn't. The Wynns had joked for generations about what he had invented because they weren't entirely sure. In fact they had no idea, but the nicknames 'William the Wicked' and 'Bellicose Bill the Bloody Rotten Badger Baiter of old Never' suggested that the house may not have been built on particularly pious foundations.

And so he had invented the sausage. And, at various times, shoe laces, buttons, ice cream and the wheel. He had also stolen fire from the Gods and sold it to the French allowing Napoleon to begin his empire building. James's father had an active imagination.

James's grandfather, also a William, had been a scientist in the government's employ. In the 1950s he had been working on prosthetics. That's as much as James knew.

But as always there was more to it then James knew.

The less bellicose but no less mysterious William Wynn was provided with a steady supply of limbs from the recently deceased. He also received lots of material imbued with, and capable of imbuing, atomic energy. It was hoped that recently deceased limbs could be reanimated and transplanted to the armless and legless thousands created in the 1940s.

His work stopped sometime in the 1950s. It's fair to assume 1957 or 1958, as another project began to devour funding. This was not before thousands of body parts had been experimented upon and injected with all manner of substances. Some had been incinerated in the small tower behind the main structure which had been William's laboratory, but that had created strange smoke and stranger smells which drew unwanted attention to the project. So it was decided to bury the limbs in the grounds of Ivy Arch.

The rear garden was still sunk by a metre because it had not been filled with the same macabre ballast as the front.

James stood in the shadow cast by the evening sun surveying his front lawn. With a sudden determination he leapt onto the lawnmower and fired the engine to life. The buried limbs, filled with experimental energies, almost certainly didn't stir at all as the mower passed back and forth.

Tilda stood at the window and watched as James tried, not wholly unsuccessfully, to stripe the lawn. She had eaten the sausages. No point in going hungry.

Chapter Seven

The next morning James was ready. Sleeping was still a problem for him but early on in a job it was important to create a good impression. He was proud of the fact that while he had had a lot of jobs he had always made it past the first month.

And so he was waiting at the gate, packed lunch in hand, when Frankie pulled up. Tilda stood in the gateway. James had decided to let her stay outside for the day. It seemed unfair to lock her in the house, away from the sunshine. He waved goodbye as he got into the van.

As they drove away James noticed that the driver looked a little disappointed. 'What's wrong?' James asked.

'I like your house.'

'Someone's got to,' quipped James.

'I've always liked it, ever since we were kids.'

'Oh, right.' James couldn't remember Frankie ever coming to his house.

'I used to come with Eddie whenever I could,' said Frankie. 'Whenever he'd let me that is. You probably don't remember.'

'I do, I do,' James lied hastily. He was a little taken aback; this was the longest conversation the two of them had had. He took a risk on a personal question. 'Eddie means a lot to you, doesn't he?'

'Yes, he does.'

'Why doesn't he trust you?' James blurted the question out. It had puzzled him since the night in the Pipe, and his mouth was quicker than his brain again.

'Same reason no one trusts me,' Frankie answered matter-of-factly. 'Except Bub.'

'Same reason?'

'I forgot. You weren't here for the Splash were you.'

'No. I saw the aftermath though. My parents were pretty upset: I'd only just moved to Grimsby, only child just flown the nest and all that, and then their house and garden gets wrecked.'

'The front garden looks alright on it,' Frankie pointed out.

'It didn't reach the front garden. The back took the brunt of it: the trees were damaged, the sheds were ruined and the kitchen got flooded but the water only reached half way through the arch.'

'You were lucky. A lot of people really did lose everything.'

They drove in silence for a while.

'I saw it.' Frankie said this flatly, almost uncaringly.

'The flood?' James asked.

'Yes, and something else.' Frankie stopped talking as he drew the van to a halt. The two men pulled themselves from the van.

'Something else?' James repeated as they unloaded their gear.

Inside, Frankie rolled a cigarette while James prepared to mix plaster. 'Something else?' he coaxed.

'I saw it crash.' Frankie lit his roll-up.

'It? 'It' what?'

'The ship. The spaceship.'

James stared at Frankie who didn't look happy, who never looked happy. He returned the gaze without flinching.

'Erm...' James had no idea what to say or what to do or where to look. Conspiracy theorists and truth seekers were rife in the area. Everyone knew those theories, and while the crashing spaceship was by far the most popular, no witnesses had ever come forward that James knew of. No witnesses because there was nothing to witness, James had always assumed.

He looked into Frankie's eyes and saw, behind the resigned acceptance, the deepest sincerity he had ever seen.

Barbara was ready for the workmen. She let them in, filled the kettles and then fled to her study.

Yesterday the plumber, Titz, had continued to press her about her about personal details. She didn't want to answer his questions. She had never kept the details of her work from anyone before. Titz knew that she was a writer, she'd admitted that much, but there was something about him that made her assume he would see her work as dirty, sordid even, and she didn't want to give him those thoughts.

In stark contrast Ziggy had been delightful; she would never have guessed that someone could make tearing apart her kitchen fun. She had been dreading the moment that it would happen. The kitchen had been Grandma's and it had a special place in her heart. Ziggy had sung songs that she hadn't heard for more than a decade. She had been quite the rock chick in her teens and listening to Ziggy belting out Iron Maiden, Motorhead and Black Sabbath had revived fond memories. For a while she had sung along but when she saw Titz watching it put her off. Not for any good reason, she just didn't want him to see her like that: exposed, enjoying herself.

Ziggy wasn't with them today. It looked like he had been replaced by a woman.

Grabbing her mobile, Barbara thumbed it open and dialled her best friend.

'I am supposed to work sometimes, you know,' said Diane immediately but not harshly.

'I can't work with hairy arsed blokes poking into every corner and hole.'

'Do I need to put an 'oo-er' on that?'

'You know what I mean.'

'Can we talk about pipes and plugging leaks?'

'No.'

'Loving the workmen, then?'

'It's horrible. One of them in particular…'

'Bit too friendly?'

'Yeah,' Barbara sighed. 'There's a woman with them today. She's black and she's gorgeous, even in her overalls.'

'And what colour are the others?'

'Erm…' Barbara realised that she had dug herself a hole.

'Funny how you feel the need to point out the one who's black.'

'Don't start. You know what I mean. You can assume that someone's white.'

'I don't think I assume anything about people. I don't think I think anything about them. About their colour anyway,' Diane added naughtily.

'Well, if I didn't tell you that she was black, you wouldn't know!'

'Why do I need to know? I didn't *need* to know that the hairy-arses are white. Do I need to know the colour of the hair on those arses? Is it safe to assume that there's no ginger hair present?'

'Alright, alright point taken.'

'Why are you on about her now, anyway?'

'She wasn't here yesterday. She's replaced that Polish guy, Ziggy.'

'Ziggy's Polish, then?'

'Yes…' Barbara stopped herself.

'So we can assume that your black sex Goddess is a joiner,' the voice stated confidently. 'Careful she doesn't use a spear.'

'Ha, ha.'

'And make sure she doesn't steal anything.'

'Do shut up.'

'It's in their genes you know.'

There was a knock at the study door, a little too hard for politeness but not hard enough to be rude.

'Gotta go.'

'Hanging up on me again? I hope whoever it is, is worth it.'

She opened the door to find Titz standing there. *It really isn't*, she thought.

He was leering. It could have been leering. She was trying to give him a chance, trying not to judge. She stood her ground.

'Just to let you know, we're gonna be turning the water off now.'

'Erm... okay. Thanks for telling me,' she managed. Titz beamed. No he didn't, he grinned slyly. *Undressing me and then trying me out in several outfits with his eyes*, she thought. The efficiency of the lechery was almost impressive. She'd written characters like Titz countless times, the schmoozer, the flirt, the cocksure hunter forever chasing skirt, the man who thinks doggy is an exotic position. In her stories they generally got their comeuppance.

'What kinda writing is it you do?'

'Fiction!'

'Romance?' Barbara ignored the glint in Titz's eye.

'Some,' she admitted. 'Anyway, I must get on.' And she closed the door on that odious smile.

She went back to her desk and tried to work. She couldn't, she kept remembering her best friend's accusation. She suddenly remembered Bub. *Bollocks*, she thought, and threw herself at her work.

She bounced off.

James mixed the plaster. Frankie smoked his roll-ups. The house was nearly finished, an hour or two after lunch would see the job done. Scrape, scrape, smooth. Scrape, scrape, smooth.

Barbara was in her kitchen drinking a cup of tea, and feeling awkward around Jane. The joiner had a confidence that matched her looks. She was Hollywood.

'You're the joiner, then?' Silly question.

'Yes.' Jane smiled and immediately put Barbara at ease.

'How does a woman like you get to be a joiner?'

'A woman like me? How do you mean?'

'I just mean that you're... Put it this way, if I looked that good in a pair of overalls I wouldn't fancy getting splinters all day.'

'As my dad said, looks won't last but a properly dovetailed drawer unit will stand forever. That and have two trades and never get dressed at the top of the stairs. Dad had rules to live your life by.'

'Sounds sensible. What's your second trade?'

'If I told you I'd have to kill you.' Barabara was a little taken aback. 'Sorry, I think my dad wanted a boy. Raised me like one and I got some of his sense of humour. And I've been hanging out with Bub too much.'

'I hope your dad appreciates it now. Too many parents and kids losing out these days.'

Jane nodded. 'He does. I can cut hair.'

'Eh?'

'My second job.'

'Oh, you'll have to have a go at my mess.'

'Only if you want it to look like a drawer unit.' Barbara laughed. 'So, you live alone?'

'Yep, just little old me.'

'Happy that way?' Barbara nodded. 'Good.' Jane shifted her head into the cupboard. Her voice was muffled. 'Eddie said you were a writer.' Jane had raised her voice. 'What sort of stuff?'

'This and that, boy meets girl, that sort of stuff.' Barbara raised her voice a little to get through to the cupboard.

'Romance?' Jane grunted as she shifted about in the cramped space.

'I write erotica mainly.'

'Erotica, eh?' Titz sauntered into the kitchen. 'Lovely.' He leered. He really did leer.

Shit, she thought.

'I must get on.' She made to leave but Titz stood in the doorway, immoveable.

'What is it, then, sex, sex and more sex?' He looked her up and down thoughtfully. 'D'you write from experience?'

Barbara felt helpless, caught in this man's misconceptions. People like Titz made Barbara want to swear, and in her mind she put on her best fuck-you glare. It slid off Titz like joy on misery.

'Leave it, Titz.' Jane had slid out of the cupboard and her voice carried a warning.

'What? Just being friendly.' He still hadn't moved.

Barbara stood her ground, but she wasn't advancing. *This is my home!*

'What's going on?' Bub was standing in the back doorway. He wore a Spiderman t-shirt. He looked at Barbara, then at Titz, suspicion in his eyes.

'Nothing, just asking after the lady's profession.'

Titz retreated.

Barbara let out a breath she hadn't realised she'd been holding. She tried to control the relieved gasp. Then her anger grew when she realised just how relieved she was and the gasp turned into a splutter of rage.

Bub watched the now-empty doorway for a few moments before turning to Jane. 'What happened?'

Jane looked to Barbara, then back to Bub. She scowled. 'Titz being Titz.'

Bub sighed and looked to Barbara, his hands already raising to a placatory position.

Barbara could have chopped those hands off. 'I want him out of my house, now!'

'Now, Miss, he didn't mean any harm. I'm sure –'

'I know exactly what he meant, and I want him out now.'

Bub's hesitation incensed Barbara further.

'Now!'

Bub nodded and started for the bathroom. 'And tell Eddie I'll be wanting a word,' she called after him. Jane looked at Barbara and smiled.

'This kitchen won't fit itself!' She snapped and immediately regretted her words. 'I'm sorry...'

'No.' Jane cut her off. 'It won't.' She smiled at Barbara and returned to her work.

'A spaceship?'

Scrape, scra…

Frankie turned to James. 'A spaceship.'

'Anybody in it? You know, little fellas, skinny arms, eyes like rugby balls.'

'It wasn't very big so there was maybe one, two or three depending how big they are,' said Frankie. 'Maybe more depending how little they are.'

'You don't know then?'

'No, why should I?'

James shrugged. 'I don't know, I just assumed...'

'Assumption brings the tourists in. All I saw was a spaceship crash. That's it, nothing more. I've never seen anything come from it except for the flood.'

'How do you know it was a spaceship? Couldn't it have been a meteor or a comet or...' James sought for alternatives. '... a weather balloon?'

'Comets're big dirty snowballs trailing gas and dust. That's what gives them a tail. Meteors are just shooting stars. Meteo*rites* are bits of asteroids that hit the earth. I take it you're not bothered about the differences between achondrites and chrondrites?'

'Erm...'

'Didn't think so. Meteorites sometimes cause craters...'

'Or big splashes?'

'Or big splashes,' Frankie conceded, 'but this wasn't a meteorite. It was a space ship.'

'You mean you're assuming it was.'

'Yes.' Frankie smiled. 'But I know it was.'

'Right,' said James cautiously. Frankie seemed like a man with a plan. Frankie seemed like a man with a lot of plans, and all obsessively ordered into their priorities. *Probably written down*, thought James. Monday: plaster the village hall; Tuesday: smoke more. Wednesday: stop aliens. Thursday:

James didn't know about Thursday. He knew very little about Frankie. He smoked - a lot; he plastered - very quickly; and he liked to wear black and white. And one more thing: he believed that he'd seen a spaceship crash into the Humber. He believed it passionately, stubbornly, obsessively, obstinately, uncaringly.

It was a shame Frankie hadn't been a bird watcher, twitching his way up and down the country looking for lesser spotted something or others; Frankie would have made a good watcher or spotter. James supposed he was really; it was just that he couldn't tick varieties off in a guide book. James considered what an alien watching book might be. Page one: alien spaceship crash landing. Tick. Page two: little green men. No tick yet but Frankie waited, pen poised.

James couldn't help but feel sorry for him. He gave the impression of not caring what other people thought, but was that true? James didn't think so. People didn't want to be seen as weird and everybody looked at Frankie and saw one thing: a chain smoking, fast plastering, black and white wearing, alien-crash witnessing nutter. And that was all he showed. He'd been building a wall, brick by brick for the last seventeen years. James looked at those bricks and saw that they were a waste of time: no one was going to bother scaling that wall.

Frankie sighed.

'Sorry Frankie. I didn't mean to pry. If you say you saw something, then you saw something,' said James. He decided to change the subject. 'Town played on the day of the Splash, didn't they?'

'Yeah,' Frankie answered with a smile. 'Wrexham, we won 5-1.'

'Birtles hat-trick,' James shot back. 'I was there. McDermott scored an own-goal. I stood in the Imperial Corner. I'd got in free because I was twenty minutes late, just as Town scored the first goal. Great day.'

'Yeah it was,' Frankie agreed. 'But it wasn't an own goal.'

'Wasn't it?'

'No. Wrexham player. Can't remember his name.'

'Really?' James replied. 'Funny how you remember things.

Frankie nodded, some small hint of understanding evident. 'D'you still go?' he asked.

'No, gave up years ago when they got rid of the corners and put seats in the Pontoon. Never could get used to sitting down to watch football.'

'Yeah, prob'ly why most people watch in pubs now. I miss standing. I miss Birtles, too!'

'A couple of seasons, eh? Amazing what you get used to. Still, there's been decent players since.'

Frankie screwed up his face at that. 'Some shit ones too.'

James nodded. 'I take it you still go.'

'Season ticket.' Frankie gave a mournful look. They both grinned.

'You've brought pack-up?' Frankie asked.

James nodded.

'You'd best let Eddie know so he doesn't bring you another bun. Have you got his number?' James shook his head and Frankie pulled a very modern-looking mobile phone from his pocket. 'I'll give you it.' He looked expectantly at James who didn't move.

'I don't have a mobile.'

Frankie gaped at James. His thumb was a blur as he composed a text. 'And people say I'm weird.' He lit a roll-up taken from behind his ear.

James smiled; he was used to this reaction. Seconds later the phone snapped shut and Frankie returned to his work. He whistled.

Scrape, scrape, smooth. Scrape, scrape, smooth.

James smiled as he mixed the plaster.

Eddie arrived at lunch time. As they sat down to eat he looked down his nose at James's carefully prepared sandwiches, especially eyeing the salad poking out from the sides. Egg yolk and grease dribbled from his giant bap.

'You two'll be finished here today,' said Eddie. 'Frankie, I'll need you to fill in on the plumbing side of things from tomorrow; I've got some trouble on Bub's job.'

'So, you're a plumber, too?' James asked Frankie.

Eddie overrode his brother. 'Yep, I like my team to be multi-skilled. Frankie'll cover for Titz, and Bub'll do the bits of plastering that Frankie had to do for the rest of the week.' He said all this very proudly. 'Sorry, Jimmy, that means I don't need you for the rest of this week. I'll try to get you more hours next week. You haven't got any skills, have you?'

'That's fine, the no work thing I mean, and, no, I don't have any skills.'

'Shame. I've no cover for Jane other than meself and Bub. And neither of us are as good. Anyway, are you coming to the Pipe tonight? Darts practice. The match's been called off 'cause the Six Bells can't get a team up.'

'Could do,' James replied hesitantly.

'Titz'll probably be there, but you can't hide in that fucked up house of yours forever.' Frankie nodded his agreement. Eddie glanced at his brother with some surprise.

'Ok, then,' said James. 'I'm pretty good at darts.'

'We'll see,' said Eddie stuffing the last of his bap in his mouth.

People in white coats surrounded the cage. Errol looked up at them fearfully. Anyone who thought that scenes like this were tragic would be very upset right about now. Those men in the white coats didn't look like they wanted to study Errol; they looked like they wanted to study what was inside him. They couldn't use their knives because they weren't exactly sure what, if anything, was inside him, and so, for now, they were stuck for what to do. So they studied.

Chapter Eight

The dark tunnel of Ivy Arch yawned behind Tilda. Her wary eyes, glowing in the sun, were trained on the ever-open gateway.

There, Dog stood monstrously still. Forming a triangle behind him were two Rottweilers, their huge powerful black and tan bodies taut, ready.

Tilda stood her ground, her head held high.

If the dark formation launched, they could arrow down the driveway and be on her in seconds, tearing her to pieces. She wouldn't stand a chance. She stood firm; it wasn't time to run. Not yet.

A horn sounded from the road. Tilda cocked her head as she listened. The three beasts glanced to their left and then stepped forward, very nearly into the gateway. They returned their murderous gaze to Tilda. A car moved slowly across the gap. It was red and shiny clean. Three dark reflections passed along its body.

They launched, dust and gravel raised in their wake. By the time Tilda had turned and started to run they were already nearly halfway down the drive. She sprinted into the archway and burst out the other side, past the kitchen, the small tower, the sheds and the garage, and into the morass.

The three burst through the arch, skidding to a halt in the circle of sparse gravel. They scanned the space, their noses in the air. Dog nodded and the Rottweilers lumbered to either end of the edge of the encroaching garden. They were swallowed by the green tumult.

Dog moved to the back door. He sniffed at the edges and pawed aggressively at the UPVC panelling leaving scratches in the white plastic. Giving up, he went to the sheds. The cracks and gaps in the wooden structure were invaded by his nose, giving his snuffling an echoing, maniacal cadence. He pawed in frustration at the unyielding wooden doors, his claws leaving deep scratches in the wood.

He ran across to the garage.

Sniff, sniff!

He growled and snapped at the vegetation wrapping itself over one door. He snarled again at the other door, his claws trying to find purchase but they just screeched along the implacable metal.

He sped to the smaller tower and quickly circled the base of the structure.

Sniff, sniff!

The brick was perpetual. With a grunt of frustration, Dog turned and ran through the archway.

Tilda stayed low, trying to keep her breathing shallow and her movements to a minimum. The wind tossed the already wild plants above her head. They had not found her yet. There was a good chance that they wouldn't find her at all. Tilda had long since made a den of this canine paradise. She knew it like the back of her paw. She had chased mice, rats, cats, foxes and birds through the under and over growth. Her scent was already on and under every centimetre of ground and plant. She just had to wait quietly and it would be okay.

The Rottweilers moved through the confusion of greenery, like sharks following blood, wolves searching their prey, Rottweilers ready to bite.

The wind covered the noise as Tilda crouched lower, but it carried wisps of her increasing fear. She couldn't give in to that fear and let it power her legs to carry her away. Not yet.

Dog had made his way around the house and tower, sniffing, looking, listening, pawing, clawing. He attacked the front door, desperately gouging the wood with his claws, his hind paws digging deeply into the gravel as he pushed at the unyielding portal.

Defeated, he headed back through the arch and to the edge of the tossing waving garden. He raised his nose to test the wind. He barked a deep guttural command. Moments later the Rottweilers emerged and joined their leader. Dog moved forward and the three entered together.

Tilda had to be ready.

Dog followed his nose, his lips drawn back, his teeth bared, saliva dripping from his fangs. He smelled the fear. They pressed on.

Tilda began to pant and to shake; control was difficult. She wanted to bolt now but it wasn't time. She needed to wait.

They were almost on her. Dog could smell her easily now and his ears were pricked as he listened for her above the wind.

Wait…

Dog's nose thrust through the choking plants and weeds. The dogs at his sides pushed forward eagerly, too eagerly. A snarl from Dog saw them return to their supporting positions.

Wait…

Dog knew that he was close. He could hear her panting now. He bore down on his prey, sure that these were his last few steps before the hunt was complete. The Rottweilers pushed forward, almost level with him.

Wait...

She couldn't. Three dripping muzzles with teeth bared poked through the wall of greenery in front of her. Tilda backed up, backed up. The vegetation behind her was dense, too dense to allow escape.

Wait!

Dog saw his target. Drool dripped in a line from his teeth to the ground, pooling at his feet. He snarled with rage as the Rottweilers surged forward.

Now!

Tilda shot toward the space left by the advancing dogs. The gap wasn't quite big enough. Dog snapped as she bolted, taking a chunk out of her hind leg. Blood splattered to the ground and coated Dog's front fangs, colouring his frothing saliva. Head and tail down, Tilda darted through the tangle. With a roar the three were after her, blood in their nostrils and their febrile brains.

Ignoring the pain in her leg, Tilda ran. She was faster than the three but that leg wouldn't hold up for long. Dog's fangs had left a deep gash and the blood flowed freely. She sprinted out of the garden, through the gravel circle and under the arch.

The three were hot on her heels, their pants and snarls sending streamers of drool from their mouths and hideous echoes that reverberated through the archway.

Tilda ran as fast as she could up the drive. The empty road was seconds away. Empty. She had gone too early. She slowed, the pain in her leg suddenly flaring.

Dog saw her falter and doubled his efforts, leaving bloody froth and Rottweilers in his wake as he charged his quarry.

Tilda was close to panic as she neared the road. She could feel the thud of Dog's paws on the drive, and his breath on her wound.

And then a white transit moved slowly into view, its side door wide open. Tilda's heart rose.

Dog almost had her, his head thrust forward, his jaws loomed large.

Tilda leapt into the van which was accelerating even before she was aboard.

Dog's teeth were an ellipse of deadly white as he leapt after her. He hit the side of the vehicle. His bared fangs left scratches and a red stain of Tilda's and his own blood as one of his fangs flew from his mouth. He was thrown onto the verge by the impact and rolled to the wall of conifers.

Immediately he was up and sprinting onto the road, the Rottweilers again at his side. The van sped away, quickly outdistancing the brutes that, while their fury might drive them until their bodies failed, were not built for speed. The van angled around the horse-shoe bypass and away.

Coming to a halt, the blood from Dog's mouth fell into a pool on the concrete road. He turned his burning gaze on the Rottweilers. They panted in the summer heat and lowered their heads.

James and Frankie stared at the shed door.

'This isn't like her,' said James. 'She's a soft thing really, daft as a brush most of the time. I've never seen her do anything like this.'

'You haven't seen her do anything this time,' Frankie pointed out.

'Well, no, but what else could've done it?'

'"What", indeed.' Frankie mused. James stared at him. He was beginning to think that he preferred the laconic Frankie. They had spent the afternoon talking football, and James had never seen him so animated. As a result he had decided to invite him in for that drink. It had been Frankie who had spotted the blood on the gravel circle and the scratches on the back door. He also claimed to be able to identify signs of a chase in the once gravel driveway. James had looked at him sideways at that.

'A chase?' James had asked. He was annoyed with Frankie for constantly making him ask questions. It felt like he was being slapped and had to keep asking why, especially about things that should stay in fictional universes. Any person's ability to identify spaceships and tracks and God knows what else will always be taken with suspicion. These talents are reserved for Middle Earth and galaxies far, far away. So thought James and most people unfamiliar with seeing what was in front of them.

'Yes. At least three dogs, maybe four,' Frankie replied.

'Really, *Tonto*.' Frankie had merely nodded, but James had been incredulous. 'So, Tilda's had her mates 'round and trashed the place; things got out of hand, there was maybe some drinking, an argument, some furniture got damaged, and now she daren't show herself. Typical, you show a little bit of trust, and look what happens. Well, she'll have to stay inside from now on.'

'Can you ground a dog?' Frankie had asked. 'Might get a bit smelly.'

James and Frankie stared at the shed door.

'This really isn't like her.'

'Shall we check the front?' Frankie asked. James noted the eagerness in his voice.

'Have you ever thought about talking to whatsisname?' said James as they headed for the arch.

'Who?'

'That guy.'

'That doesn't narrow it down.'

'The Splash guy, the one who set up Splash Land and made Never "the Roswell of Europe",' James waved his fingers in the air to indicate the quotation marks. 'Woodman, is it?'

'Howard?'

'Yeah, Howard. Howard Woodman.'

'What about him?'

'You could talk to him about what you saw.'

'No.' Frankie ended the conversation.

They emerged from the arch, Frankie pushing ahead. Arriving at the front door they saw the gouges in the wood. Frankie pointed out the troughs carved into the gravel path a metre and a half or so from the door.

'What?' said James.

'That'll have been her back paws; she really had a good go at it.'

'She really did.' James was beginning to feel a little guilty about leaving her outside all day. He had thought she would prefer it to being cooped up. These feelings were washed away by the thought of all the repairs that would be needed. He glanced at Frankie and saw that he was staring at the gouges, staring and more. He was studying them, analysing the length and the depth, going over all the possible causes his avid mind could come up with.

James was wrong. Frankie didn't seem particularly imaginative; he didn't need to be because he took things at face value. That was how he *saw* things.

'Are you sure you don't want to go see Howard? You could put on a good show in that visitor centre of his. They had a guy in there from Star Trek a couple of weeks ago.'

'Which guy?' said Frankie.

'Can't remember,' said James.

'Which Star Trek?'

'Can't remember.' They stared at the marks for a while longer 'Shall we have that drink?' James prodded. Frankie nodded.

As they headed for the arch a white transit pulled into the drive.

Eddie filled the cab like an over-sized goldfish. He leant forward, his huge head looming over the steering wheel, his eyes peering ahead.

'Does he need glasses?' James asked Frankie.

'Yeah, but he won't admit it. Too vain.'

'Driving like that doesn't exactly make him look gorgeous.'

'Nope.'

As the van drew to a stop, James and Frankie both took an involuntary step backwards.

'Now then, Jimmy,' Eddie boomed as he squeezed out of his cab. The van rocked and rolled as the big man got out. 'I wanted to talk to you about tonight.'

'Come on in, I was just gonna put the kettle on.'

In the kitchen James prepared three mugs of tea. Eddie and Frankie sat at the table.

James placed two of the steaming mugs in front of his guests and took one for himself before joining them at the table. 'What's up then, Eddie?'

'That spot of bother,' Eddie began. 'It was with Titz. It's put his back up. He's in a mardy, and I don't want you getting it in the neck.'

'Or the nose,' James replied ruefully. The pain was all but gone, and the bruises were just beginning to yellow at the edges. One on his eye, his nose and his chin. And above his kidney, and one of his left ribs. Not *all* the pain had gone.

'Titz can be a prick,' Eddie admitted. 'In fact he *is* a prick. But he's a bloody good plumber.'

'Has he got it in for me then?' asked James. He felt strangely calm about the whole thing, lucid even. He'd been terrified on Sunday, but now James saw him for what he was, or at least for what he was to James: unimportant, irrelevant. He was even absurd.

'In the past he's got his claws into people, and...' Eddie seemed embarrassed, lost for words. James had never seen this before.

'Danny,' Frankie interceded. Eddie glared at his brother, and then nodded in agreement.

'Danny?' James raised his eyebrows. Eddie looked uncomfortable.

'Danny used to work for me, labouring. He's just a young lad but Titz wouldn't let up on the poor kid, and in the end he quit.'

Frankie stared at his brother who eventually continued. 'I mebbe could've done more to help him.'

'You *should've* done more.'

'Alright, Frankie! Jesus, when'd you get so gobby?' Eddie turned to James. 'I *should've* done more, Frankie's right. Danny was a good worker but he was a leery gobshite all on his own, forever complaining about me using Poles and whoever instead of giving him overtime. At first we all thought he needed bringing down a peg or two. I s'pose I let Titz wear him down, toy with him for a while; he got on everyone's nerves, you know? And, to be honest, we're better off without him.' Eddie sighed, a huge hand rubbed against his bristly chin. 'Problem is Titz thinks he can do what he wants, thinks he's got a free hand to take the piss. He always has done but now he's worse. I could've used Danny to rein him in, and that would've helped the lad out at the same time.' he glanced at Frankie. 'Anyway, I didn't.'

'He's out of control, Eddie,' said Frankie. 'You just won't admit it.'

'Good plumbers don't grow on trees, Frankie, you know that. And neither do good plasterers.'

'Titz isn't a problem,' said James.

'Really?' Eddie was suspicious.

'Well, he might be a problem. I'm just not bothered about him. I can't spend my life hiding from people like Titz; he's not going away so I may as well...' James sought for a word other than confront, 'be in the same room as him.'

'If that's right,' Eddie answered as he looked James up and down kindly but disbelievingly, 'then it's darts night.'

'You coming, Frankie?' James asked.

'He doesn't come out Tuesday nights!' Eddie jumped in.

'Why's that?' said James.

'Where's that dog of yours, Jimmy?' asked Eddie.

'Gun club,' said Frankie.

'Lovely dog that.'

'Gun club?'

'What kind of a dog is she?'

'Gun club,' said Frankie.

'Some kind of collie, mebbe?'

'What, proper guns?' James was yet again slapped into asking questions of Frankie. 'In a club with bang, bang, plastic goggles and a sore shoulder?' James was proud of his implicit reference to recoil; it represented his sum knowledge of firearms.

'Was it her that scratched your front door?' said Eddie, not giving up.

'Pretty much,' said Frankie to James. 'No hand guns, though. And a few bring their own. Mostly air rifles.' Frankie sniggered at this.

'Did I notice a few scratches on the back door, too?'

James stared at Frankie. Guns. He'd never held a gun, never seriously thought about holding a gun. James knew why Eddie was trying to steer the conversation away from firearms. People didn't feel comfortable with people who liked guns. The uncomfortable ones knew almost nothing about them, and thought that the comfortable ones, who seemed nothing short of fascinated, knew too much about an implement that, ultimately, had only one purpose.

'I'm not sure,' James had turned to Eddie, 'a brown one is pretty much all I know.' James forced a laughed. Eddie didn't.

'She's a Border collie.' Frankie was as terse as ever.

'Nice dogs. Shame about your doors,' said Eddie.

'And the sheds too,' James added.

'Didn't want to be left outside, then,' said Eddie. 'At least she didn't take a dump on your doorstep!' Seeing James's face, Eddie added. 'Did she?'

'Er... no.'

'Well, if you need any repair work I know a few builders and the like!' Eddie laughed, his rumbling chuckle filling the kitchen.

'Have you got any guns, Frankie?' James's curiosity was piqued as the gun's fascination reached out to him.

'Course he hasn't!' If Eddie had been playing football, his statement would have been two footed with the singular intention of taking James out of the rest of the game. 'Guns? Where would he get guns?'

'No,' deadpan Frankie confirmed. 'No guns. The club's got a good selection.'

'But you said that some people brought air rifles,' said James.

'I've just bought a new bat,' said Eddie. 'You wanna take a look?'

'Well,' Frankie looked sheepish but proud. 'I've got one or two shot guns.'

'It's in the van. You can come *outside* and take a look.'

'Shot*guns?*'

'Yep.' Frankie recognised the glint in James's eye.

'A cricket bat. Just got some new pads too.' So did Eddie.

Frankie drove through the arch and away. James and Eddie watched him go. James looked down at the sparse gravel.

'What are you looking for?' said Eddie.

'Blood.'

'Eh?'

'Well, more blood to be precise.'

'Don't be daft, Jimmy. What blood? Where?'

James pointed. The big man strolled over and bent his head. 'Where?'

'Right there,' James answered. Eddie stooped lower, scanning the ground. 'Where?'

'There!'

'Don't get mardy with me, Jimmy,' Eddie warned. 'There's no blood. You're being daft.'

James walked over and pointed to the splatter of blood. Eddie stooped and bent and finally crouched lower.

'See it?'

'Yeah.' Eddie straightened. 'Found any more?'

'It's all up the drive and probably through the arch too. Can't tell for sure 'cause of the shadows.'

'Looks like you've got dog troubles, Jimmy. Shame. Anyway, I'll see you tonight down the Pipe.'

'Okay.' The two strolled through the arch to Eddie's van.

'Good to see you've kept that kitchen nice.'

'Eh? How d'you know?'

'Fiss Fixin's fitted it, you moron. What else?'

Eddie climbed into the van's cab, the suspension rocked and rolled anew as he forced his way in. His pink head glowed through the windscreen as he leant over to retrieve something. He waved it out of the window. It was a brand new cricket bat.

Chapter Nine

Bub and Jane left with a forced cheery goodbye.

Barbara closed the front door. She regularly used such mundane observations in her work. Plenty of sex and not too much plot meant a character's emotions were often measured by their actions: a door could be slammed or thrown open, burst through or peeped around and, of course, it could always be ajar.

Barbara closed her door gently, unhurriedly. A keen observer might have noticed that the knuckles of the hand that gripped the handle were white.

Later, in the front room, she opened a bottle of wine. Her phone was clamped to her ear by her shoulder. Her hair swung wildly as she juggled and jiggled with the corkscrew and bottle. She grunted and swore the corkscrew into the cork and began laboriously turning.

Tosser, she thought. *Shithead*, she added. *Arsehole*, she concluded.

'Is this turning into a dirty phone call?' said Diane. 'I don't mind if it is.'

Barbara's grunting intensified as the corkscrew finally bored deep enough and she pulled.   'Hello?'

With one last grunt the cork was out. Barbara stumbled and red wine spilled onto her trousers. The phone flew free scattering and clattering across the polished wooden floor, coming to a rest in the doorway to the entrance hall.

Barbara grabbed a glass, stooped for the phone and stomped to the living room.

'Bit fed up?' asked Diane.

'Yes,' said Barbara. She placed the bottle and the glass on the coffee table before perching on the edge of the huge soft settee. She stared at an unopened box of cigarettes that were sitting on the coffee table. A clean ashtray and a brand new, bright pink, disposable lighter sat innocently next to it.

'Are you still there?'

'I'm still here,' Barbara sighed.

'Are you alright?'

'Been a rough day.'

'Did those characters of yours misbehave? Been dumping your humping? Did you venture into plot again?'

'I haven't written a thing. The workmen have been too noisy.'

'Well, it'll soon be over, and then you'll have lots of shiny things to cook and clean with. Of course that would mean learning to do something other than wine and toast. Speaking of which, what are we having tonight?'

'A Modra Frankinja.'

'Not very summery. We *have* had a bad day.'

'It was the plumber. He came on to me, or he was just flirting. I don't know, but it scared me.'

'Don't you know any fancy kicks to deal with randy plumbers?'

'That's not what the classes are about. But yes I do know a fancy a kick. Three or four even. But you know what? It didn't even occur to me.'

'What did he do?'

'Nothing in particular, it's just the way he did it.' Barbara reached for the cigarettes. 'And it was in my own home, you know?'

'People are nasty, people are nice. Now that you've let a few into your house, you're going to find this out.'

'I'm not that sheltered!' The phone was clamped to her ear again.

'But this is the first time in God knows how long there are some people you can't keep at arms' length.'

Barbara couldn't think of anything to say to deny it. She turned the cigarette box over and over in one hand while she turned her glass red with the other.

'Ah, the booze flows. So, what did you do about the perilous plumber?'

Barbara took a long gulp. 'I kicked him out.'

'Really? Was he on his own?'

'Well, I told the others that I wanted him out.'

'Well done, you!' said the voice. 'How's the wine?'

'Just right.'

'And the fags?'

Barbara stopped turning the box, her hand frozen mid spin. 'I don't know what you're talking about.' She quickly put them back on the table.

'I'm sure you don't. How's James? Have you spoken to him?'

'No,' Barbara was hesitant. 'I didn't like to call, just in case…'

'In case what? He sounds as sappy as you. Probably been waiting for the phone to ring, and now he's convinced that you've changed your mind and he's drowning his sorrows with that dog.'

'D'you think so?'

'Of course. Although it's not him I feel sorry for. At least he's got the dog to talk to.'

'I've got you.'

'I could hang up.'

'But you won't.'

'But I could,' Diane teased. 'And I might.'

'He doesn't even have a mobile!'

'Neither did you a few years ago. How did you survive? Or have you only been *alive* for the last five years? Were the previous thirty nothing more than instinctive existence just to keep your body operational until you could send a text message?'

'You've thought about that a lot haven't you?'

'I might even have rehearsed.'

'I'll ring him.'

'Only if you want to.'

'I'll ring him!'

'Go on then.'

'I will!'

The conversation stopped. Barbara took another gulp and reached for the cigarettes.

'That wine's going down well.'

'Mmm...' Barbara was careful not to handle the box too much. She held it lightly in a pincer grip as she sought the small tab sticking from the clear wrap. Finding it, she slowly unwound the plastic strip. As her hand orbited the box, not a whisper of sound escaped.

'What are you going to say to him?'

'Mmm?' Barbara was slowly sliding the top portion of the plastic sheath up and away from the box. With the slightest of sounds the clear film dented as it moved. Barbara held her breath, her tongue on her lip as she concentrated on the task.

'Where are you, B? In a field not so far away perhaps? Near a house that combines the Addams Family and the Munsters in one untidy but potentially fantastic home?'

'I've never said that I see it as a potential home,' said Barbara. The plastic top was off. She began to ease the lid back.

'No, you haven't. Would our knight in rusty armour run for his horse if he realised?'

'Of course he would.'

The lid was open. The foil wrapper blazed in the early evening sun that streamed through the window. The south tower of the

Humber Bridge could just be seen. It watched as Barbara's fingers hesitated at this final barrier.

'Ah, men!' said Diane.

'And so would I in his position.' The foil remained intact, Barbara's fingers hovered. 'So would I in *my* position.'

'Ah, women!'

Barbara coughed to cover the sudden pulling away of the foil wrapper. She held her breath for a moment.

'The conversation has flown again. Not to the fields or the house, then.'

'I don't know what you mean.'

'It's gone to the nearest Macmillan ward. That's a nasty little cough you've got there. It could be bigger and nastier.'

Barbara threw the open box, a cigarette halfway out, onto the table. Grabbing her wine, she retreated into her settee. 'Alright,' she breathed.

'You're still on the phone to me,' the voice pointed out. 'Give him a ring. Take your mind off things.'

The phone rang. James was in his kitchen just starting to prepare his evening meal. He took a nearly boiling pan off the heat and headed to the phone, past the freshly filled bowl of water on the floor.

'Hello?'

'Hi,' said Barbara.

'Hello,' James repeated.

Barbara panicked; he didn't recognise her. She was disappointed, deflated even: *the shit!*

'Is that Barbara?'

She re-inflated like a sheet in a wind tunnel. 'Yes.' And because she didn't want to appear terse or isolated like some oaf who didn't even own a mobile phone, she added, 'It is.'

A moment.

'How've you been?' she asked.

'Fine,' he replied calmly. 'I got into a fight,' he added in that same calm tone. So calmly in fact that she was a little unnerved.

'Do you often,' she hesitated, 'get into fights?'

'No. Never.' James fell silent for a moment. 'Ever.'

'Good,' she said quickly. 'I mean erm…'

'It's okay. I wouldn't want to go to someone's house if I thought they were the fighting type. Especially alone,' he assured her. 'At night,' he added.

'No,' she said, suddenly nervous.

'That's why I'm telling you about it now. I wouldn't want to scare you on Friday night.'

'Scare me? Why?'

'Well...'

'Does that mean you lost? Is your face a mess? Are you okay?' she fired the questions at him rapidly, her voice rising with each one.

'Of course I lost. I've never been in a fight before. Except for Andrew Farmer. But that doesn't count because his sister was helping him.'

'And the other guy had?'

'Who, Andrew Farmer?'

'Who's Andrew Farmer?'

'A kid I had a fight with when I was eight.'

'What's that got to do with Friday night?'

'Nothing.'

'Oh.' Barbara stopped for a moment. 'So the guy you had a fight with this week had fought before?'

'Yes.'

'It was a guy?'

'Yes.'

'No one's sister?'

'No. Although his sister was involved. Sort of. I made a joke about her being a whale.' James always admitted to his mistakes. He liked to think of his honesty as disarming, but it just gave people reasons to dismiss him – employers and friends. Winning and losing was very important to people. Victories made people more attractive and James had never been a winner.

'I get the impression you only open your mouth to change your feet, Copierkicker guy.'

'Yeah.'

'Shall I get the boys together and go and have a word?'

Barbara was not a winner. She wasn't a loser either. To winners she was something much worse: Barbara was an achiever. Not in everything, she wasn't an over-achiever, which was the bottom of the pile as far as people were concerned. People who considered themselves winners detested achievers, while all people detested over-achievers. People were weird.

'Do you have 'boys'?'

'I could rustle some up. What do you reckon, Glaswegian kiss followed by a good kneecapping?'

'Darts,' said James, steering Barbara away from extreme violence.

'In the eyes?' Barbara grabbed the wheel.

'Erm…'

'Too much?'

'Maybe a little?'

'Okay. What about 'darts'?'

'I'm playing tonight.'

'What's that got to do with kneecapping?'

'Not a lot, but the guy's gonna be there.'

'Really! I hope he plays nice.'

'Probably not. He was bollocked by the boss today. In a foul mood, so I hear.'

'I might've got someone in trouble today. He was a proper idiot,' Barbara sighed. 'I can't wait to get all this work finished and have my house back.'

'Workmen are a pain,' James sympathised. 'I had thought I was going to surprise you on Monday. I've got a job with Eddie.'

'You've got a job! What do you do?'

'Whatever I'm told,' James replied. Barbara giggled. 'I know the guy you got in trouble. Don't worry, he deserved it. What did he do to you?'

Barbara told him.

'And now he deserves a bit more,' said James. There was menace in his tone. Barbara didn't admit it, she barely even realised it, but she liked it.

The interior of the Rat swallowed James whole. They were all there: Eddie, Bub, Jane, Gal, Ziggy, Baz, Len. And Titz. Not all, Frankie would be at his gun club.

Eddie beamed, Titz sneered and the rest shifted uncomfortably, apart from Bub who waved a cheery hello. He wore a Danger Mouse T-shirt, the one-eyed heroic rodent smiling at James as he approached the bar.

'Can I get anybody a drink?' James asked. Enough people replied in the affirmative for James to order four pints of lager, one of which was for Titz. As James handed it to him he asked, 'Had a good day?'

'Better than your face!' the Londoner snapped.

'My face'll be better quicker than your personality.'

Titz lurched forward. Eddie moved between the two men, an implacable lump of meat. Titz stopped. James just smiled.

'We're here to play darts,' Eddie's voice was not loud but it was heard clearly by all. It carried a promise that the only thing thrown would be those darts – and at the board.

'Right, we're only practising so it's five games of three-oh-one,' Bub announced. 'Two teams: Jane, Baz and Titz versus meself, Ziggy and Jimmy. Gal'll keep score.'

'Aren't you playing, Eddie?' asked James, innocently.

'No, darts is for kids,' Eddie laughed. James thought that it was forced, faked even; it jarred with his otherwise genuine personality. A few looked away, covering smirks. James laughed dutifully to cover a smirk of his own.

The match was organised into games, each of which was made up of three legs. There would be five games. People liked to compete, even when they were only practising; there was winning and losing at stake.

Bub's team won the first game 2-1. He and Ziggy had beaten Titz and Baz while James had lost to Jane. She had been deadly accurate.

'Thought you were good at darts?' said Eddie, laughing.

'Just warming up,' James replied, sipping slowly at his still-full pint.

'Another?' Ziggy asked, nodding at his glass.

'No, thanks.'

In the second game Jane beat Ziggy and Bub beat Baz, this left a decider between James and Titz. The Londoner squared up to James over the oche. James stepped aside to let him throw.

Titz launched his darts quickly with an angry determination: 20, treble 5, double 20.

'Seventy five,' Gal announced as Titz took a long pull on his pint, all the while glaring at James.

James threw carefully and deliberately: 20, and treble 20, and 20.

'One hundred.'

Titz strode to the oche, and again the darts were rapid and buried deep into the board: treble 20, 5, 20.

'Eighty five.'

Titz lit a cigarette as James took up position. He threw carefully: 20, and treble 1, and 20.

'Forty three.'

Titz sniggered before he threw, his cigarette hanging from the corner of his mouth: 20, 20, 19. He grinned as ash tumbled down his shirt front.

'Fifty nine.'

James steadied himself on the oche: 5, and 1, and treble 20.

'Sixty six. Titz needs ninety two.'

Titz took a huge drag of his cigarette and placed it in an ashtray. A stream of smoke followed him as he took his position. He launched the first dart: 20. A look of disappointment passed across his face so quickly it was only seen by two people. His second dart: 20. There it was again, that look, and still only fleeting. This time James noticed too. Titz hesitated. His third dart: 20. He nodded grimly.

'Sixty. Jim needs ninety four.'

James stared across the 2.37 metres from the oche to the board. The bull was just about level with his eye. If he didn't win it now then Titz was in a great position. The first dart: double 20. James tried not to smile. He failed. The second dart: double 11. 'Yes!' he said it quietly, but inwardly cursed himself all the same. The third dart: 16. An audible 'oooh,' from those watching. Bub turned away in disappointment while Jane smiled.

'Seventy eight. Titz needs thirty two.'

Titz was ready before Gal had even finished. First dart: miss. The point buried itself in the number sixteen. Second dart: 16. 'Ooh,' from the crowd. Bub, Jane and James leant forward as Titz launched his last dart: double 8. 'Yes!' Titz shouted, and glared at James with venomous triumph.

'Thirty two. Titz wins.'

'There's winners and there's losers,' Titz growled at James. 'You ever even seen a winner, fanny?'

'All the time,' James replied. 'But some days I have to look a bit harder.'

Bub and Jane both heard this and smiled. 'Unlucky, Jim. Another one?' Bub asked as he moved to the bar.

'No, thanks.'

The next game went to Jane's team. She beat Bub while Baz lost to James and Titz won again, this time beating Ziggy. Jane's team were 2-1 up and Titz revelled in the reversal. He knocked back another pint.

'And a short, Lenny,' he crowed. 'No need to save myself tonight,' he gestured to Bub and his team. 'Not for this shower of shit!'

Jane's team needed one more game to secure the match but Bub, James and Ziggy all won, besting Titz, Jane and Baz respectively. James let Jane buy him a pint to celebrate his second victory and the opposition captain's first defeat.

'Staying sober won't save you, wanker!' Titz called across the pub. The group stopped for barely half a second while the few other patrons openly gaped at the comment. Titz's aggression had grown steadily as he drank. Eddie watched this boozy belligerence.

In a repeat of the second game Ziggy once again lost to Jane, and Bub beat Baz to complete the older Pole's miserable night. He had lost every one of his legs. The match would be decided by James and Titz.

The Londoner swaggered to the oche and hurled the first dart: 20. It had struck just a millimetre below the treble, barring that route. He turned to the nineteen; 3, 3.

'Twenty six.' Titz snarled as Gal announced the score.

James threw carefully: treble 20, and double 20. A pause, a narrowing of the eyes: bull.

'One hundred and fifty.' There was an interested murmur around the pub; more than just the practising team were watching. James smiled, not exactly directly at Titz, but certainly within his field of vision.

Titz seethed as he returned to the oche. First dart: miss. It struck the wire around the twenty and bounced away to land at the feet of Baz.

'The way your luck's gone tonight, I'm surprised that didn't land in your toe!' Bub called out to the amusement of everyone but Baz. His English wasn't quick enough for the pace of the rhetoric.

'Shut the fuck up, Bub, or you'll be needing a real eye patch!' Titz hadn't laughed either. Everyone stared at him. Everyone but Baz who was chuckling merrily because Ziggy had just told him what Bub had said. Ziggy was now trying to shush him and tell him what Titz had said.

Eddie spoke. 'Just throw your dart, Titz.'

Second dart: 1. Titz grabbed his drink and guzzled the remainder, just over half a pint in all, gone in a second. 'Another one, Lenny!' he barked at the bar. Third dart: miss. The point was buried into the board just above the double twenty.

'One.'

There was an embarrassed silence as Titz turned a full circle to glare at everyone in the pub. Jane was visibly disappointed in her teammate. She, James and Eddie were the only ones not to turn away.

Titz sharked his way to his fresh pint as James returned to the oche.

'Jim needs one hundred and fifty one.'

James paused with his first dart ready. Taking a breath, he launched his arrows one after the other: treble 20, and double 20, and 19.

'One hundred and nineteen.'

James suppressed a smile. The onlookers were confused; had James tried to win?

Eddie smiled.

Wiping lager from his lips with the back of his hand, Titz staggered to the oche, staring balefully at James all the way. Outwardly he readied himself as he stared across the distance to the dartboard.

The pub was quiet as everyone watched the first dart.

Outer bull, just below the twenty.

Double 3.

Miss.

The point entered the wooden mounting below the board then drooped and finally dropped, landing impotently on the floor.

Gal stared at it, as did the rest of the pub, Titz included. No one wanted to look at the Londoner.

'Thirty one,' Gal finally announced.

Titz retrieved his darts, his glare daring comment as he stooped for his errant third.

'Jim needs thirty two.'

James stood ready. Double sixteen, that was all he needed. One dart and the leg, the game, the match was his, Bub's and Ziggy's. *Tosser*, he thought. Miss the double and hit the sixteen, doesn't matter, just move to the double eight; two darts and he, Bub and Ziggy would win. *Shithead*, he added. Miss the double and hit the eight, doesn't matter, just switch to the double four; three darts and Titz loses. *Arsehole*, he concluded.

He had been careful to take it this far. He had toyed with Titz, who was already as mad as a yard of dogs. And now he had got himself good and drunk and angry. A flicker of regret entered his mind; he didn't need to do this, he could have already finished him. He didn't need to be the cat.

'Are we playing, or what?' Jane called out. He turned to her, smiled, and turned back to the board. He threw.

Double 16.

'Yes!' James shouted, a little too loudly. Titz glared. Bub and Ziggy cheered. Jane and Baz joined the others and clapped. Eddie was poised.

'Thirty two. Jim wins!'

'A pint and a short for that man, please, Lenny,' Bub shouted to the bar. Titz glared as he finished his drink. He swallowed it quickly, his teeth visible through the bottom of the glass.

James smiled as Jane shook his hand. 'There's a place on the team for you,' she said. 'What do you reckon, Bub?'

'He can throw, he's on!' Bub confirmed handing James two drinks. 'We've a game in Barrow next Tuesday against the Six Bells. We'll murder 'em with you on side!'

Jane looked over to Titz. 'C'mon, Titz, game's over, we lost. We'll all be on the same side next week.'

'Fuck you, monkey girl!'

Jane was so quick to head for Titz that James was surprised he managed to catch hold of her arm. 'He's not worth it,' he whispered to her.

'I think he just might be,' she hissed back and shrugged his arm off, ready to advance.

'That's enough,' Eddie rumbled, and moved towards Titz, ahead of Jane. 'That's too far.'

'That's right. Fat faggot like you'd always side with a boom-boom-fucking-banana,' Titz drawled drunkenly. No one averted their gaze. Jane's eyes blazed, but she held back behind Eddie.

He walked up to Titz as softly as a tidal wave. 'There's no more work for you, Titz. Time for you to go.'

Titz sneered up at the big man. 'Who's gonna do your plumbing? Your mental brother?' He laughed into Eddie's face, which clouded immediately, everyone in the pub but Titz could see it. 'You can't get ridda me.' He jabbed his finger at Eddie. 'You *need* me, you shrimp-eyed queer fucker!'

The tidal wave hit Titz as Eddie swept him up and out. After a split second's stunned silence, the boys and girl of Fiss Fixings rushed to follow.

The sun was just setting as they all piled out to see Titz ranting and raving and spitting venom at an immovable Eddie.

'You're done, Titz,' said Eddie.

The Londoner glared at his dumbstruck audience. His wild eyes settled on James and his hatred grew.

'You! It's all you! C'mon, me and you, now!'

James didn't move. 'C'mon, c'mon get happy, Titz.'

'Nothing to settle,' Eddie told Titz, never taking his eyes off him. 'Now get gone.'

Titz switched his glare from James to Eddie and back again. He panted in anger and drunken exertion. Spitting onto the car park gravel he turned and walked away.

Nine pairs of eyes watched him go.

The ninth pair was hidden deep in the bushes that bordered the car park. Dog watched Titz leave then turned his attention back to James as he followed the others back into the pub. Later he would follow him home, but neither he nor James would see Tilda.

The phone rang.

'Hello?' said Barbara.
'Got him,' said James.
'You took him all the way?'
'Yep.'
'How was it?'
'Aces.'

Chapter Ten

Errol settled in the cage. His body was restless but his mind was at peace. Or, as we know, it was in pieces, and any bits that weren't at peace were fenced off and ignored.

There was only one white coat watching him now. The rest, either bored or sulking at the lack of scalpel action, had left this one, the youngest, to keep watch.

She was annoyed by her treatment. The older white coats made her make all the drinks, and it was always her who had to go to the shop for cigarettes and crisps. She took some pleasure in imagining their hearts and lungs dying, but this didn't give her the immediate satisfaction that she craved.

And they didn't listen to her. And they made her wear a badge. They said it was traditional, and that she had to wear it. The badge was a trinket, a gift shop stalwart. It was in the shape of a shark and bore the legend: 'Check me out, I'm Deep!'. It was from the gift shop for the tourist attraction *The Deep*.

The design of *The Deep* was supposed to represent the prow of a ship jutting dramatically from the ground. To some of those involved in the design it didn't matter what it looked like. The important thing was that the tip of the prow was exactly the same height as the tip of the spike above Ivy Arch.

The young white coat – we'll call her Susan – didn't like the badge or the people who made her wear it. She'd considered violence, and immediately dismissed it. She wasn't equipped for the task. Not necessarily physically, a person could achieve a great deal of bloody mess with just a biro and a bad mood, but Susan just wasn't the sort to see it through. One or two stabs, maybe three or four, and her bad mood would give up. She needed to belittle them through the job. And so she had determined to find out all she could about Errol and, through him, all of the dogs of Humberside.

The fleeting violent fancy had been caused by a dog. Not Errol, another meaner, leaner dog; a Doberman pinscher had followed her when she fetched crisps and cigarettes. She didn't know this for sure, she couldn't, but she had seen it on the way out of and back in to the secret entrance to the complex behind a public toilet on the plaza outside *The Deep*: a three-metre plastic shark marked the spot next to the brown waters of the Humber.

A door led to two flights of stairs which led to a lift. Susan had often muttered to herself that it was almost a cliché.

The underground complex, nicknamed The Warren, was reaching the end of its recent renaissance. A top secret, high priority operation, Project Eden's Aegis had begun in the late 1950s, fallen out of favour in the 1970s and ultimately failed in 1990. Then the building of The Deep in 2002 signalled the operation's revival as a scientific and technical project. But the idea of actually using Eden's Aegis was fired back into life by the dogs of Humberside.

Did the Doberman pinscher follow her on her way to buy crisps and cigarettes? Yes it did. We know that, but Susan couldn't be certain. An unattended Doberman was strange and to think that it was following her was stranger still. But in her canine obsessed mind this made sense: the Doberman was watching her and Errol was listening to her. Susan was right about a lot of things.

But back to Errol. Susan had been given the job of studying the animal, and study him she did. Every aspect of the dog's behaviour, every pattern during waking and sleeping hours, the dog's intake and output, and every scan that could be performed were performed, with the results meticulously recorded and analysed.

And from this mountain of data Susan was on to something: every eight hours Errol changed.

James stood at the open back door of Ivy Arch, a mug of coffee in hand. He had a day off, which was nice. He was worried about Tilda, which wasn't nice. He had never worried about her before. He had never worried about anything much before.

The angry purple of his bruises was beginning to fall back before the yellow encroaching at the edges. He was a little bit worried about Titz, too. He had no idea what the Londoner might do. *Where is that dog?*

He went back into the kitchen and changed the water in her bowl, then he threw out the food he had put down last night. When she turned up he would give her a fresh helping. He flicked the kettle back on and pushed bread into the toaster.

She might not turn up. She might have been run over. It wasn't a busy road but there was traffic, and most of it considered the long straight piece of concrete to be a drag strip. Tilda's body could've been squished, her broken body wiped and spread along many metres of roadside verge, the grass so bloody that it grew out of an HG Wells novel. He imagined carrying her down the road back to the house. The sun would be setting while he dug a grave under her favourite tree.

James had no idea of her favourite tree, or if she even had one. He sighed. Death was so much worse when it required one's own shovel.

He tried to imagine a dying Tilda still physically whole and able to rest her head on his lap. She would whimper once, lick his hand and pass peacefully on. That would be better.

He sat at the empty table in the empty kitchen and ate his toast.

Barbara let the Fiss Fixings team in. Bub was wearing a t-shirt with Lando Calrissian's face and the legend: 'I've got my own problems'.

'Morning, Miss,' said Bub. 'This is Frankie,' he nodded to the man dressed head to toe in black and white. 'He's gonna be doing the plumbing.'

Frankie nodded. He was particularly white, almost as white as the stripes in his shirt.

'I was at Blundell Park a few years ago when West Ham played,' she told him nodding at his shirt. 'I was living in Sheffield. My friend's a West Ham fan. And it was more than a few years now; it was back in '96!' Barbara shocked herself with the passage of time. 'Do you remember it? FA Cup? Fourth round I think. Wasn't there something to do with an Italian?'

'Yes,' Frankie smiled. 'Town won 3-0. The manager had broken the Italian's cheek bone the match before.'

'That's right. My friend wasn't happy.'

Apart from the smile Frankie's face held a serious mien and intense eyes.

The three of them went to work. Bub took Frankie upstairs to the bathroom. Jane went straight to the kitchen. 'I'll be finished today,' she said. 'Your kitchen will be all yours and ready to use. Bub'll finish the last bit of wiring later. And the plumbing was already done downstairs,' she added almost apologetically.

'When will the bathroom be finished?' she asked Bub as he came back down the stairs.

'Mebbe tomorrow,' he said cheerfully. 'But prob'ly Friday.' He smiled awkwardly.

'Okay. Eddie said it might take all week. Shall I put the kettles on?' Bub beamed his assent.

'Now then,' said Eddie as he pulled his black Ford Ranger up alongside James who was standing on the grass verge.

'Nice,' said James admiring the big shiny truck. 'Is it new?'
'Cert'nly is. Bit comfier than the old Transit!'
'I'll bet.'
'Enjoying your day off?'
'No. Not really.'
'Oh?' Eddie replied. 'Can I help?'
'I've lost my dog.'
'That's a shame. Lovely dog that. Tell you what, let me do this plastering job,' he nodded into the back of his truck, 'and then this afternoon I'll come help you look.' He dug a mobile phone out of his pocket and peered at its display. 'If you haven't found her by then, that is.' A car was creeping past his truck, two wheels bumping over the grass verge. 'What's your number? I haven't got it in me phone,' said Eddie, seemingly oblivious to the other driver's difficulties.
'I don't have a mobile.'
Eddie stared at him for a moment. 'I forgot,' he said. 'Get one.'

Dog was in the field across the dyke hidden among the crops. The two Rottweilers were with him. They watched the black truck pull away.

Barbara sat at her desk and stared at the monitor. She was having trouble with an in-car sex scene. The idea was to have the driver be an American boy racer, and then she could talk about the hot rods inside and outside the girl. She thought it sounded silly, which it did, but she hated to reject an idea without seeing it through.
Sighing she reached for her phone.
'Hello?' James answered. His bright white kitchen was a stark contrast to his gloomy mood.
'Hi!' said Barbara.
'Oh, hi.' His tone lightened dramatically on hearing her voice.
'What's wrong?' she asked.
'Still no sign of Tilda.' James sighed.
'Shall I come and help?'

Titz didn't know it but he was taking a risk, a huge risk.
Dog was watching him. He watched Titz because Titz watched Ivy Arch. Nodding to a Rottweiler to stay, he took the other and started for the bridge so as to skirt round and watch from the other side of the road. He paused as a car approached. It was a red Mini Cooper. It slowed and pulled into the driveway.

The Rottweiler watching Titz saw his animated reaction to the driver. The dog had no idea who it was, just that it was female and if it was in a car any bigger it would have shrunk even further into insignificance.

James stared out of the kitchen window. He was waiting. He sighed. Not a big sigh, just a small expression of impatience and repressed excitement. He didn't like waiting.

Pretending he wasn't, he flicked on the radio and began to wipe down the already clean work surfaces.

"Now to my engagements. This morning, I had meetings with ministerial colleagues and others. In addition to my duties in the House, I will have no such further meetings today or any other day," said Tony Blair through the radio. Laughter greeted his words.

James wasn't really listening. He wiped and he cleaned. He emptied the tray from the bottom of the toaster.

He wished that Barbara had agreed to have lunch; it would've given him something to do. He hadn't eaten anything himself. Her impending visit had taken his appetite. He started on the oven.

"...that the definition of socialism that he has just given – that it is for the many and not the few – is one that I wholeheartedly share..."

The roll of tyres on gravel brought James's attention back to the kitchen window.

He watched Barbara step from the red Mini Cooper. Her long hair was tied back and she wore trainers, blue jeans and a white vest. She was gorgeous. That was a word used too often, James realised. He thought that he might never use it again.

Seeing him watching, she waved as she swung the car door closed. He rushed to the back door to welcome her in.

"...increased the amount of money for our coastal defence protection to, er, something in the region of six hundred million pounds a year..."

'Drink?' James asked as he led Barbara into the kitchen. He looked awful. His battered face topped a cheap-looking plain blue t-shirt and blue jeans. Barbara could imagine a body as shapeless as his clothes hiding beneath.

"...the only way of bringing stability and peace..."

'Tea, please.'

"...is a two state solution..."

She smiled as he busied himself with the kettle; he wasn't hiding behind it.

"...and not merely in terms of its territory, but in terms of its institutions and governance..."

'So,' Barbara began, 'you haven't seen Tilda since yesterday morning.'

'That's right.'

They stared at each other across the kitchen, each in the glow of their own skylight. Barbara tried to keep her mind on Tilda. James wasn't trying at all; the two women in his life shared his thoughts, but not equally.

"...people want to see a situation where hostage-taking and violence are a thing of the past, and the two groups..."

'Your face doesn't look too bad.'

'Yeah it does,' laughed James. 'But thanks.'

They sat down to their drinks. They were like a pair of oddly-shaped cushions: uncomfortable and comfortable at the same time.

"...those two elements that we're fighting, we're fighting the world over. We will not beat them by giving in to them. We will only beat them by standing up to them..."

'So, was it good?' said Barbara.

'What?'

'Titz.'

'Yeah, I told you last night.'

'I know. But is it still good?'

James paused. Barbara smiled.

'Yes and no,' he said.

'I know what you mean. In the cold hard light of a Wednesday morning victories tend to shrink, and life grows and reasserts itself. Do the ends justify the means? And will they always?'

'Did you say you were a writer?'

'Was that a bit much?'

James smiled and nodded. 'Spot on though,' he said, taking a sip of his tea.

'Anyway,' said Barbara. 'Tilda. Has she got a favourite place to go? Does she ever hide or go walk-about? Anyone in the villages know her?'

There was laughter from the radio. The braying rang in James's ears. He reached over and flicked it off.

'Erm...' he said. 'How's your kitchen coming?'

'Nicely. Jane and Bub say it'll be finished today. It'll be good to have it back. Not as good as this though,' she said, gazing with renewed admiration at the modern space.

'The same people fitted it.'

James suddenly realised that Titz had been in his house, had known it intimately. He suppressed a shudder, and then berated himself. *He's only a plumber.*

'Although maybe not Jane,' he added. 'She's only been here a year or so I think, and I'm pretty sure the kitchen's older than that.'

'Shame you missed out on Jane; she really is gorgeous, but then you don't need me to point that out.'

Shit. James stared at Barbara. He had no idea what to say.

'I thought we could walk the fields, maybe she's out there somewhere,' he said, desperately. 'I've already checked the verges all the way to Never.'

'What about the other way, to Barrow Haven?'

'Not yet. We can walk down there and circle back through the fields on one side. Then we can cross over to the other and check out the ones between here and the river. We'll have to skirt the car park but she sometimes comes back muddy, which suggests the Humber bank.'

Barbara nodded her agreement to his plan; it certainly sounded sensible. She was glad she had worn trainers and not sandals if they were to tramp across fields. She let his avoidance of Jane slide. It was an uncomfortable question to have asked and she knew it now. Diane was right: she'd not had enough practice at this.

James wondered if he should feel guilty that Tilda's plight meant that he could spend time with Barbara. He didn't feel guilty at all. He wondered what Barbara would think of him if she knew this. Then he wondered if he would feel silly calling Tilda's name in the middle of a field. He wondered if he would feel happy, silly and guilty all at the same time, the gamut of emotions making him dizzy and leading him to faint through the heat and exhaustion, the field spinning like a drunkard's bed. Barbara looking down at him…

The kitchen dimmed. They looked to the skylights. Clouds raced across, their undulations visible in the light grey shadow. In the kitchen lights flickered on. Barbara looked round in surprise.

'Photosensitive lighting,' James told her. 'They come on when it gets dark.'

'Sounds wasteful,' said Barbara. 'And also quite cool.'

'They go off if they don't detect movement in thirty seconds.' He waved his arm in the air.

'Still sounds wasteful. I mean, it's not that dark in here.'

'No it's not. I'll turn the sensitivity down.' He operated a small control panel set above the work surface. The lights went out. 'Better?' he asked.

'Much,' Barbara replied, and swallowed the last gulp of her tea. 'Shall we go?'

James nodded. 'Have you got your hay fever stuff?'

'Yep.'

'Let's shake, rattle and roll.'

Dog and his companion hid among the conifers. They watched James and Barbara walk down the drive and listened to their conversation.

'Are you sure you'll be alright?' James asked.

'I've got more drugs in me than a rock star in rehab.'

'Okay, then,' said James.

They walked in silence for a few steps.

'I didn't know you smoked,' said James.

'I don't. Why?'

'Saw a packet on the dashboard of your car.'

'Ah, caught out. I don't smoke, but it's only been a few months, and I'm struggling a bit. Keep feeling like I'm gonna have a relapse.'

'It's difficult,' James nodded. 'Can't be that bad though, you sound pretty calm with your "few months".'

'Alright then, two months, three weeks, and four days.'

'Hours and minutes?'

'I'm not that bad!'

James and Barbara laughed as they joined the road and passed out of Dog's sight. Staying hidden, he and his companion removed themselves from the conifers and trotted after them.

Titz was watching too, and he in turn was watched by the other Rottweiler, its black fleshy face pointed at his back.

The Doberman, whose given name was Scud, watched Susan approach the rear door of the public toilet on the plaza outside of *The Deep*. The three-metre plastic shark kept watch from its vantage point on the roof. The wind was picking up, and she held her light jacket over the badge that she had probably forgotten to take off. She had a plastic carrier bag filled with crisps and cigarettes. Stopping at the entrance, she looked up at the gathering clouds as the wind rustled her back. She passed inside.

Scud looked up to the sky and sniffed the wind. He stood next to the river, the Humber Bridge framing his powerful body.

Once James and Barbara had disappeared toward Barrow Haven, Titz left his hiding place, crept down the bank of the dyke, leapt across the steady stream of water, scrambled up the other side and hurried down the road toward Never.

'Tilda!'

'Tilda!'

James scanned the fields, his eyes always moving, and his head turning this way and that, ostensibly looking for Tilda. He was starting to feel guilty: Barbara seemed to fill his vision.

And he felt silly. He was irked by the dog, and he was worried for the dog. He remembered the blood on the driveway, the angry furrows created by more than one set of paws and claws. Was that blood spilled by tooth or claw, or both? Was it Tilda's blood alone? Was it even Tilda's blood? In a surprisingly insightful moment James imagined dark monstrous hounds stalking and attacking his faithful companion. He dismissed the image as ridiculous. Insightfulness was wasted on most. His eyes fell on Barbara again, and again he snapped them away.

Barbara glanced at James. She was worried for him. She assumed he was worried for Tilda and trying to cover it up. She was also happy to receive his glances. James's gaze was currently enjoying her weekly trips to the gym, Pilates classes and Tae Kwon Do lessons all wrapped in her figure-hugging blue jeans and white vest. She wondered if she'd worn them on purpose. She didn't think so.

Dog kept his distance. He had sent his companion away, back to Ivy Arch, nervous that the searchers would spot the massive creature. Dog's smaller body snaked through the crops, careful not to make too much noise. He was confident; he could smell the lust on both of them. They were too wrapped up in each other and their half-hearted search to notice him. That was no reason not to be careful though.

The clouds had swarmed and now formed a great grey blanket that lowered and glowered like old slate roofs stretching across an eternal row of terraced houses. Dog was glad of the shade. His dark coat was hot and the promised deluge would be a relief.

'Can I have a picture?' Barbara asked James.

'Erm, okay'

She held her phone out toward him. James had never had his picture taken with a mobile phone before, and the chocolate brown tablet didn't look like any kind of camera he had ever seen. So the picture showed him peering in confusion and mistrust at the lens, like a dog confronted with a friendly cat.

As Barbara showed him the image he missed what she had said to him.

'What did you just say?'

'I said there's a storm coming in.' Barbara looked up at the grey sky.

James sighed. 'I know.'

Mr Tricks padded down the main street of Never; he had taken up Titz's trail. The Rottweiler had returned to Ivy Arch as it was well known in the village and couldn't roam free yet. Titz led Mr Tricks to a house. The Spaniel waited while he disappeared inside. Soon he emerged with a younger man in tow. They seemed to be arguing. Mr Tricks couldn't make out what they were saying except the young man's name, Danny. It was clear that Titz was winning. They climbed into the cab of a flatbed van and drove away, Danny at the wheel looking thoroughly miserable. Mr Tricks, unable to follow, watched them go.

Scud roamed the anonymity of the city. He walked at the water's edge along pathways not made for him. He stared at the Humber Bridge two miles upriver. The lowering darkening cloud blurred its edges.

The Rottweilers watched Ivy Arch from across the dyke. A flatbed van arrived with a micro digger and a compressor secured to the back. As it disappeared into the drive they decided to cross the road. Not confident of the dyke's sheer sides they went to the bridge. The same one used by James and Barbara three days ago.

Settling into the conifer wall, the dogs sniffed at a sky so low it seemed the charcoal cloud would be slashed by the tips of the wind-tossed trees.

The micro digger was on the ground with Titz climbing aboard. He shouted and gesticulated at Danny who watched with apprehension as the inimical Londoner began.

He used the scoop to slash and stab, churning the lush lawn of the front garden. Leaning out of the window he shouted at the younger man and pointed to the truck. The dogs had not noticed at first that there was a pneumatic drill on the back. Danny jumped on the rear of the truck and started up the compressor. He hauled the drill down and, still looking thoroughly miserable, he attacked the driveway, methodically working his way down the middle. The noise was incredible. The Rottweilers didn't like it at all.

Up and down, Titz gouged and scarred the ground, he attacked the trees, he joined the young man in assaulting the drive, and he moved from under the tower's gaze and rammed into the tumult, twisting and tangling the vegetation so that if it ever healed it would grow back more wild and furious than ever.

The rain started to fall, lightly at first but steadily heavier, the volume of water growing exponentially with every drop. Lightning flashed and thunder boomed concomitant to the assault of James's land.

Danny ceased his drilling and took shelter in the cab of the van.

As the rain grew and the cloud did not break he went to the micro digger. He was soaked in seconds as he waved desperately for the maniacal driver to stop.

Water dripped and soon poured through the conifer canopy onto the dogs as they watched the two men wrestle the micro digger onto the back of the van before they climbed back into the cab and drove away, the rain pounding on their vehicles.

The dogs, unable to follow, watched them go. The rain hammered into the trees, weighing them down and making their movements ponderous and mournful as they shook their branches in protest. The Rottweilers waited, grounded gargoyles in the shadows.

They had laughed at the first few drops of rain, and been excited by the first few flashes of lightning and rolls of thunder. The weather seemed to match their tumultuous passions and desires. So thought Dog with distaste; he kept his canine body firmly under control, as he believed others should. He watched them get wetter and wetter.

James's recidivistic passions were not dampened by the downpour. Barbara stood in the rain, hands on hips with her head cocked, listening.

'Can you hear that?'

James tried not to stare. He moved his head this way and that but his eyes stayed still, refusing to leave Barbara's flat stomach, the smooth curve of her back, her breasts.

'Gah?' he said.

'I thought I heard road works.'

'Gah?'

James snapped his face to the low sky, the rain a cold shower.

'I mean, what?' he said.

Barbara looked at James. His blue t-shirt made a silhouette of his flabby torso and his undefined arms, his hair was slicked to his forehead, around his ears and his neck, not unattractively, but it made his chin look even smaller. She sighed as the rain sluiced down her face.

'It's getting heavier. Maybe we should head back?' She didn't want to abandon Tilda but this field would soon be a quagmire.

'Definitely,' he agreed. He had to spit the rain away from his mouth as he talked.

They turned and headed back to the road. As they laboured through the sucking mud Barbara's hair swayed across her back, a sodden rope. James's unfit body felt heavier and heavier. They were soaked to their underpants, and James's loins had finally cooled.

Their arms were cold, the mud rose higher and higher on their trousers and the field clutched and grabbed and pulled them back. They looked to the heavens, desperate for signs of a break in the charcoal grey. But the thunder rolled over them time and again, leaving their ears ringing while the lightning grew brighter and brighter, the whole grey sky illuminated by flashes that highlighted the craggy underside of the continuous cloud, allowing shadows to leap into life for the briefest of moments before hiding once more.

'Fuck me!' James cried dramatically into the sky. They laughed, the glow of desire, of friendship, of the new was rekindled. They forged on.

Finally they reached the sunless black road. Their feet splashed in a deep film of water. Mud was rinsed from their shoes with every step and the footprints created were blotted and blurred as soon as they were made. But compared to the field they were walking on air, and so when the black truck pulled up, lightning flashing along its flanks, the rain drumming on every centimetre, every millimetre of it, the relief, while present was not quite palpable.

'You two kids're very happy for being so wet,' said Eddie as they climbed giggling into the cab. Even a fresh boom of thunder didn't give them pause.

They sat in amiable silence as the truck powered through the weather.

'Did you find your dog?' said Eddie.

'No.' James tried to wipe the smile from his face as he rubbed the rain away, but he couldn't.

As they pulled into Ivy Arch, he had no trouble.

Tilda tested her leg. It was healing well; the man had bandaged it assiduously and there had been no need for stitches. Soon she would be fully fit and able to go out again. The canine body, so unsuitable in so many ways was just useful enough to be priceless. If only more dogs could be kept from the others. Their monopoly was beginning to tell. But they didn't have a man yet, we were the only ones to have succeeded there. Perhaps that would be enough.

Chapter Eleven

'What's happened?' Barbara asked, bewildered. She, James and Eddie were sitting in the black Ford Ranger, just inside the gateway to Ivy Arch.

No one answered. James's once fine lawn was a shattered mess. The pounding rain smoothed the jagged edges of the mud and withered and beat what little grass could be seen. As they stared down the shattered driveway the noise of the rain, which just about drowned out the idling diesel engine, was finally broken by James. 'I don't know,' he said.

'Did your dog lose her bone?' Eddie tried a joke. 'Sorry.' Whether he was sorry for the poor taste or because no one laughed, James and Barbara would never know.

'No,' James and Barbara said together. Then James carried on alone. 'Oh well,' he said. 'I'd best put the kettle on.'

Nodding, Eddie shifted the van into gear, the engine suddenly clearly audible above the rain and edged forward over the broken ground.

Dog joined his companions amongst the conifers in time to see the truck lurch slowly over the jagged driveway.

'I reckon cricket practice'll be off tonight,' said Eddie as they emerged from the arch at the rear of the house. 'Night in the pub then!' He looked like a schoolboy who had lost a Playstation and found a Nintendo.

'Shame though,' he continued. 'I've got all the gear in the back: me new bat and some new pads for me and Frankie. Plus a helmet,' he mused. 'Has the back been done over as well?' He peered through the windscreen. James and Barbara scrutinised the soggy chaos.

'I don't know,' said James, tilting his head to see if a new angle would tell him.

'I don't think so,' said Barbara. The other two looked at her. 'It looks the same,' she explained. 'Only wetter.'

'You put the kettle on, Jimmy,' said Eddie, opening his door, 'and I'll check out the damage.'

'We may as well come with you,' said Barbara. 'We're already soaked.' The three of them climbed out of the van and dashed to the arch.

They passed through the tunnel and back into the downpour.

'What was that?' Barbara exclaimed whirling around to face the conifers on her right.

'What?' said Eddie, squinting into the garden. The rain ran in rivers down his bald head and plastered his white t-shirt to his body making him look like a butcher's carrier bag.

James craned around the two of them to see what Barbara was looking at. 'I can't see anything,' he said.

'In the trees,' she said in a calmer voice. 'I could've sworn I saw something move.'

'I can't see anything,' James repeated.

'Nothing there,' Eddie boomed. James looked at the squinting giant and wondered if he could even see the trees. The two men continued down the drive. Eddie surveyed the damage, while Barbara continued to scan the trees.

'Looks like your tower's taken a beating too,' said Eddie. The big man suddenly hopped across the churned muddy ground toward the base of the tower, his boots gaining an inch of mud on the way.

'It's alright,' he called out. 'Just scratches. I reckon they're from turning it round.'

'Turning what round?' James shouted back, shielding his eyes from the rain.

'Micro digger. Someone's driven a micro digger all over your garden. They really slung it about, too.'

'How do you know?' James shouted through the rain.

'The tracks,' said Barbara pointing to the nearly washed away indentations of caterpillar tracks. 'Right?' she shouted to Eddie.

'Give that girl an ice cream!' he bellowed back.

'Everyone's a scout,' said James.

'Eh?' Barbara asked, confused.

'It was Frankie who saw the blood on the driveway.'

'Ah.'

'Some of this goes pretty deep,' Eddie called over; he had moved away from the tower and was gesturing to the rents in the ground. 'Whoever it was really went for it. They've gutted your lawn! Gone down three or four feet in places. Definitely more than just scraping the scoop and I'd say the bastards've used a drill on your drive! Right up and down the middle of it!'

'I told you I heard road works!' Barbara cried to James.

'I never said you didn't,' said James. 'Anyway, there's nothing we can do about it now. Let's go inside!'

'Good idea,' Barbara agreed, spitting water from away from her mouth. The two of them turned and headed for the arch.

'Hang on!' Eddie cried, seemingly oblivious to the weather. 'There's something buried here!'

James and Barbara paid no attention. 'Leave it for now. Whatever it is we can check it out later!' James called over his shoulder, not trusting Eddie's eyes in the mud and the rain.

The kitchen was dark as they entered. The three of them had removed their sodden shoes and all but aquaplaned onto the tiled floor of the room. James waved his arms, but the lights stayed off. 'Trouble with your motion sensors?' Eddie asked as he dripped onto the floor.

'Probably the light sensor,' he replied. He threw a grin at Barbara who only just caught it in the gloom. She smiled back. James went to the control panel and the lights flickered into life.

'Once you find a setting that suits you, it's best you leave it,' said Eddie, ''cause when you start messing about with 'em, you can never get 'em right.'

'Yeah, but they were wasteful before.' James grinned at Barbara. 'Anyway, I'll get towels.' He disappeared into the house.

'Nice bloke Jimmy,' Eddie said to Barbara with a grin of his own.

'Yeah, he is,' she replied. They both smiled broadly.

'What?' James asked as he returned and threw each of them a towel.

'Nothing,' said Eddie, already rubbing himself down.

Barbara lifted the towel to her hair, taking a crafty sniff on the way. It was clean. 'Nothing at all,' she said as she rubbed vigorously at her hair.

James offered them dry clothes. Eddie wasn't bothered so it was just the two of them that went to get changed. It was the first time that Barbara had been into the house proper. She was relieved to find that the interior wasn't as bad as the outside suggested but it was still a letdown after the kitchen.

Everything was in gloom. An open doorway on the right led to an unused dining room, and on the left another door stood closed. At the bottom of the stairs, next to the large and dirty front door was another room. This was a messy but comfortable-looking sitting room.

'Just up here,' said James, already halfway up the stairs. Barbara followed.

At the top of the stairs James turned left around the banister and back toward the front of the house. Barbara looked right. There were no windows in the corridor that stretched to a dark and seemingly open space. There was a closed door two thirds of the way down on the right, and in the distance she could just make out the steel shaft in the centre of a column of grey light.

'You coming?' James called out. Barbara nodded. On her way she passed two closed doors on her right. James waited at an open doorway across the landing. 'In here,' he said.

The open doorway led to a bedroom, probably *the* bedroom, James's bedroom. Barbara could see the bed, the mess, the innocent look on his face.

'Erm...' she said.

'What?' James asked, his head full of nothing but clean dry clothes.

The bedroom was big. It held a big bed with big bedside cabinets, and it had a big dressing table, two big wardrobes and a big bookcase. It was a big mess. An open doorway led to a white-tiled room that currently reflected the grey day.

'Sorry about the mess,' said James as he hurried to open the curtains. The grey oozed into the room as he threw the curtains aside. The cheerless illumination did nothing more than highlight the lack of highlights.

'It's fine,' Barbara began. 'It's very nice... very comfy.'

'No it's not,' James laughed. 'Well, it is. Comfy I mean, but it's not nice. When I moved back in I meant to redecorate.' He shrugged. 'Haven't got round to it.'

'No, really, it's fine, it's...'

'A bedroom for an *old* generation!' James mocked the advertising jingle.

'Charming, rustic, retro, characterful...' Barbara countered. 'And...' she floundered.

'Clothes,' James rescued her. 'That's mine,' he pointed to one of the wardrobes. 'Would it be weird to offer you my mum's clothes?' he added, pointing to the other.

Barbara eyed the other wardrobe filled with ghosts. James saw her reaction; he wasn't that shallow.

'Don't worry about it,' he said, 'just thought I should offer. Check the drawer at the bottom of mine; there's some drawstring pants and t-shirts. Grab what you like and you can get changed in the bathroom.' James nodded to the open door. 'Sorry again,' he added.

Barbara just nodded and went to the drawer. Bending over she selected a pair of black pants and what looked like a plain white t-shirt.

Her still-wet clothes outlined her body into even sharper definition. James snapped his eyes away and when Barbara turned he was staring out of the rain-soaked window. She fled to the bathroom.

James went to his wardrobe and selected dry clothes: fresh jeans and a t-shirt. He began to change.

Barbara pulled the cord to turn on the light. The bathroom was lovely. Like the kitchen it had been recently refitted and it was a bright modern space with a huge bath and separate double shower. The circular windows at the front told her that she was above the arch. From outside the unfrosted glass would be glowing white eyes, and if she were to stand at one of them then the arch would look like a pugilistic cat, with one good eye, and one milky white. There was another door which she assumed was the one she had seen from the top of the stairs.

The white t-shirt wasn't plain. It was a polo shirt with a badge on the left breast. She recognised it as the same crest as that worn by Frankie. She checked herself in a full length mirror. The t-shirt was almost down to her knees and she had rolled the bottoms of the pants up so that she could see her feet. Her hair was a mess. Rummaging in a cabinet she found a brush. *His mum's?* she thought. *What the hell, it's only a brush.* Hurriedly detangling her hair, she padded over to the door. Opening it she saw that it did indeed lead to the tower. After a few more furious strokes she replaced the brush and retied her hair.

Slipping out of the door she crept toward the tower. She soon found herself on a two metre-wide walkway of steel grating. The edges of the strips of metal dug into her bare feet uncomfortably. To her right were wooden steps up to a closed trapdoor, and to her left another in the floor which she assumed led to steps down. The middle of the room was empty except for the steel shaft which sank into the dark depths and soared through a two metre hole in the otherwise solid ceiling. Barbara was reminded of a fireman's pole, although, looking over the handrail, it would be a long way to slide.

She was disappointed; it was just a circular space with a walkway. She tried to catch a glimpse of the glass roof but she could only see a sliver of it as something bordered the hole blocking her view. She could hear the rain clearly, though, the eternal rhythm beating on and on.

Looking below she could see nothing. She leant out further, the hand rail crushed against her chest as she strained for a better look and waited for her eyes to become accustomed to the darkness after the bright bathroom.

'Boo!'

'Jesus Christ!' Barbara flailed against the handrail as for a split second she thought that she might fall.

'Sorry, sorry,' said James making a grab for her. 'Sorry, sorry, sorry!' He withdrew when he realised that her new, and very loose fitting clothes would easily come away in his grasping hands.

'You idiot!' Barbara pushed herself away from the handrail and turned on James.

'...sorry, sorry, sorry, sorry...'

'You're not right in the head!'

'...sorry, sorry, sorry, sorry...'

'I could've fallen!'

'...sorry, sorry, sorry, sorry...'

'Could've broken my neck!'

James giggled.

'It's not funny!'

'What's going on?' Eddie lurched into the tower. James was still giggling.

'Stop laughing!'

'What?' demanded a bewildered Eddie.

James stymied his giggles. 'I'm sorry,' he said and then started laughing again.

Eddie looked to the stony-faced Barbara and then to James who was holding his sides. 'What? What's funny?'

'Nothing's funny!' Barbara snapped.

'What did you do, Jimmy?'

'I made her jump, that's all' he managed. It had been a daft thing to do, he knew, but the absurdity of withdrawing his help because her over-sized trousers might fall down fuelled his giggles. And he knew that she wouldn't have fallen because she was just too short to go over the handrail.

He saw that Eddie was on the verge of laughter. This helped him bring his own mirth under control. *Don't laugh*, he willed. *Please don't laugh.*

'I really am sorry,' he said to Barbara, his face almost straight. 'I was just having a bit of fun and I didn't think. But you were never gonna fall off.'

'How do you know?' she demanded.

'Because you're too...'

Barbara waited as James stared at her open-mouthed.

'Too what?' she said. She wanted to tap her foot with impatience but the steel grill was not the surface for it.

'I grew up in this house. I know when someone's gonna fall over the rail, and you were never gonna fall. I promise you I knew that before I did it.' James smiled and held out his hand. Eddie watched. Barbara looked at the proffered appendage.

'Let's have that cup of tea,' she said and strode past him ignoring his hand and the discomfort in her heels from the floor. James watched her go, the neat-again line of hair swaying to and fro across her back.

Back in the kitchen Barbara already had the kettle on by the time James and Eddie caught up. 'When are you calling the police?' she asked James.

'I don't know,' he replied.

'Best to do it sooner,' she said.

'I know, but...' James paused and then plunged on. 'They're gonna ask me who I think might've done it, and I'm not sure I want to tell them.'

'Titz,' Eddie and Barbara said together, and then Eddie added, 'Although I don't know where he got the digger and drill.'

'Yeah,' said James. 'Titz is a prick, and I think I'd rather just forget about it, move on. You know how it goes, I tell the police and it never stops, it'll be constant tit-for-tat. A merry-go-round.'

'But without the merry bit,' Eddie agreed.

'A misery-go-round,' Barbara chipped in, trying to put her annoyance with James behind her.

'Exactly,' James nodded.

'You can't let him get away with it, though,' said Eddie.

'We don't *know* that he did it,' said Barbara. 'I mean he might not have done it. We're assuming a lot. He's a prick, but is he that much of a prick?' James and Eddie looked at her. 'Alright, yes, he did it,' she admitted.

'So what are you gonna do about it?' Eddie demanded.

'I honestly don't know,' sighed James as he landed on his chair.

'Sugar?' Barbara asked.

'No, thanks,' James replied.

'Four, please,' said Eddie sitting down next to James. Barbara spooned sugar into Eddie's mug. The two men sat in silence as Barbara made the drinks. She hitched up her pants several times.

The three sat at the table, mugs of steaming tea in front of them. The lights went out. The drops and rivulets of water on the skylights were suddenly clear. James and Eddie both waved their arms. Nothing happened.

'Told you,' Eddie chuckled. James grumbled his way to the control panel, and the lights came on driving the rain away just a little.

'Well,' Eddie started. 'There's always violence.'

'What?' said Barbara. A nervous giggle drifted from her mouth.

'A good kicking might sort him out, keep him away.'

'Don't be ridiculous!' Barbara retorted, the giggle gone.

'Yeah, you're right,' Eddie conceded. 'Guy like Titz'll keep coming back for more, no matter what you do.'

'That's not what I...'

'Never gonna happen,' James cut in a little too late but better than never. 'The last time me and Titz did any of that the result wasn't a fluke.' James pointed to his face.

'I'd, you know, help out,' Eddie offered. 'And I reckon Frankie'd be up for it. Mebbe we could do enough between us to keep him down. For more than just a week or two I mean.'

'For Christ's sake, I can't believe I'm part of this conversation!'

'Don't worry, Barbara, it's not gonna happen,' James soothed.

Eddie shrugged holding his hands out generously. 'If you change your mind,' he offered.

'Call the police, James.' James nodded to Barbara's demand and went to get the phone.

Dog watched from the conifers as James, standing beneath an umbrella, talked with the police officer. Eddie was there too, he had had one massive hand on the police officer's shoulder for a long time while he gestured toward James. The officer scribbled in his notebook while the damage was pointed out.

Dog had sent the Rottweiler back to his yard and he would have to go soon too, but there was no need to rush; he had already exposed himself once today and didn't want to repeat his mistake. James, Eddie and the police officer disappeared through the arch. Dog let them go; it was time for him to return.

As he left the trees he threw a glance at the Humber Bridge, its grey towers camouflaged by the gloom.

'You should've told him about the assault,' Barbara berated James. The three of them watched from the kitchen window as the police car turned around in the circle of gravel.

'No,' said James as the car disappeared into the arch. 'That's done with.'

'Don't worry, Roger'll take care of you,' Eddie boomed clapping James on the shoulder. 'Anyway, I'm off. Can I give you a lift, Miss Bean?'

'No, thanks,' she replied gesturing out of the window. 'That's my car, there.'

'Terrible weather for driving,' Eddie commented as he checked out the red Mini. 'A little thing like that might struggle. Been raining for hours now, and you know what the Barton road's like for flooding.'

'Um... no I don't,' Barbara admitted.

'I could give you a lift,' James offered. Eddie stood back smiling and winking.

'You drive?' Barbara didn't know why but she was surprised. She ignored Eddie.

'Yes,' James nodded. 'Just the thing for this weather, too.'

'You kids sort it out,' Eddie said cheerily. 'I'm off.' And he was gone. They watched him stride through the weather toward his truck, his t-shirt soaked anew by the time he climbed aboard.

'I'll be okay,' Barbara said eventually. 'You stay here, there's no point in us both going back out in it. Besides I'll need my car for the rest of the week.'

'Doesn't matter,' James said cheerfully. 'I got wet all over again talking to the police. Tell you what, why not let me follow you home just to make sure you're alright?' he said. 'I can see where you live, then,' he added with a smile.

Barbara sat in her car. She had wiped away the rain that had quickly gathered on her arms and face in the dash from the back door. James had run to the unencumbered garage door.

He was only just opening the large metal door after struggling with the key and handle. Barbara laughed at him from the dry comfort of her Mini. James disappeared into the garage. She started up the engine and was about to turn around when she heard the noise. It was a deep bass grumble exacerbated by the confines of the breeze block building. Barbara shifted her car back into neutral and fished an earpiece from the clutter on the passenger seat. She watched the garage as she fitted it to her ear and placed her mobile in the bracket attached to the dashboard. The grumbling got louder but never groaned, as the vehicle edged into the open. It quieted to a hungry rumble as it left its confines. The badge on the aggressive grill declared it to be a Mitsubishi, and that was as far as Barbara could go. It was big, it was black, shiningly, sleekly black. It looked mean, it looked angry. Its huge tyres seemed to grind the gravel out of the way.

'What is that?' Barbara asked rolling her window down as James pulled up next to her. She had to look up and the rain drenched her face. James looked down on her, a cocky smile on his lips. 'It's a Mitsubishi Montero Sport,' he informed her. '2002,' he added.

Barbara shook her head. 'Why?' It was all she could think to say.

'I think dad was having a crisis,' James laughed.

'Saves you having one,' she said eying the polished finish.

James laughed. 'I like to keep it clean,' he admitted.

Barbara turned her little car around and made her way cautiously up the drive. Under the small wheels the damage seemed worse. She was able to go around the worst of it but she still lurched from hole to crack to fissure, to gouge and back to hole again. Behind her James's monstrous vehicle looked to tackle the ground with ease.

Reaching the road, she turned westwards and was able to accelerate away from the lumbering behemoth, but it soon caught up. She slowed down, and wrapped the earpiece around and inside her ear.

'Not the weather for racing,' she said out loud as the wipers fought vainly to keep the windscreen clear. She noticed, with a certain amount of satisfaction, that the driving rain and the mud of the driveway had combined to de-sleek the black car. She reached out and operated her phone.

'Hello?' the voice of Diane friend reached her ear. 'How's the sex? Get plenty done? Have any?'

'No and no,' Barbara answered concentrating on the wet road, barely visible through the downpour. She slowed down some more.

'Oh dear, never mind. What are we drinking?'

'Nothing yet.'

'What's all that noise?'

'The weather. I'm in the car.'

'Not driving?'

'Yes.'

'You're driving and talking to me while it's pissing down, and has been pissing down for hours now?'

'Yes.'

'Well, mind that ark. Noah's a nice fellah but he gets pretty annoyed if you bump his boat. Flood rage they call it.'

'Mmm.'

'Hey, you and your new squeeze could be the human bit of the old two-by-two. You'd mebbe have to kick Noah and his missus off, but that'd be alright 'cause then the boat's yours.'

'What are you on about?' Barbara stopped the rant. 'Anyway, he isn't really a country boy; he's spent the best part of twenty years in Grimsby.'

'Very cosmopolitan,' said the voice, wholly unimpressed. 'Never mind. Where is the country hunk? I assume you're out there?'

'Right behind me.'

'Really? Sorry about the sheep comment, Jimmy.'

'Not behind me, *behind* me. He's following in his car.'

'He can drive, then.'

'Yeah, I was surprised. Don't know why.'

'Two cars? You environmental terrorist, you.'

'As far as the environment's concerned it's three! Great big bloody thing right up my arse.' Barbara regularly checked her mirror. James's car seemed to fill it, a shadow on her green conscience. The voice had gone silent. 'You still there?'

'I'm refusing to pass comment on your previous statement.'

Barbara cast her mind back several seconds. More silence.

'Anyway,' the voice continued. 'Have you got a picture to send me yet?'

'I have. Hang on, I'll just pull over.'

James peered ahead at Barbara's car. He felt protective like he wanted to get close, but he kept his distance. Memories of the four second gap had surfaced, and now he had a mantra that he was certain lasted four seconds, if he said it slowly: Where. The hell. Is. Tilda? Barbara past a tree: Where. The hell. Is. Tilda? James passes the tree. Perfect, he thought. He couldn't get much closer anyway. The bonnet of his ridiculous but quite cool car swallowed Barbara's little red runabout.

She pulled over. James drew to a halt just behind her. His car loomed in the rain, the water bouncing off the black body, the white light of the headlamps clearly visible on an early evening in June. He waited a moment and when she didn't move on he went to see what was wrong.

Barbara pulled her hair free, shaking it quickly as she wound her window halfway down. James bent down to speak to her, the rain already running down his face and dripping off his nose. He screwed up his eyes against the water as he spoke to her. 'What's up?'

'Nothing,' she replied, leaning back to avoid the rain blown into her car by the wind. Her hair covered her ear piece.

'Is he at the window? He is isn't he! In all that rain too. He must be soaked!'   'Why have you stopped then?' said the soaked and wind-buffeted figure of James.

'Just to...' Barbara paused.

'He's very keen isn't he.'

'... get a cloth,' Barbara finished.

'A cloth?' James wiped his face, his fingers squeezing water from his eyebrows, his hair plastered to his forehead.

'A cloth?' said Diane. 'You'll have to give him more than that. He's very handsome. If you ignore the bruises.'

'To wipe the window,' Barbara explained. 'And it was at the bottom of all my junk.' She nodded at her passenger seat. 'Thought I'd best stop to fish it out. Safety first and all that!' she added with a forced chuckle.

'No, you wouldn't want to cause an accident,' said James. Barbara thought he looked peeved. She was right.

'The camera doesn't exactly love him, though,' Diane continued. 'Seems to have missed off his chin.'

Barbara giggled just as a car sped by throwing a wall of spray over James. The wind, the rain and the spray had combined to petrify his face. 'Sorry,' she said. 'I wasn't laughing at you. I was...' Barbara gave up as her best friend cackled in her ear.

'I'll get back to the car,' said James. Barbara nodded her approval; she was getting quite wet herself. As he made to go something caught his eye. 'Are you on the phone?' he nodded at the illuminated mobile fixed to her dashboard.

'What, when I'm driving in this?' Barbara indicated the weather. 'Safety first, remember?'

'That really would be a stupid thing to do,' Diane pointed out. 'Good job you're not that stupid...'

'Why's it on, then?' James asked suspiciously.

None of your business, thought Barbara. 'You have made him stand in the rain,' her best friend reminded her.

'Sat-nav!' Barbara exclaimed. 'It's on to tell me if any roads are closed.'

'Oh, I didn't know mobiles could do that,' said James. 'Good idea' he added approvingly.

'You lying bitch!' the voice teased. 'Poor simple county hunk. Imagine his face when he finds out about electricity. Of course, we've got to get him through steam power first.'

'This one can; it's new,' Barbara nodded to the phone urgently to cover her too-straight face. James smiled at her, misunderstanding why she was trying not to laugh.

'Right,' he said, rubbing his face to a different sheen of wetness. 'Lead the way.' He dashed back to his car.

'That man'll be soaked to his arsehole,' said Diane as Barbara wound up the window.

'Yes he will be,' Barbara agreed, shifting her car into gear. 'I'm gonna go. The roads are not getting any easier; I'd best concentrate.' Barbara hung up and eased out on to the road.

Tilda was impatient by the time the man returned. Her body ached for the outdoors, but she couldn't risk it alone, and now with this weather it seemed unlikely that the man would take her out.

We were lucky to have him, lucky that he was so willing, lucky that he knew what he knew. In just two days things were going to get difficult and we had to decide whether or not to let everyone else know. If we did then the others would find out too, and they would probably realise that it was us that had told everyone.

The man spoke to Tilda of the weather, a very popular subject. Hot, cold, wet, dry all of it enthused about with a miserable passion: nothing was right and everything was wrong. Take all those adjectives and put 'too' in front of them. In all our time with men and dogs we never knew what constituted good weather. *Whatever it wasn't*, we supposed in the end.

The man spoke while his wife prepared the evening meal, which Tilda would share. Our presence was kept from his family, but Tilda was more than welcome.

Barbara drew to a stop in the driveway of her pleasant semi-detached house. Through the violence of the weather James could see that it was neat and tidy and organised: the antithesis of Ivy Arch.

Jumping out of his jeep he dashed over to Barbara.

'Should've brought my brolly,' rued James as he tried to help her. She struggled out of the car, pretending not to have noticed his proffered hand. James dismissed it as being down to the weather. They hurried to the front door. James sheltered gratefully under the overhanging porch as Barbara rummaged in her bag. Producing her key, she fumbled it into the lock. As she opened the door Frankie loomed into view, a plumber's trappings slung about his body. James wasn't used to seeing him without a layer of dust.

'Oh, hi,' said Barbara, slightly startled. In the excitement of the afternoon she had quite forgotten that someone might be in her house. 'You're here late.' The clock in her hallway showed the time to be half past six.

'Yeah,' said Frankie. He was staring at her chest. The damp polo shirt hung heavily from her narrow shoulders and breasts. He snapped his eyes back up to her face. 'I wanted to give myself a good chance to be finished tomorrow, or Friday dinner at the latest.' He nodded as he sucked his lips. 'Anyway, see ya.'

'Okay,' she said, noticing Frankie's attentions but guessing them to be directed at the badge on the shirt rather than its contents. James thought that it was both. Frankie left.

'Well, thanks,' said Barbara to James when they were alone. She used her body to block the doorway.

'Oh,' said James halting abruptly. Her small body was as effective as brick. 'Err… that's okay. Anytime.'

'I'd invite you in but I've got loads to do after this afternoon…'

'Well, yeah of course. Thanks for all your help,' said James as evenly as he could manage, trying to mask his disappointment. 'I'll see you Friday?'

Barbara merely nodded and closed the door.

James turned and slunk back into the rain. He trudged to the end of the short driveway as a familiar small white van pulled up. 'Alright, Jim?' asked Frankie, ignoring the rain battering his face through the open window.

'Yeah, fine.' James forced a smile through the rain.

'Drink? We'll be there at eight o'clock. No cricket practice in this."

'I saw you staring.'

'What?'

'Staring at Barbara's…' James didn't finish the statement.

'No I wasn't. I saw the badge on her t-shirt.'

'Yeah, right.' James turned and walked to his car, making no attempt to hurry through the rain.

Chapter Twelve

Barbara closed the front door. Just that, no problem, it was closed. She leaned against it, her head lolling against the frosted glass.

She went upstairs, showered, changed. Back down, she headed for the kitchen; and shrieked with delight. Her new kitchen was spread before her. The beech work surfaces, the cream cupboards, the glass cabinet, the silver appliances, the new table – it was gorgeous.

"Of course, you'll have to learn to cook." The memory of Diane's taunts threatened to ruin her mood as she opened and closed every drawer and every cupboard and cabinet door. She turned on the taps and then turned them off again, on, off, on, off, giggling at the clear water and the way it flowed differently than from her old taps. She opened the fridge that was too big but she had just had to have it. She marvelled at the chilled cavern. Excitedly she grabbed a mug left on the draining board by one of the workmen and filled it straight from the fridge. She sipped at the icy cold water as she opened and closed the fridge door. It was so big that the frigid light filled the kitchen.

She dashed off and came back with the kettle. 'Where, where, where…?' She put it next to the sink, under the window, next to the back door. 'Ah!' She placed it right in between the doorway to the hallway and the sink, halfway along a stretch of beech worktop. Screeching with excitement, she dashed out and dashed back, out, back, out, back until the kitchen was filled with her things. For some she found homes quickly but most were piled high on the kitchen table.

James thumped down the stairs in his third set of clothes that day. In the kitchen he started to throw together a meal. He slammed pots and chopped a little too vigorously, placing his fingers in jeopardy.

It had stopped raining. James stared up at the dark grey. The sun must have poked a few holes in the cloud and the top of the tower was shining in the glare of soft spotlights. James glanced down to the tunnel of the arch. It yawned empty. Still no Tilda. He put fresh food down for her.

Tilda sat with the man. He was engrossed in the television which showed the film *Invasion of the Body Snatchers*. The night before he had watched *Star Trek: The Motion Picture*. The man watched both avidly even though none of the scenes seemed new to him. Tilda was unimpressed. He would go out soon and then the man's wife would select a film. Tilda looked forward to it.

I can do it, Barbara assured herself as she poured over a recipe book. The book was old but pristine in a dusty flicked-through-once style.

'So what are we cooking?' Diane asked. Barbara had her ear piece back in. She took a sip of red wine.

'Fried mustard-and-herb-coated chicken!'

'Sounds nice.'

'Oh. No, forget that, it's fried…'

'There was a clue in the title.'

'… in an *inch* of oil!' Barbara resumed her flicking.

'What did the country hunk think of your new kitchen?'

'He didn't see it.'

'Why not?'

The riffling stopped. 'Here we go: *Simple Stroganoff.*'

'Sounds suitable.'

'I've only got stewing steak, though,' Barbara mused.

'Stroganoff is fillet steak; strips of fillets steak. What you have is lumps.'

'Lumps'll do!' Barbara declared. She went to her old fridge still sitting in the front room.

'Well?' said the voice. 'Why didn't he see the kitchen? Or shouldn't I ask?' Barbara was in awe of the way her friend could wink through a telephone.

'I didn't let him in. Onions? Onions?' Barbara sorted through the boxes of ready meals stacked on the wire shelves. 'Ah!' She returned to the kitchen, her arms loaded with packets of meat, mushrooms, sour cream and onions.

'Why not?'

Barbara studied the book. 'Wait a minute; I need to use white wine or cider.'

'White wine it is then.'

'Oh yes.' Barbara went back to the old fridge grabbed the three bottles of white wine and returned to the kitchen. She put two bottles in the new fridge – they looked lonely in the cavernous space – and left one next to the hob.

'Well?' the voice tried to bring her back to James.

'Hang on; I need to cut the onion into half moons.'

'Which recipe book is it?'

'Delia.'

'A name you can trust.'

'Hope so. Okay. Half moons.' Barbara glared at the page fiercely as if trying to make the book do it for her. 'Forgot the saucepan!'

'Important in cooking.'

Barbara swigged at a glass of red wine and grabbed a saucepan from the table. She placed it reverently on her new gas hob and began to fumble with the controls.

'Anyway!' Diane dragged her away from the newness. 'Why wasn't the podgy Adonis given the chance to ogle your new shiny bits?'

The gas ring flared to life. Barbara had squatted to see underneath the pan and her mouth formed into an impressed o. 'Oooo,' she said.

'Oi!' Diane demanded.

'What? I just didn't want to invite him in. What's wrong with that?' She cast about the kitchen. 'Butter? Butter?' She dashed to the old fridge.

'Not aces. You should have built an extension instead of a kitchen, made that house of yours into a proper tower. Time to wake up, sleeping beauty.'

James, shoulders slumped, prepared his meal. The sun bounced from the tower top to the kitchen window and created speckles and blemishes of ever-changing light. James cast shadows on unwashed pots left in the sink. Crumbs fell to the floor. Work tops were left greasy. A place for one was set at the table.

Barbara hurried back with butter. She sliced off a corner and dropped it into the centre of the hot pan. It sizzled as it slid to the edge, melting and collapsing as Barbara swung the pan to and fro to cover the bottom with hot spitting butter. Diane waited for Barbara's reply. 'I don't know,' said Barbara. 'Maybe we're going too fast.'

'You've only seen him twice! Any slower and your mating ritual would be in double maths with a date in the canteen for the first round of fumbles,' said the voice, and then added: 'Mmm, pink custard on chocolate concrete.'

'Don't be ridiculous,' Barbara retorted. 'It's brown custard on chocolate concrete.'

'Each to their own. Puddings aside, I don't think you could describe your romance as 'whirlwind'.'

'You know what I mean: I've been in his house; I've eaten in his kitchen; I've got soaked in a field with him; I've been in his bedroom…'

'Oooo.'

'… got changed in his bathroom; I've worn his clothes; I've rung the police with him; I've been followed home by him…'

'Talked with him, laughed with him, shared with him, snotted on him, plotted with him…'

'Listened to him consider violence.'

'Really?'

'Him and Eddie, Eddie Fiss, the big builder guy, we're talking about sorting Titz out.'

'Was this James's idea?'

'No, Eddie's. And James quickly squashed the idea.'

'So what's the problem?'

James sat alone at his table and ate his meal. He opened a bottle of wine and poured himself a glass, drank it quickly and poured another.

'I know, I know. I'm being stupid.' Barbara dropped the half moon onions into the pan. 'Wooden spoon?' She scanned the kitchen. 'Wooden spoon!' She dug into the pile on the table, snatching a drink of wine as she did it. She retrieved a wooden spoon and set about the onions desperately, afraid that she might have burnt them. 'It's just that he seemed to be…' she trailed off as she stirred the onions. The edges of the half moons and some of the layers in the middle had browned. She had no idea if that was right or not.

'What?'

'I don't know. When we met on Sunday he seemed hopeless and nice, and today he seemed…' Barbara gave up again.

'Hopeful and not nice?'

'No. Well, yes. I don't know. He's still nice. Maybe it's the dog.' Barbara made to tip the onions onto a plate and stop herself mid-tip. 'Plate? Plate!'

'What about the dog?' Diane asked. Barbara sipped wine and rummaged for a plate. Returning the hob, she rescued the onions once more.

'He had Tilda with him on Sunday but not today. She's a lovely dog.'

'Lovelier than him?'

'No. He's nice with or without the dog.' Barbara poured the onions onto the plate and then returning the pan to the hob she turned the heat up to full, the flames leaping at her command. 'But is *nice* enough?'

'It helps. And don't you think that this lack of hopelessness might have something to do with you? You've brought him out of his shell.'

'Well I want to put him back in a bit!' Barbara wailed as she dropped the lumps of meat into the pan. They flashed and sizzled and spat as she attacked them with her wooden spoon.

'That's ridiculous.'

'No, his jeep is ridiculous; it's a tank! And I didn't need him to follow me…'

'Nice of him, though.'

'… and he was getting judgemental over the phone…'

'You did lie to him.'

'Whichever! I didn't need him there; it was only a bit of rain. I can do things for myself. I'm a big girl!'

'Really? Aren't you supposed to be at the gym tonight?'

'Shit! I forgot.' Barbara pushed, prodded, stabbed and stirred the meat with a new fury. She grabbed the onions and poured them back into the pan. 'And why do I want to get together with a guy from school who I can barely remember, except that he followed his best mate's girlfriend around like a lost puppy? And so what if he's nice? I don't care about nice.'

'You don't care about much.'

'That's not fair.'

'Have you heard from your mum and dad? Have you heard from anyone but me and James?'

Barbara sighed. 'Cooking takes too long. I'm hungry now,' she moaned. 'Salt and pepper?' She drank more wine as she sorted through the table.

'At least he's thinking about you,' said Diane.

'That's how it starts,' she replied, vigorously shaking salt and pepper into the pan. 'It's like that time with whatsisname.'

'Who?'

'You know, thingamabob.'

'Oh, him.'

'He started out nice and attentive, thoughtful even. And then he bought me shoes for God's sake! And to top it off he talked in the cinema!'

'Bring back hanging!'

'You can't talk in the cinema,' Barbara stated flatly.

'It is rude,' Diane conceded.

'Rude? It goes past *rude* and all the way to wrong!'

'But you did give whatsisface two weeks.'

'Two weeks and he's buying me shoes? Control freak or gay. Or both.' Diane was quiet while Barbara poured the white wine into the pan. She stirred the mixture together, the heat still on full.

'Are you still going on Friday?'

'I think so,' said Barbara, refilling her glass with red wine. 'Be silly not to; he's nice.' They both laughed. Barbara stirred her Simple Stroganoff as it was brought back to the boil. She looked to the book wondering when she was supposed to add the mushrooms. She read the words 'simmer for an hour and a half'.

'Oh bollocks!'

Tilda settled her head on the man's wife's lap, relaxing as she stroked her head. The wife had put a new DVD into the machine. It was *Only You* starring Marrisa Tomei and Robert Downey Junior. Tilda liked it, just as she had enjoyed *When Harry Met Sally* the previous evening. The wife talked to her throughout both films, explaining the need for the characters to meet, fall in love, fall out of love, and finally come together for the happy ending; this was very important. That these films seemed to deal with lies and deceit and identity crises, and that the fog of romance and the haze of sexuality clouded everything didn't seem to bother the wife; the cloud was cleared by the chase. This seemed to be as important as the happy ending, in fact it *was* the happy ending: a glorious but desperate charge down the home straight and the affections of your loved one the ribbon.

All this superfluous nonsense was worth it for the chase. Without the dramatic tremors to their relationship, the sight of Billy Crystal running through the streets of New York to Meg Ryan on New Year's Eve would have been trivial. The wife promised Tilda that there was another chase at the end of *Only You,* and that it would include cars and an airport and the revealing of identities. Tilda looked forward to it.

Barbara sprawled on her sofa, her chin on her chest, her eyes staring sulkily at her open lap-top sitting smugly on the coffee table. An empty ready-meal packet sat next to it. She was struggling, she was tired and she had written nothing all day. She couldn't go to bed until she had written something. She leant forward and typed 'something'. The word was pasted on the screen. She flopped back sighing then sat up again and highlighted the word. She stared at it for few moments and then hit *delete*. Flop. Sit up. Flop. Sigh. Sit up. Deep breath. She reached for the keys.

Friday: should I go? Of course I should. Why wouldn't I? He's a nice guy. More than nice, he's sweet, and not in a disinteresting way. And it's great that he's gaining confidence. If I'm honest a man of his age without some confidence would be a bit of a squib. I think he's been a squib in his time; he's certainly been a waster. I guess that's how nice guys stay single till they're thirty five, by squibbing their way through life. Do I have time for a squib? I think that he's been there and done that as far as wasting and squibbing go and this business with Tilda is helping sort him out. Not sort him out, that sounds bad. Help him I mean. Not that he needs help…

Yes he does. We all need help to get on, to get past things, to live without things, to not let talking in a cinema rule our lives.

Forget that, some things can never be forgiven.

I'll go on Friday and I'll enjoy myself. He will be charming and witty and engaging and interesting. We *will enjoy ourselves.*

Should I book a taxi?

I might not need to…

Barbara smiled at the screen.

With only half an hour or so till dusk the sun gave up as the grey returned in force. It grew darker in James's kitchen. Extra lights were supposed to come on. He sighed and moved, slightly unsteadily, past the empty wine bottle to the control panel. He had decided against a night in the Pipe; he couldn't face the interrogation from Eddie, and Frankie, he'd seen enough of Frankie to last a month.

Spaceships. The man was clearly unhinged.

James returned to his washing up and attacked the pots with a sponge. He glanced up at the pitter-patter of rain against the kitchen window. Water droplets had already formed and were quickly running together, reflecting the kitchen's light. The outside was gone.

Dog watched the pathetic figure of James move about the kitchen. He didn't make any effort to conceal himself, only using the arch as minimal shelter from the rain.

Dog knew that while drunk, James's defences, such as they were, were down. He knew that he could just step inside; it would be that easy, as simple as putting one paw in front of the other. He watched James bend over the sink. It would be easy. Thousands had fallen foul of such temptation, and some had died. So many of those who had tried were still too weak to leave home, that great yard trapped in the dark. The yards of the houses of Humberside were so much smaller, so unimaginably smaller, but they were open and free compared to that vast space. What was the point in infinity if you had nowhere to go? Dog stared at James and swallowed the temptation. *Not yet*. There were those who were working on a way, but if they didn't find something by Friday... well, there weren't enough dogs to go around. Some, he knew, had reasoned that their best weapon might be their own existence. Dog thought that that was a waste and didn't think it would achieve anything.

He watched James. He also knew that he could whine at the back door and when James opened it, he could knock him down, tear his throat out and let him bleed to death. He could call on the Rottweilers and have them make such a mess of his corpse that no one would ever know who he was – ever. But what would that achieve? They needed access to James and his house, not his blood or his meat. Dog watched as James finally gave up on the washing up and staggered through the kitchen to the house.

Chapter Thirteen

James stared at the ceiling of his bedroom. The sun had not yet hit the window so it was early, cloudy or still raining, or all three, or just two. He had no idea.

Had it rained last night? He looked at the ceiling. Would it look so dirty if it were lighter in here? He strained to hear rain on the window but he couldn't be sure. James filled his head with trivial thoughts in an effort to ignore the pain, to prolong getting up. Hangover. Another hangover. *This is no good*, he told himself. *Stuff to do. People to impress.*

Out of bed, into dressing gown, down the stairs. Slowly.

He shuffled into the kitchen, squinting in anticipation of the lighting. It remained off. James opened his eyes gratefully. He put down fresh water.

Kettle. Sit. Stand. Make coffee. Sit. Slowly.

He sipped at his drink. The vast wooden table stretched before him.

James fell out of the shower and stumbled to his bedroom. It was still dark, the curtains still closed, the ceiling still a shadow that covered the details of the real dirt and dust.

Stuff to do. He was unsure of how it had happened. He was standing in the dining room with a duster in his hand, staring out of the window. A white van moved along the road, past the front gate. James thought that it wasn't moving very quickly, that it seemed to be just setting off. James's thoughts weren't to be relied upon at the moment, and so he didn't. He bent to his task, dusting and rubbing his way into Barbara's affections, when movement caught his eye making him look out of the window again.

Tilda was picking her way down the drive.

James spotted the bandaged hind leg. Apart from making her way across uneven and suddenly unfamiliar ground, she was making her way confidently, jumping over puddles, not at all bothered by that bandage. She walked as if nothing had happened, as if she hadn't been missing for two days and was now returning wounded but recovered. James dropped his duster as Tilda trotted under the arch. The day's first drops of rain hit the window as James turned and headed for the back door.

'And just where have you been, young lady?' he asked as Tilda walked into the kitchen and straight to her bowl. She slaked her thirst then walked into the house. 'Hang on,' he called after her. 'Where've you been?'

He followed her through to the sitting room where she climbed onto the settee and turned on the spot until she was satisfied and lay down. James watched her settle. If he didn't know better he would say that she looked like she was making sure she could see the television.

'Welcome home,' he said and went back to his dusting.

Susan sat, slumped, on a steel chair. Her head lolled. We were amazed, surely she was too uncomfortable for sleep? But sleep she did. Errol watched the slow passage of drool from the corner of her mouth.

Scud watched Susan go home. She had worked the night shift. A quick turn-around that she wasn't happy about. Her silent sulks and quiet tantrums had made for a vaguely interesting study - any sign of discontent was surely a good thing; the more these people wanted the less they needed to be offered. But she was increasingly unimportant. Friday night was the problem and, other than realising something was going to happen, she knew nothing. Scud was beginning to think that something would have to be done. It was his turn to be inside tomorrow. Perhaps an extraordinary demonstration for Susan's benefit would bring someone more aware of what was going on. If it was serious then he would need to make sure that the Doberman was safe – and available.

He looked across to the Humber Bridge the source of their woes and the cause of an incredible opportunity.

Barbara opened the door to Frankie. 'Just you today?' she asked him.

'Yeah,' he said. 'Bub's busy on another job, and Jane's done her bit.'

'Yes, I love my kitchen!'

'Well, I can't take any credit for that,' said Frankie, almost sheepishly. 'Did you cook yourself a nice meal last night?'

'Sort of,' she said. 'Anyway, I'll let you get on. Shall I put the kettle on?'

'Yes, please,' said Frankie, slowly and perhaps carefully. He had stepped inside and now stood awkwardly in the entrance hall while

Barbara went to the kitchen. She glanced over her shoulder; Frankie was just making his way to the stairs.

Later Barbara sat in her study staring at her monitor. She had taken a drink to Frankie and her suspicions had been confirmed. She sighed. She sighed again at her sigh, frustrated that that was all she seemed to do lately. She grabbed her phone and dialled quickly.

'You writing types don't do a lot of writing,' said Diane.

'I've got a problem,' said Barbara quickly. 'The new plumber's gone doe-eyed.'

'Is he nice? Is he fit? Is he old, young, clever, dumb? Short, tall, big, small?'

'Not the point,' said Barbara. 'Although he is, fit I mean. I think.' Barbara pondered for a moment. 'He's weird.'

'"Weird"? Sounds interesting.'

'Not weird. Odd.'

'Odd sounds interesting too.'

'Not odd. Intense. Determined. Driven. Focused…'

'Not necessarily negative things.'

'Not necessarily, no. But he seems a bit empty with it. There doesn't seem to be a point to his intensity. He doesn't seem ambitious or dedicated to plumbing. Should there be some direction to that kind of focus?'

'Probably.'

'I don't think he's…'

'What?'

'He doesn't seem real.'

'Why not?'

'Don't know.'

'Still sounds interesting.'

'I think he might be crazy.'

'Hey there,' said James into the phone as Barbara answered. He was in the kitchen in Ivy Arch.

'Oh hi,' she said cheerily. 'Is it Friday already? Am I late?' she forced a laugh. *Lame*, she chided herself.

James panicked: *she thinks I'm hassling her.* 'Tilda's back!' he blurted out quickly.

'Really? That's great!'

'Yeah, she came back this morning.'

'Is she alright?'

'She seems to be, but she's got a bandage on her back leg, so she's been in the wars.'

'Who bandaged it?'

'That's just it, I don't know. She trotted up the drive this morning as if she'd never been gone. I felt a bit miffed truth-be-told, cheeky little thing just sits and looks at the telly.'

'Maybe she's been kidnapped by the media in some brainwashing experiment to get pets watching the telly. Or a dog food company made her watch ads over and over and they stuck pins in her back leg if she chose the wrong brand. You've seen *Clockwork Orange?*'

'Yeah someone's taken over my dog to make her into a model citizen and buy the right tins!'

Tilda watched from the doorway to the house.

'She's here now. I'd swear she was laughing at me!' James guffawed into the phone.

The two chatted easily on the phone. James relaxed.

James stood on the landing outside his bedroom door, a bright purple vacuum cleaner held limply in his hands. It had been a busy day: the dining room, entrance hall, sitting room, stairs and landing had all fallen under his brutal new regime. He had dusted, scrubbed, polished, tidied, vacuumed, shifted, vacuumed some more and cleaned like a man possessed, which of course he was. Not by us but by a need to impress. And now that need had brought him to the threshold of his bedroom and its clutter and dust and dog hairs. A decision: clean the room and not need it or leave it and not dare to use it. Putting the decision off, he headed for the tower, dragging the vacuum cleaner with him.

Tilda settled onto the settee. She was full, pleasantly full after her tea and ready for one last peaceful evening. James looked at her impatiently; he had just told her to come down from the cushions he had slavishly de-haired that afternoon. Tilda had no intention of obeying; she was comfy and she was hoping for more of the head rubbing thing dispensed by the man's wife. James reluctantly accepted that he wasn't going to win this particular stand-off.

He pulled a DVD from a shelf on the wall. Tilda raised her head, her interest piqued. James put the disc into the machine and came to settle next to Tilda. She shifted herself to get her head on his lap and still have a view of the television. James put a hand on her head. He smelled clean and freshly showered after his day of domestic labour.

The screen flickered to life. *Two Weeks Notice*. We soon forgot the missing apostrophe as we acquainted ourselves with Hugh Grant and Sandra Bullock.

Dog watched the lights from the television flickering on the window get brighter as the evening wore on and the rain continued to pour. The sun had not been seen all day, and now the roads were streams and the fields huge puddles. Dog's own yard was centimetres deep that afternoon when he went back for his meal. The family had even allowed him to eat inside because of it. They had soon sent him back into the rain afterwards.

She was in Ivy Arch. Dog knew, he could smell her.

He wondered across the front garden to the former lawn so impressively dismembered by the angry man. If his level of bitterness and hatred could be harnessed then it could useful. Dog went to the spot pointed out by Eddie Fiss the previous afternoon.

As he investigated, a plan began to form.

'Are you finishing today?' said Barbara to Frankie. It was half past four and she had tentatively stepped into the bathroom for the first time since bringing him a drink that morning.

Frankie looked apologetic. 'Sorry, no,' he said. 'I'll need to come back in the morning.'

'Oh, okay.' She scanned the bathroom; it looked finished to her. 'Can I use the bath?' She indicated the half-full pristine tub glowing beneath gleaming tiles.

'Not yet,' Frankie shook his head. He looked her up and down as he did it. 'The grout's not dry. You should leave it for at least a few days till it's dry and make sure it's settled.'

'Why's it half full?'

'There's some who'd say it was half empty,' Frankie said and cast out a chuckle that was obviously alien to him. Barbara didn't join in. 'It's to get the give in the sealant,' he said, swallowing his chuckle. 'Put the silicone down with an empty bath and the first time you fill it up it splits.'

'Ah,' Barbara nodded. 'Good idea.' She sucked her lips and left.

Later, when Frankie had gone, she checked the bathroom. It definitely looked finished: the tiles shined, the toilet and the bath

117

gleamed. The man was coming on Monday to lay the lino and it was definitely ready for him. There was a single floorboard raised. She peered into the shadows of the unfamiliar stratum that existed without her ever realising. Dust, dirt, and timbers surrounded water pipes that definitely looked finished.

Chapter Fourteen

The phone was ringing when James hauled himself and several fit-to-burst carrier bags into the kitchen. Keys swung from his mouth as he looked across the table to the phone clinging to the wall. He lugged the bags onto the table. The phone was still ringing. He took the keys out of his mouth and dropped them next to the bags The phone was still ringing. He walked around the table. The phone was still ringing. He reached out to pick up the receiver. The phone stopped ringing. *Typical.*

James noticed Tilda standing in the doorway to the house. 'Hello,' he said. 'Have you been out since you got back?' Tilda walked to her bowl and drank. 'Well, the door's open.' James set about the shopping while Tilda ventured outside.

An almighty barking raised James from the bags and he dashed outside. Tilda stood in the middle of the gravel circle, her head and tail low. James came out shouting and hurried to Tilda's side. He spent a second looking her over before glancing down the driveway; three dogs reached the front gate and fled onto the road.

'Who were they?' he asked Tilda. He reached out his hand to her, the hackles on her rain-soaked neck all stood on end and she quivered from nose to tail.

'Are they the ones that hurt you?' he asked. He stroked her head and her back, trying to soothe her. Eventually she calmed down and came back into the house. James closed the back door. *Mystery half solved*, he thought. *We know whodunit but not whydunit.* James shook his head; they were dogs, and dogs fought. There's no mystery. He made a mental note to see about getting the front gate fixed to try and discourage such visitors.

The shopping put away, James ate his lunch and considered what he should cook for Barbara. He had gone shopping without a plan which, he knew now, had been a mistake. He had rice, pasta and potatoes, cabbage, peas, and carrots, beef, chicken and pork. He had basil, thyme and coriander, peppers, chillies and onions, red wine, white wine and beer – lager and bitter. He hadn't bought any soft drinks. 'Maybe she'll get a taxi,' he said to Tilda, who was sticking by his side. 'Maybe she won't need to.' He smiled.

After lunch he was standing on the landing staring into his bedroom again. He carried two large empty wine glasses. He turned and headed for the tower.

Tilda settled herself in the living room. She felt better now, less nervous. She had followed James around for a while but his own nerves and the stench of pheromones was putting her on edge all over again. Tonight would be difficult enough, she knew. She settled down to rest before the action began.

It was still early afternoon when the phone started ringing again. James was halfway down the stairs and still enjoying the sensation of clean carpet on his bare feet when it started. He hurried into the living room.

'Hello,' he said into the receiver.

'Have you got that mobile yet?' Eddie sounded irritated.

'I'm not all that bothered about...'

'Get one! I need to get hold of you if you're gonna be working for me!'

'... having one,' James finished lamely.

'Jane and Bub've gone home ill,' Eddie's tone suggested that illness was something that shouldn't happen to his staff, 'and Frankie's still not finished at your would-be bird's house. I need you to help out this afternoon.'

'Well, I would but I'm kinda busy. I'm cooking...'

'Buy her a kebab; she'll love you for it. Right now I want you at...' Eddie's voice flooded over James, washing away all resistance. He found himself dutifully scribbling an address onto a piece of paper and agreeing to be there within half an hour.

'What can I do, though?' he asked a little desperately.

'You can help out!'

And that was that. James pulled on his shoes and trudged across the puddles in the gravel circle. The rain had eased off a little so he wasn't quite soaked by the time he got the garage door open. He made another mental note to put the lawn mower away when he got home. It had been outside for a week now. He climbed into his jeep and set off.

The afternoon's work helped the time pass quickly for James. He fetched, he carried and he got to drive Eddie's Ford Ranger. It made the decision of what to cook easier too: he would have just enough time for a curry, probably a jalfrezi.

Eddie worked like a demon as he picked up the slack left by Jane, Bub, Frankie and Titz. James sensed a temper in him that was building as he muttered about having to work Saturday. But James was impressed at the single-minded dedication. His work was a wall for his frustrations with his crew.

'That's about it, then,' said Frankie to Barbara. She looked around the bathroom; apart from the floorboard being replaced it looked no different to last night. 'It's all yours,' he continued. 'Sorry it took so long and sorry again about the business with… well, you know,' he finished awkwardly.

'That's okay. None of that was your fault,' said Barbara. She thrust her hands into her pockets. 'Well, thanks for everything. Does Eddie send the bill, or should I settle up now, with you?'

Frankie raised his eyebrows, and for a long moment didn't answer. Barbara regretted her choice of words.

'Eddie'll deal with it.' Frankie was holding his bags rigidly, gripping the handles tightly. He looked like he was building to something. Oh shit, thought Barbara. *Don't do it*, she willed to him, *not now, not here. I don't want to hear the confessions of my plumber.* Frankie was opening his mouth.

'Anyway!' Barbara jumped in. 'I'll let you get on. You must need to get on. You must be so busy what with having to cover for… for…' she was jabbering and now stammering over Titz's name. 'Anyway. Busy. You must be very,' she took a deep breath, 'busy.' She smiled and left the bathroom.

She was down the stairs and holding the front door open before Frankie had even reached the top step.

Errol looked at Susan from behind the mesh of the cage. She had switched back to the day shift, and now, with sleep that could be counted in minutes, she felt harried and rushed.

The greyhound was not as strong as the Doberman, but here in this cage that didn't really matter. He could feel the power in the dog's legs. It would be interesting to make Errol run.

Errol sighed. Inwardly he was torn between laughing at this wretched woman and howling in frustration. *Look at me!* he silently willed to her. She was buried in her notes and printouts. He made the dog paw at the mesh and cocked its narrow head. He knew that this looked cute, that it would be enough to distract her if she would only look. Paw down, other paw up, head cocked to the other side. Still no reaction. Another sigh, this time from down below. He waited.

Although he'd been in captivity for several days, Errol's previous diet had left an indelible stain on his digestive system. As he waited for a reaction, Susan riffled through her papers and jabbed at her keyboard. She was glaring at her monitor when it hit her.

'Jesus Christ! What are we feeding you?' And finally she looked directly at the caged dog: head cocked, one ear up, paw held out. She stopped what she was doing.

'What are you doing?' she asked a dog. Did she expect an answer? She checked her monitor and the fresh printouts. She looked back to the dog that now had its front paws on the mesh and stood on its hind legs. 'You're doing... stuff,' she breathed. Errol barked. Susan jumped and excitement glazed her eyes.

'Guns,' James repeated to Eddie.

'What about them?' The big man asked. He had avoided the question the first time, James was sure.

'Has he got any?'

'Who?'

'Frankie.' James was cautious. He knew that Eddie was sensitive about his brother. More than sensitive, Eddie thought that his brother was a loon just as much as everyone else and those fraternal feelings were getting in the way. It was a problem for the whole group.

'He told you: he's got two shot guns.'

'Yeah I know, but he mentioned hand guns.'

'No he didn't.'

'Yes he did.'

'No, Jimmy, he didn't.'

'So he hasn't got a gun? Other than the shot guns?'

'No. Why?' Eddie's defences were up. He was suddenly very tall.

'No reason,' said James, and bent to mixing the plaster. It was strange doing the same job with Frankie's brother. The work was the same but it was an altogether different experience. Eddie chatted, whistled and sang.

They worked in silence for several minutes.

'Not even under his bed?'

'How the fuck would I know what's under his bed?'

They worked in silence for several more minutes.

'You've never looked then?' James asked innocently. Eddie stared at him, his shoulders squared.

'Listen, Jimmy,' Eddie began firmly. 'Frankie's a funny bugger: aliens, guns, football, fags... he obsesses about things, we all know that. But he's harmless.' Eddie raised a hand to forestall James's protest that he had never suggested Frankie was harmful. 'He hasn't got any guns. I don't need to look round his house to know that.'

'Don't you live together?' asked James, surprised.

'No,' said Eddie, simply. Was there something in that 'no', thought James.

'You both live in Never, though yeah?'

'We live next door but one with us mum in the middle,' said Eddie. 'Right in the middle of the main street.' James wasn't surprised at that. Baron Fiss and his family would need a central location to keep an eye on the fiefdom. He bent back to his mixing.

'I mean how could he get a hand gun?' Eddie threw the question into the air, not caring where it might land. 'And even if he could get one, what's he gonna do with it? There's nothing he *can* do with it! Can't shoot it anywhere, so what's the point?'

'Unless he's got one with a silencer!' James blurted out, and immediately regretted it. Eddie went back to his wall and James to his mixing and watching. Scrape, scrape, smooth. Scrape, scrape, smooth.

They worked in silence for several minutes.

'Why don't you bring Barbara out with us tonight?'

'Bit much for a first date don't you think?'

'Well, there's only me, Frankie an' Ziggy goin' now. Could do with a couple extra.' James understood Eddie's recalcitrance. A night out with a laconic Englishman and a heavy metal Pole didn't sound like an evening of wit and entertaining conversation.

'You'll be alright,' said James. 'Lose 'em in a gay bar.'

'I just might.' Eddie sighed heavily.

'Of course, you could be doing some writing,' said Diane. 'You know, work, your chosen profession, your bread and butter? Think of all the sex those characters aren't having - they must be going out of their minds!'

'Never mind that,' said Barbara. She stood in her bedroom in front of a full-length mirror. Her hair was tied back revealing the ear piece. 'What am I gonna wear?'

'Who for, Mr Nice or Mr Interesting?'

'For me,' said Barbara indignantly, and then added flatly, 'For when I meet Mr Nice. And Frankie's not interesting, he's…'

'Crazy?'

'I don't know. Anyway, forget about him, tonight's about me and James.'

'So you've not fallen out with him? Or are we merely keeping the doves alive for the pot?'

'No. And I never did fall out with him.' Barbara shrugged her shoulders at her reflection to deflect the accusation. 'He just needs to...' she paused.

'What?'

'Lighten up and tighten up.'

'Eh?'

'Well, you know, he's a nice guy so he doesn't need to be so nervous. I mean it's endearing at first but then it's like, okay stop now. I like you, you like me, so, yay!' Barbara waved her hands above her head for her reflection's benefit. 'That'll do. It's not a game. But at the same time he needs to stop acting so rashly, so like a... like a... tit.'

'Not much then.'

'Hey, the man's got potential, and that's a good place to start. How many single men in their mid-thirties can you say that about?'

'He's not a house waiting to be redecorated. You can't walk in and say this'll do but I need to change the fireplace.'

'Yeah I can,' said Barbara holding a dress up for her reflection. 'And he does need the fireplace changing, maybe even ripping out, but I'm not talking about gutting the place, his house is mostly sound.'

'You're a cold woman.'

'No, I'm a thirty five year-old woman,' Barbara retorted. She held up a shirt and skirt for inspection. 'And you were right, I'm alone. I'm a first-time-buyer who can't afford to be too choosey.' She sighed. 'If the house isn't bad and the renovation isn't gonna cost too much then it can be a home. I've got to go for it.'

'That's the wrong reason. That's a lot of wrong reasons. We're really taking the rom out of your rom-com.' The voice fell silent for a moment. Barbara held up another outfit. 'And the com too,' Diane added.

'Look at me,' she said to the voice in her ear. Her reflection held a t-shirt and jeans. 'I've lost the week because some guy who happens to be nice happens to pay some attention to me. We *both* need to grow up.'

Susan was treated to an incredible half-hour. Errol was put through his paces as she ran simulations, studied data and tested the dog.

'Lift your left paw,' she said with the triumphal flourish that comes with successful repetition. The printer clicked and clacked away, producing a substantial account of the half-hour. He didn't sigh as he lifted the left paw for the seventh time. He had lifted its right paw six times, shaken its head six times and nodded its head six times. The cycle never changed: left, right, shake, nod. It was demeaning but that didn't matter; this would work. 'Lift your right paw!' He could hear the exclamation mark. He lifted the right paw. Seconds later he shook his head.

James was home. He had washed off the afternoon's dust and dressed. He wore a pinny to protect a pair of trousers and a casual shirt.

It was half past six. Under the glare of the clock he chopped and sliced like a maniac: peppers, chillies, onion, garlic and chicken all juggled and arranged into a jalfrezi – he hoped.

He stopped. Tilda was watching him. He fed Tilda.

'Am I being silly?' he asked the dog as he fired the gas hob to life. Tilda ate. 'Am I too old for first dates?' James tutted to himself and shook his head. 'I'm thirty five not ninety.' He put a frying pan on the hob and poured in oil.

'Ginger…' he muttered to himself as he rummaged through a cupboard. 'Ah, ginger!' He placed the oddly shaped root on the work surface next to his chopping board. 'Turmeric?' He checked his spice rack and produced one jar, then another. 'And chilli powder.' His hand paused. 'Salt?' he asked himself. 'No, no need.' He went to a different cupboard and returned with a tin of tomatoes.

He dropped the onion and garlic into the oil. He liked that bit, the beginning when the first pieces of food landed and began to sizzle. He stirred the onions and garlic to fry them evenly. Quarter to seven. Tick tock, tick tock.

They hadn't set a time for Barbara's arrival. To James Friday night meant seven o'clock, but she could be here at any moment. His plans had gone awry and now not everything would be ready when she arrived.

Is it anal to want everything to be perfect? James stopped. He had no idea if he had said that aloud. He looked at Tilda who was heading back into the house.

The chicken was added to the pan and began its own sizzling journey from raw to cooked.

James stirred the whitening meat into the onion and garlic and added the turmeric and chilli powder.

Ten to seven. Still not Friday night yet. He stirred the contents of the pan and added the tin of tomatoes. He stirred until it came back to the boil, then he lowered the heat and covered the pan.

James stared out of the kitchen window hoping and dreading to see a red Mini Cooper. Turning back to his cooking, he lifted the lid from the pan. A column of steam rose as he wondered whether or not Barbara would bring one or two bottles of wine. One bottle meant one thing, two bottles something else. James hoped and dreaded for something else. It was five past seven.

'What are we drinking?' the voice asked.

'Nothing,' said Barbara. She sat at her little kitchen table, a bottle of red and a bottle of white in front of her. She held the phone to her ear. She was dressed in brown trousers and a stripy colourful shirt. Her shoes matched the brown of her trousers and were on the casual side of smart low wide heels. She felt comfortable about the clothes.

'Alright,' the voice conceded. 'What *will* we be drinking?'

'A Cabernet Shiraz...'

'Nice choice.'

'... and a Chardonnay.'

'Very nice.'

'Should it be *or* a chardonnay?'

'Well, two bottles says taxi to me. And out there in the sticks that means you won't have a convenient get-out; you can't flag a taxi on Nowhere Lane. But it's got to be a taxi because driving with two bottles of wine's a bit erm...'

'Like hanging my knickers off the aerial,' Barbara finished for her best friend.

'Yeah.'

'A taxi means I'm promising nothing,' Barbara mused.

'True.'

'But if I take one bottle of wine and my car and only sipped,' she ignored the snort from her best friend, 'then I've got my get-out.'

'You could always not take wine.'

'Seems rude.'

'He's entertaining you. Let him provide.'

Barbara sighed. 'But I *want* to take some.'

'Ah.'

'What do you mean 'ah'?'

'You know, *ah*,' said Diane smugly. 'You've decided.'

'Decided what?' said Barbara innocently.

'He's a nice guy: respectable, trustworthy, nervy but in a cute way rather than wet. Don't you think *Jim* would help with the lightening and tightening?'

'Yes it would,' Barbara agreed.

'Anyway,' said the voice getting back on track. 'You get to decide how this evening ends and I think you've decided.'

'Don't be ridiculous!'

'Freudian slip, my precious. You're already considering your knickers.'

'This isn't Bridget Jones.'

'And he's not Hugh Grant, not with that chin. Maybe Colin Firth, he's a bit of a drip.'

'I want to take wine because I want to share something I enjoy with him. That's it.'

'Is the taxi booked?'

'Yes, for midnight, and I'll drive myself there.'

'Red *and* white, then.'

Barbara glanced at the clock; it was quarter past seven.

Chapter Fifteen

'This had better be good.'

A promising start, thought Errol. The voice was impatient, superior, mistrusting. It belonged to a man whose hair was greying, let's call him Jones, Dick Jones, because that was what Susan will call him. Errol had never seen the man before because he hadn't been here when the dog was first studied, but he knew about him; this was the one who would rather cut than study. Good, they could use people like him.

The man breezed into the round chamber. Susan, trying to maintain a smug, triumphant exterior, was tossed in his arrogant wake. 'It's better than good,' Susan panted. 'It's fantastic! That's why I brought you here.' The man raised his eyebrows at her attempt to claim some authority. 'You'll have to see it to believe it,' she insisted.

The two stood in front of the cage. The dog looked up at them expectantly. 'He looks like he wants a biscuit,' said Dick.

'And he can have one once we've been through the tricks. I'm just re-setting the equipment for another run.' Susan was breathless with excitement as she dashed around her small work area. 'First let me show you the bio information.' She handed Dick a wad of printouts which he quickly flicked through.

'What am I looking at, Susan?' Disdain dripped from his words. 'All this shows is that a dog had a steady pulse and body temp for thirty minutes.'

Susan was clearly rankled by Dick's attitude but she pressed on. 'Look *how* steady,' she enthused. 'That's one cool dog, especially for one who has performed a series of tests eight times with a one hundred percent success rate!'

'What tests?'

'I'll show you,' Susan said as she turned to the cage. 'Raise your left paw.' She said it with the confidence of one who assumes success. Errol simply wagged his tail, glad of the attention and hopeful of a biscuit. 'Raise your left paw,' she repeated a little more forcefully and a little less confidently. Dick Jones looked from the dog to his subordinate. 'Raise your right paw!' Susan tried desperately.

'It's not Crufts, Susan,' said Dick. 'We're not training them to do tricks. We're here to find out what's behind their odd behaviour, not be the cause of more of it.'

'But that's just it!' wailed Susan. 'It's not *their* behaviour! Look, forget about the tricks, it doesn't matter if he does them now or not. I have him on tape doing the tricks and the bios can easily be matched up. Some*thing* is making him, *made* him,' she corrected herself, 'do these things. Whatever it is, is making him, making them all,' she waved her arms in the air, 'behave oddly!'

'The theory that whatever caused the Splash has affected the local fauna is currently prevalent, as well you know. But a few party tricks are not enough to prove it. That will come tonight.'

'What *is* happening tonight?' Errol listened intently for the answer to Susan's question. The greyhound cocked its head and lifted an ear. Neither Dick nor Susan noticed. 'What's so important?'

'We've turned Eden's Aegis inward and we're going to point it at the Splash site. Whatever is down there will be *wholly* contained.'

The dog pricked both ears at that. *Trapped!* He knew that he must get away and that he had to warn the others. But how would they keep it a secret when there was no time for caution?

'Is that even possible?' Susan was incredulous.

'We've been working on the modifications for two years. Ever since we returned to the *Warren*,' said Dick, shrugging his shoulders as if the details were unimportant. Susan looked livid.

'Two years? What am I *doing* here?' she demanded. 'Why wasn't I involved on the modifications?'

'We needed somebody to watch the dog,' said Dick, simply.

'I've been here six months! We've only had it,' she gestured at the caged dog, 'for five days! You've had me twiddling me my thumbs while everyone else gets to work! I *knew* that this place was a waste of time!'

'It still might be,' said Dick with another infuriating shrug of his shoulders. Errol was enjoying the show. He wondered if Susan's neck could get any redder. The colour had risen to flush her cheeks and was making a break for her forehead. 'The shield didn't work, so who's to say that the net will fare any better?' Dick added.

'You've brought me here to watch a *dog* and now you're telling me you need a net to contain whatever's affecting them? What if that,' she indicated the greyhound, 'and whatever's in it isn't contained, then aren't you closing the door after the horse has bolted? I've studied the thing night and day. Read my data because it *will* be useful to you.'

'Yes, I noticed your self-imposed shift change,' said Dick, his eyebrows raised.

'Never mind that,' Susan was panting again. 'This dog is not the same dog. I've studied it every minute of the day and I would swear it's not!'

'Not the same? What are you talking about?'

'It's the same *dog*, but it's not the same…' she had probably rehearsed this speech for days, and she still had no idea how to express what was essentially the right answer. '… the same… mind,' she finished weakly.

'You mean that its mind is affected by something.'

'No, I mean that it's altered or *in*fected by something.'

'Infected?' Dick looked at the dog. Errol allowed himself the luxury of looking directly back at him. 'I didn't see anything on the bios,' he said as he flicked the printouts once more.

'Not virally,' she said, exasperated. 'Or any other way that we can detect - at least not for certain,' Susan sighed as she pointed at the greyhound and went on. 'This dog is possessed.'

'Don't be absurd,' Dick retorted. 'It's affected, perhaps even altered in some way. And I'm willing to accept that, for now, we cannot ascertain how or why, but after tonight we will have plenty of time to study the gaps in our research…'

'What research?' Susan interrupted. 'You've been messing about with the shield. You're not studying, you're tinkering!'

'… and,' Dick looked pointedly at the beetroot Susan. 'We have no need to resort to *exorcisms*.' His face remained hard as he continued to talk down at her. 'Perhaps I've left you down here with our four-legged friend too long. Your dedication to its study has been acceptable but your energies obviously require stricter direction.'

'But my research! Check it, it adds up. I've got the dog on video performing like a seal while reacting like a stone; you can match it up. That dog's a vessel, a robot, a…'

'I'll look it over on Monday,' he held up a hand to silence her. 'Tonight's a busy night and *you* need to go home, Susan.'

Her protests began anew, but we'll never know what she said; Errol was just a greyhound again.

Barbara emerged from the arch juggling an umbrella and two bottles of wine.

James was rinsing ginger root from the grater, and ghee, cumin, cilantro and ground coriander from his hands. The meal had only to simmer for a little while longer and it was ready. *Not bad*, James told himself, *not bad at all.* He watched Barbara walk to the back door through the rain that had, for now, slowed to a drizzle. She looked fantastical as her clothes and hair were whipped in the wind. She hurried through the drizzle, dodging around the ride-on lawnmower, which James still had not put away. It was quarter to eight.

'Hi,' said Barbara as she stepped through the back door that James had left wide open in welcome. She closed it against the rain.

'Hello,' he said. 'Come in, come in. You look great!' He went to greet her. *Do we kiss? Of course we do.* He leant in to kiss her on the cheek. She was soft and warm, almost flushed, and James lingered as long as he felt he could, which was probably longer than he should. He felt a little flushed himself.

Barbara was impressed; James looked good, and the kiss was just right: confident and firm, yet gentle enough to take his time. She had almost reached up to caress his cheek but the dazzling brightness of the kitchen helped to keep her feet on the ground. Whatever he was cooking smelled gorgeous and she realised how hungry she was. She looked at James pointedly, and he laughed as he stepped aside to let her in. As she entered she noticed that the great wooden table was not set.

James watched her sweep into the kitchen. 'We're not eating in here,' he said as he took the wine off her. 'Are you drinking? I mean did you drive?'

'Yes, please,' she smiled warmly. 'I did drive; the car's parked at the gate. I didn't want to risk bringing it all the way down what with the holes and the rain. And I've got a taxi booked for midnight,' she explained.

'Well then, Cinders,' James returned the smile and the warmth. 'Red or white?'

'Red, please.'

'I've got one breathing,' James nodded to an open bottle on the side. Barbara raised her eyebrows, impressed. 'Shall we start on that and I'll open yours for later?' She nodded her ascent. James opened the Shiraz that she had brought and poured two glasses from the bottle on the side. Barbara craned her neck to look in the pan on the hob.

'I thought we could go upstairs,' he said to her as he handed over her drink.

'Upstairs?' she said uncertainly. 'Thanks,' she added as she received the glass.

'Yeah, c'mon.' And he headed into the house. Barbara paused. She hadn't had any wine yet and she planned not to have more than a few sips for the next half-hour or so, so that her get-out was still an option. She stared down the well-lit hall, all the way to the front door.

James was at the bottom of the stairs. 'You coming?' Barbara set off tentatively.

She glanced into the dining room; it looked sparkling. She looked into the living room which was clean and cosy and subtly lit. Tilda lay on the sofa. 'Hello, you,' Barbara said to the dog. 'Welcome home.'

She climbed the stairs to James who waited at the top. He led her to the tower. She was glad that she had worn low wide heels as she stepped across the grating. They climbed the stairs to the top floor of the tower.

Barbara was amazed. She was astounded. She was delighted. The floor was covered in a carpet so lush that she wanted to kick off her shoes. There were comfortable chairs and a huge plump sofa. A small table-for-two had been set up in the middle of the room. The hole in the floor surrounding the steel pole kept it away from the centre. A single candle burned between two empty white plates. A wooden wall surrounded the north side of the steel pole and fanned out almost to the glass but left plenty of room to walk around. Opposite this there was a door in the glass leading to the walkway that ringed the tower. A triangle of brickwork marked the roof of the arch and a large modern-looking cupboard stood against it.

Nothing could have ruined that first impression, not even the dark, heavily pregnant clouds that pushed on the glass and the steel frame. She eyed the tops of the swaying conifers and felt like she was among the weather but protected from it, like some kind of open but impervious shelter. It was daring and safe, exciting and calm. It was wonderful. Finally, as if she had been saving the sensation, she looked up into the conical glass ceiling and out onto the spike beyond. They looked as if they might reach through the clouds, above the rain that was now sluicing down the glass, and form a tunnel to the stars. Barbara was breathless. *He's taken my breath away*, she told herself, not at all disappointed.

'Like it?'

'It's amazing.'

'Make yourself at home,' said James. And Barbara was so impressed that he could have winked and she would have liked it. He didn't. 'I'll get us our tea.'

And James was dancing down the steps and floating through the house back into the kitchen. *Doing okay*, he told himself. It was eight o'clock.

Dog watched the Ivy Arch from the cover of the conifers. The rain, as it now felt it always had, poured through the branches in a thick steady drizzle. He hadn't relinquished the bull terrier's body for six days now, another day would mean that if and when he did there wouldn't be much bull terrier left and he himself would struggle to find another to take him. And men would be ruled out for ever. He had decided that it was worth the risks days ago.

The Rottweilers were with him and so were the dogs of Never. Thirty five of them had dashed down the thin concrete road to James's house. Thirty five here and many, many more in the city.

Dog's north bank counterpart, back once again in Scud, had broadcast his findings as narrowly as possible. Dog had told of his plan to the Rottweilers who had relayed the information to as many as they thought could be trusted. It would be naïve to think that they could keep their secrets but they knew that time was running out. Tonight they would break into James's house and deal with the problem of Eden's Aegis once and for all.

Chapter Sixteen

Barbara prowled the top floor of the tower, still resisting the urge to take off her shoes. She tried the two chairs and both were luxuriously comfortable, as was the sofa which threatened to swallow her whole. Before she allowed it to she jumped up and moved to the wooden wall separating the northern third of the room.

Passing through to the other side she gasped: concave shelving stretched away from her stuffed with rows and rows of books: big, small, soft, hard book after book after book. The height of what she had thought of as a wall was unremarkable but now it looked like a sheer and dizzying edifice that loomed over her. At three metres high it more than justified the wheeled steps that could run upon the smooth tiled floor. The carpet finished a metre from the shelves. Although smaller than the previous area there was more than enough space for the two comfy-looking armchairs and the reading table with dual lamp and two bare wooden seats. She set off on a voyage of discovery. There were a great deal of science texts dealing with atomic theory, genetics, anatomy and prosthetics. They looked old and dusty and Barbara presumed them to be out of date. She passed them by and moved on to a full encyclopaedia that was almost certainly out of date and probably worth a fortune. She found fiction and non-fiction, novels and manuals and collections of stories, poetry, essays and plays, many of which she had heard of and many more that she hadn't. As she ran her hands along the shelves and caressed the spines of the books she noticed that her wine glass was half full. She was warm, whether it was the room or the alcohol she didn't know. *Oh well*, she thought, *if he locks me in I'll have plenty to do.*

She pushed the steps all the way to one end and climbed to the top-left of the shelving. Start at the beginning, she told herself. She wanted to drink in the titles, to somehow commit every one of them to memory even before she asked James if she could move into his magnificent glass loft. Barbara giggled at the thought as she swept along. She stopped at a set of paperbacks and gasped in surprise.

'Have you done a runner already?' James's voice came from behind the shelves.

'Erm, no,' said Barbara, startled. 'I was just erm… just erm…' Barbara was flustered as if she had been caught somewhere she shouldn't be.

'Looking at the books?' James came around to her side of the shelves. He was smiling.

'Yes,' she let out a breath she had been holding. 'Looking at the books. Very impressive.'

'I can't take the credit. All collected by my grandparents and parents. Anyway,' he held out a hand to the elevated Barbara. 'Dinner is served.' He bowed his head.

Smiling, Barbara took his hand and clumped down the steps. To James, of course, she glided. 'I can't wait,' she said. 'It smells gorgeous.'

On returning to the table Barbara wanted to clap in delight and she even raised her hands a little when she saw the spread. James had managed to cram a large pot of curry and another of rice onto the table along with the two bottles of wine, poppadoms, a tray of dips and a jug of water.

'I feel like I've fallen out of a pub and landed in after-hours heaven,' she said excitedly.

'Good,' said James. 'Sit down and dig in.'

She landed in her chair and began spooning rice onto her plate.

'You're smooth,' she accused James with a smile.

'I do try,' he said, and this time he winked.

It was 20:15. Errol watched as Dick supervised a dozen men and women in white coats. This was the most activity that the dog had witnessed since his incarceration. The agent from the south bank watched over the urgent hustle and bustle, white coats fluttering and flapping around the room from console to console, panel to panel, operating, measuring and recording. The power in the room was discernible and rising to a pulsating hum.

Here we were right beneath the Humber and its huge bridge. Eddie, Frankie and Ziggy were travelling across that bridge for a night out in Hull. We were trying to discern what was happening. Whatever it was it was was happening tonight and all we had were the eyes and ears of Errol. We should have been more suspicious that the others had left him for us.

Scud stalked the streets of Hull. He was leaving a trail that as many of the others as possible could follow, and as he nosed past the bus station and left his scent on a shelter, Eddie, Frankie and Ziggy jumped down from a bus. They paused as they eyed the hammering rain.

'Did you have to wear that?' Eddie said as he jabbed at the collar of the smallest.

'What?' replied Frankie.

'You know what.'

Ziggy, dressed all in black, joined in. His accent was different and so thick that Scud had to concentrate to understand. He recognised all three of these men and wanted to hear what they said. 'Why will it matter? No one is going to be seeing it.'

'Until he shows it to them. We're here to have a night out, get pissed, have a laugh and maybe have to find a taxi who'll take us home. Or, if we're lucky get the bus back in the morning. Not,' he jabbed his finger again, 'to start fights!'

'I'm not gonna start anything!' the smaller man protested. Scud thought he caught a glimpse of a wry smile. Or a sulky defiance.

'I think that's it's finishing that he's liking,' chuckled the foreigner.

As the big man began to reply they all jumped into the rain and ran toward a pub. Scud was tempted to follow, but he had a mission: he and the others had to be outside that door as soon as possible without drawing too much attention to themselves, in this world or the other. He carried on with the trail, turning to growl at a mongrel that was following too closely. He didn't know yet how they were going to get in, but they must.

'This is really nice,' said Barbara, sweating as she ate. James's face shined back at her as he beamed in response.

'I'm glad you like it,' James answered her between sips of water. 'I didn't think it would be this hot. It wasn't supposed to be. It's supposed to be tasty and spicy, not hot. Although a kick is good, but this is a bit more than a kick, more of a kick*ing*.' *Was he babbling? Calm down a bit if you are,* Barbara willed to him as she nodded her agreement about the food's delicious assault.

'It's fine.' She chewed carefully for a moment. The light from the candle danced on the steel pole nearby. 'It's tasty, spicy and it's got just the right kick.' *And a tingle,* she added to herself. She wasn't certain that it was all coming from the food; she hoped it wasn't from the food. And who are we to deny hope?

James felt the same tingle.

'Do you not read, then?' asked Barbara remembering his assertion that the books were not his. The rain fell on the glass roof in torrents and the light of the evening was almost wholly blocked. James went to turn on a lamp. The light, though subtle, was momentarily startling.

'I do,' said James defensively. 'Well, I used to; I had a thing for sci-fi,' he continued sheepishly. 'No, I don't read,' he finished honestly.

'That's okay. You don't need to feel guilty. I mean you're only ignoring my profession, belittling my career, negating my talent...'

'Okay, okay,' James held his hands up, a poppadom clenched in a fist. 'I'll read yours. Bring them round and I'll see what erotica's all about, and assure you of your undoubted talent. I mean *tell* you. You don't need assuring.'

'I don't need to bring them round,' said Barbara, swallowing another bite of chicken. She took another gulp of water and reached for the jug; it was empty. James grabbed it and stood up.

'You don't?' he said as he headed toward the cupboard standing against the triangle of brickwork. 'Why not?'

'Because you've got them,' she said, wondering why James was taking a jug to a cupboard.

'I have?' He opened the cupboard door and light flooded from within; it was a fridge. Barbara remembered to close her mouth as he looked round at her. Turning back he began to fill the jug straight from the fridge.

'I've got one of those!' Barbara exclaimed. 'I've just had it fitted!'

'They're good aren't they,' said James as he sat down and filled Barbara's glass with ice-cold water. 'Anyway, how come I've got your books?'

She took a grateful gulp of the fresh water. Neither of them were drinking their wine. They sweated and they tingled and their excitement grew. The wine went unheeded, unneeded. 'They're in the bookcase. Your mum's I suppose.'

'Really? The sly old so-and-so!' said James. 'Or they're me dad's, the dirty old man.'

'Why do you say that?'

'What? Dirty old man?'

'Yes.'

'Well, you know...' James floundered. The heat seemed to rise up a notch.

'It's not porn,' said Barbara.

'No I know...'

'No you don't.' She smiled as he squirmed. 'But don't worry about it. Why would you?'

James hid for a moment behind a forkful of curry.

'You said that you thought they were my mum's,' he said, nodding at the wooden wall indicating Barbara's books beyond. 'Is it mainly women that read your stuff?'

'My stuff? Or erotica in general?' she giggled as she leaned back in her chair. It was so hot and so close, the clouds outside, the rain on the glass and James just centimetres away across the small table. It seemed dark after the brightness from the fridge, and James got up to turn on another lamp.

Barbara was short of breath and beaming red; she was thrilled. James looked flushed; his shining face had a ruddy complexion.

It was quarter to nine.

Dog watched the light go on in the top of the tower. He turned to the other dogs and nodded them forward; there would be little chance of them being seen now. They left the cover of the conifers and stalked to the broken driveway. Dog looked to the gateway and at that moment a stream of dogs appeared. Everything from the scruffiest limping cur to a freshly pampered toy poodle trotted into the grounds of Ivy Arch. Dog nodded toward the lawn so recently assaulted and the pack fell on it with a desperate enthusiasm.

Errol was nervous now. He turned in his cage over and over again trying to find a decent breath in the breathless room. The air was thick and heavy as if the clouds that choked this small island had broken through to the Warren, wrapping the cage in smothering smog. Power. It was everywhere, in this chamber and the one with the steel spike that ran from floor to ceiling. All of The Warren was suffused with tremendous energy that was just waiting to be released.

Errol cringed. His body felt like a dam. Worse, it felt like something caught between the dam and the water, a piece of driftwood, helpless, powerless, just waiting for everything around him to break and wash him away.

His reaction made observation difficult. What was happening? It was about now that we noticed that the others had been taking more and more dogs on the north and south bank. We stayed put; we had to have faith in our plan for the dog and the man to get us out of here. We were safe in our shelter, as we had been safe for many, many years before we found ourselves at the bottom of a river. Once we gained control of the bridge we could leave, and we would take the others with us.

'Both,' said James, easing himself back into his chair. 'Yours and erotica in general.'

'Well,' said Barbara leaning forward conspiratorially. 'An erotic fiction novel is a book that contains sex, but it's not about sex. It's about the story, the characters and how they both evolve and grow throughout the pages. Very much like a *proper* book.' Barbara raised her eyebrows to show what she thought of the popular feeling on erotica. 'A story crammed with sex that's still read with both hands on the book,' she summed up with a smile.

James was blank for a moment, and then he smiled. 'Ah, like rocket ships in sci-fi.'

'Exactly.'

'So it *is* aimed at women, then.'

'Why?' Barbara fanned her body with her shirt. The tingle was undeniable now as she sweated in her chair which seemed to be humming. *Too hot*, she told herself, and shifted around to free her buttocks and thighs from the sticky seat. The silver pole gleamed, the reflection of the candle less obvious in the lamp light but still there, still dancing.

James fanned his own body as he chewed on a mouthful of jalfrezi. He wondered how the rain wasn't sizzling into steam as it hit the glass roof. Curry, passions and a conversation about sex. *Hot, hot, hot*. He was staring at Barbara. Her cheeks were aglow and her neck was damp along with a pale V of flesh at her open-necked shirt. Had she undone another button? The top three were open and James thought that it had only been two before. 'A man couldn't keep two hands on a book full of sex.'

'Yeah you're right,' Barbara laughed knowingly. 'Women it is.'

'So…' James started to speak and then popped a poppadom into his mouth. He chewed efficiently.

'What?'

James swallowed. 'Where do you erm… you know…' James laughed suddenly, cutting himself off. 'Doesn't matter. Question for the future.' He took a big gulp of water and wiped his brow.

Barbara smiled at him. 'Where do I get my inspiration?'

'Erm…'

'It's what everyone wants to ask, and quite a few actually manage to. Most don't,' she confided in him. 'They're not my fantasies. Take your rocket ship, do you think the writer fantasises about them?'

James thought for a moment. 'Probably.'

'Bad example,' Barbara agreed and then quickly changed her mind. 'No, not a bad example. Look at Star Trek, whoever wrote that – what's his name?'

'Erm...' James stuttered unsure. 'Bub'd know.'

'Well, yeah, obviously. Anyway, whatsisname probably came up with Kirk's ship – the Enterprise?' James nodded. 'Right, the Enterprise, but did he think of all of them?'

'All of what?'

'The ships!'

'Ah, see what you mean,' said James, chewing happily. 'Probably not.'

'No. He'll have had help. Or,' Barbara continued, 'think of some really nasty shit that you might've read. Something so bloody, violent, disgusting or depraved that if the author thought or fantasised like that then they're not gonna be able to function in the world. And what about the exposure? D'you think Stephen King really thinks like that? He spends his day dreaming of killing people and forming back-up plans in case they come back? And if he did would he really want to tell the world? Would he really write down his plan to kill his wife for all the world to see?'

'Probably not,' James repeated.

'There's everything *but* my fantasies in my novels. Me and Steve are together on that one, I reckon.'

'That still doesn't tell me where you get your inspiration.'

'I just sit and write and see where it goes. That and Angela.'

'Who's that?' James started on the last forkful of his meal.

'She's a mobile homeopath,' said Barbara simply, and sipped her water to cover a teasing smile. James laughed. 'No, really,' she assured him, giggling. 'She's a star, an absolute star. I got to know her years ago when I was looking for a hay fever cure...'

'It didn't work,' James interrupted.

'It does work. I just forgot to take it on Sunday, but I was alright on Wednesday wasn't I?' James had to nod.

'Why is a mobile homeopath such an inspiration?'

'She's also a...' Barbara thought for a moment and then shrugged, 'a prostitute.' James stopped, his glass held mid-sip. Barbara scooped the last bit of curry from her plate and chewed steadily while watching his eyebrows travel up his forehead. He swallowed a mouthful of water, and reached for his glass of wine.

21:00. Dick was getting excited now. He shouted and pointed and sweated. His open white coat revealed a blue shirt damp enough to cling to him. Errol spotted Susan. Had she been there all night, or had she just slipped in? The south bank agent was standing in her way, suggesting the latter.

'I work for Dick Jones,' she said. 'Dick Jones!'

Dick looked over on hearing his name. He looked annoyed but he waved her in; the agent stood aside.

Control over the dog was ever more difficult. The power build-up was now a loud continual pulsating hum, and Errol's sensitive ears made it all the worse.

Dog's head snapped round to the gateway. Through the hammering rain he had heard a car pull up. A door slammed.

'Be quiet, you fucking turd!' a voice hissed.

'We shouldn't be doing this. It's not worth it.'

'That wanker called the fucking cops on me! He's gonna pay.'

'C'mon, Titz. You've already made your point, and the cops can't touch you. Leave it as it is.'

'No! No fucker does that to me. I'm a Fitz and that means something where I'm from. Time it meant something up here in this shit…' Titz and the accompanying young man stopped dead in their tracks at the top of the drive. A Bull terrier and two Rottweilers barred their way.

'Wha the fu…' Titz was cut off as the three dogs advanced, their heads dipped, a low growl in each throat, their teeth bared. It was a warning, a promise of menace. The young man turned and fled. For a moment Dog wondered if Titz might stand his ground. It didn't matter if he did. Things needed to be settled tonight; the time for concealment was at an end. Titz's wouldn't be the first body or the last but it would be among the bloodiest. The man backed up to the gate and onto the road, glaring all the time.

'Titz! C'mon!' the young man turned and walked out of sight.

'Did you see them? There was fucking dozens of them! And they were all fucking digging!'

'I recognised 'em. They're all from the village. One of 'em was Mrs Wimble's poodle…' Doors slammed and a car's engine started.

'She has regular clients, like me, who just use her as a homeopath, but she offers an extra service, another pill to swallow, a different cure for whatever ails you,' said Barbara.

'What are you, her agent?' James laughed over his wine.

'I've never stopped being amazed by what she does,' said Barbara laughing along and taking a sip of wine. 'She's got a dozen or so clients that have her 'round anything from twice a week to twice a year.'

'How much does she make?' James sipped at the wine and used his shirt to fan his body. 'Shall I open that door?' he asked before Barbara could answer his first question.

'With all that wind and rain?' She raised her eyebrows. 'You'll ruin the carpet. It's fine,' she said fanning her own body. 'Probably just the curry,' she added saving Dog from discovery.

James nodded. 'So, how much does she make, your mobile homeopathic lady of the night?'

'I've never asked. She drives a nice car and wears nice clothes, so I assume she's not giving it away, but that's not important to me anyway. She tells me people's fantasies.' Barbara smiled enigmatically. 'There's some funny folk out there.'

James smiled casually as he leaned back in his chair. 'Like what?' he asked with faux nonchalance.

'Read the books!' Barbara barked out a laugh. 'They're all in there, most of them anyway. I'm holding back the old man who likes to be tied up at his front window wearing nothing but a bag of frozen peas while she whips him with celery.'

'Really?' James leant forward, all ears. Barbara laughed.

'Sorry, no, not really.' James smiled at his own gullibility.

'So that's the sex, what about the rest?' he asked.

'The train,' she replied. 'I get on a train, any train, go on a journey and watch the people, the ones alone and the couples. I take my note book and I watch them and what they do on my way to somewhere new.'

James nodded as he sipped his wine. 'And what do you do when you get there?'

'First I sit in the station. If it's a big one I can sit there for hours just watching. Then I'll go to a restaurant, then the shops and I'll always try to have a walk round a hotel. Not just the lobby but up into the corridors and maybe amongst the rooms. I can see if there are signs on the door or shoes on the floor, or see if the newspaper is still uncollected in the afternoon.' She winked at this last bit.

'Before I come home I always visit the nearest hospital. I like to walk the wards during visiting hours and see the love and the greed and the distaste and the boredom. Every kind of couple, every kind of story all bound up in one building.

'Sometimes I might stay over. On one of my fact finding missions,' Barbara paused as she caught James's expression. She laughed. 'It's what I call my little trips. Anyway, this one time I stayed away for more than a week: I got on a train and ended up in York. I stayed there one night and then moved on to Middlesbrough, then across to Carlisle then Edinburgh, back down to Newcastle and on to London and Bristol and I finished up in Cardiff.

'I sat in stations, I ate in restaurants, I prowled the hotels I was staying in and I visited the hospitals. I shopped for new clothes every day, leaving the ones I'd worn just once behind so that I could travel light.' Barbara shook her head at the decadent memory.

'I filled three notebooks!' she continued excitedly. 'Enough "facts" for half-a-dozen novels. I was exhausted!'

'I bet you were.' James poured them both more wine.

'What about you? Where does your inspiration come from?'

'I don't really need any,' shrugged James.

'Everyone needs something.'

James thought for a moment. 'I spent the afternoon watching Eddie's arse which was supposed to inspire me to be a plasterer. I was leaning toward a giant jelly. Maybe I could be a chef!'

Barbara looked pointedly at her empty plate. 'I reckon,' she said.

Errol whined and pawed at his prison. He wanted out, to be away from this room and the power thrumming through the space. We knew that the power was being generated elsewhere and fed into the steel pole. It was a conduit for whatever had brought us here seventeen years ago, this Eden's Aegis. What were they doing with it now?

'How have you changed it from a wide broadcast to a narrow beam?' Susan was badgering Dick.

'Susan, we'll talk on Monday,' said Dick. They wouldn't. This was the last conversation Susan would have, which was a shame because she would never have chosen Dick to hear her final words.

The agent, still standing near the door, suddenly fumbled into her pocket and pulled out a mobile phone. She quickly launched into an animated conversation.

'But you've changed it from a shield to a cage.' Susan wasn't giving up on Dick. 'An umbrella to a bubble. How?'

'It never was an umbrella…'

'But…' Susan interrupted, only to be silenced by a wave of Dick's hand. She fumed as she listened on.

'We never managed to create a shield, just a beam of energy that merely needs redirecting. The bubble is created by…'

It was hard to keep the dog calm enough to listen. A bubble? What kind of bubble? What kind of cage, and for whom? It had to be us! Not waiting to listen to the rest of what Dick had to say, we were gone. They, the government of this island, were back in the Warren to investigate the deaths, of the people and the dogs, and they knew that whatever was at the bottom of the Humber had something to do with them. How could we have been so blind?

Panic spread as quickly as the word. Some, many thousands, chose to escape, but where to? Too late we realised that the others had taken all the dogs, thousands upon thousands of them and all under their control. There were many thousands more just as trapped as us but seemingly not as scared. They had another means of escape unknown to us, and we had given them a way to time it to perfection: Errol.

They kept it under control in that cage, an iron control of the desperate with a plan. Not a whine or a whimper was permitted. It would not survive this night. They watched Dick, watched him and waited.

As he gave the order to activate Eden's Aegis, thousands leapt away before the bubble closed and we were left with only two on the outside.

There was a pulse. Scud could feel it through the pavement. Drunks revelled in their penultimate night of interior smoking. They rolled along the paths and the plazas like animated bananas, jiggling and juggling their bodies from pub to pub, unlit cigarettes in their mouths and lighters held ready in their hands so that they could smoke and wheeze from entering to leaving each pub they landed in. The rain soaked their clothes but didn't dampen their spirits. None of them could sense it, the whump, whump, whump of power building and building, awaiting direction.

Scud glowered at the people. He wondered if they were worth all this effort, worth all this time and energy to find out how, how to make them willing, how to make them their *friends*. The word sliced through him like a blade. They were weak, petty, pitiful things that herded themselves like cattle; they were unworthy of friendship. They lived their pointless lives and spread their pointless influence. Some clamoured for more, some got. They were just as pointless, just as irrelevant. Each and every life crissed and crossed and spread across this globe in a web so fragile, so fleeting that it seemed impossible that any of them could ever do anything that would last or would mean anything to anyone. Ever. This world turned and its microscopic parasites multiplied, each life briefly flaring in a dull glare that begot more glares just as dull, just as insignificant.

The Doberman looked about. It was a good world but it needed cleaning. And the people would have to do it, with a little help from their friends.

Scud shifted his gaze to the Bridge as the pulse reached a crescendo. A message was sent out at that moment. We didn't understand, but thousands of others did, including Scud. They all knew that it was time and they left in their droves, to where we would soon find out, but for now we knew not. As the bubble began to coalesce around our massive world contained by its tiny house, many panicked and bolted. There was nowhere to go. Those working in the Warren were the first. Some made it to the north bank and into the city, some the bridge and others to the small towns and villages of the south bank. But there was nowhere to go.

We saw flashes of The Warren, then nothing. Glimpses of smoke-filled rooms, then nothing. A car on the Humber Bridge, then nothing. Sometimes we heard screams. Scud saw men and women stumble from more than just the effects of alcohol. In one smoky room Frankie Fiss, fists clenched, elbows bent, shoulders squared, was saved from a beating as his would-be assailants were suddenly overcome, overcome by something that Frankie would love to know about.

Eddie noticed nothing as the man behind him in the queue for the bar collapsed, he just stepped aside as the bouncers removed the man whose face was bloody from its impact with the floor.

And Ziggy. Ziggy danced with a fervour that delighted the women near him: they clapped and laughed and danced along.

Then he collapsed.

The women laughed some more and whirled away to another eager to impress.

James and Barbara stared across the table. Tilda could be heard barking downstairs but they were too wrapped up in each other to pay attention.

It was so hot. Barbara had slipped off her shoes and James had rolled up the sleeves of his shirt. The conversation had stopped, their glasses were empty, the bottle was spent.

'White wine and ice cream, Cinders?' asked James, remembering her midnight taxi.

'Just the ice cream I think,' she replied while fanning her face with her hand. The pause was over.

'Plenty of time,' James nodded at the clock. It was half past nine. He went to the fridge. 'I've left it downstairs,' he tutted.

'Never mind, we'll have it another time.' Barbara smiled.

'I'll nip down and get it,' said James. 'I think we could do with it.' His face shone as he smiled back at her. 'And I'd better see what Tilda's barking at.' He disappeared down the steps, the trapdoor trembling slightly at his passing.

Barbara leaned back and sighed as she burrowed her toes into the carpet. It was a good night, she decided as she contemplated cancelling her taxi. Tilda continued to bark as Barbara got up and padded about the room, listening to the rain and turning on all the lamps. The room was ablaze with light. From outside it must have looked like a beacon in the storm. She turned them off again and was about to return to the books when she realised that James was taking a long time to get ice cream. Maybe he was planning a surprise. She moved to the edge of the room, close to the door to the gantry and imagined him climbing the tower's ladder. An umbrella covered string quartet in the drive. She chided herself and, not bothering with the view from the window, turned away and switched the lights back on.

James skipped down to the ground floor where a frantic Tilda awaited him.

'What? What is it?' Tilda danced around James, barking desperately. This was where we made a mistake. But Tilda knew that something was wrong and on seeing the dog's state James said the one thing that he was always going to say. 'Wanna go out?' he said cheerily. Tilda went into frenzy as we objected. 'Okay, okay, I'll let you out.' He strode toward the back of the house, the spring in his step lending him speed. On the way he flicked off the hallway light, confident that Barbara would be impressed with his green thinking.

The whole of the downstairs was plunged into darkness.

Tilda barked and whined and tried to bar his way. She knew there was something wrong at the back door. 'Bloody hell, dog! If you wanna go out you'll have to get out of my way.' He reached the back porch and saw that the door was open. He assumed that neither he nor Barbara had closed the door when she arrived. We wanted him to close the door. That's all. 'The door's open, you daft thing. Get yourself out there,' he said. Tilda shrank back and growled. 'It's only a bit of rain, not worth getting worked up about. Anyway, it's up to you, the door's open.'

Under pressure, Tilda ran over to the door. We tried to close it but it was held open with a hook. The level of control we exerted over her meant that we couldn't undo it. Such actions required complicated motor skills and to force those upon her might cause irreparable damage.

Just as we were beginning to think that it was worth the risk, James was realising that the light hadn't come on in the kitchen. 'Typical,' he said but without any real bitterness; he wasn't going to let it ruin his mood. And the weak watery light from the tower provided some illumination. His foot kicked something across the tiled floor. It was cold, heavy and solid but soft. Whatever it was it was long and slim and it struck the base of the cupboard with a heavy thump. The light from the tower was extinguished. The kitchen was almost black. 'Tilda?' he called out. 'Have you been leaving your toys out?' He peered into the shadow. He could see a long misshapen tube, bent in the middle and splayed at one end. He dismissed it and went to the freezer. No light came on when he opened the door. 'Why do you get a light in the fridge but not the freezer?' he asked no one, and began foraging through the drawers.

Tilda reached for the hook and then stopped; she smelled something, something alien, unknown, and whatever it was it was already in the house. She reached for the hook and turning, twisting and stretching she pushed with her snout. Dropping back down, she tried to push the door closed but something barred her way.

James carried on searching through the freezer. He was about to give up when a faint light shone through the skylight. It was just enough to locate the ice cream. 'Thank you, Miss Bean,' he said glancing up at the top of the tower.

He turned away from the freezer and the cold plastic tub fell to the tiled floor, dropped by James's fingers suddenly numb with shock and fear. The lid pinged off and the tub came to rest upside down. The silence was broken by James's short heavy gasps and Tilda's scrabbling efforts to close the back door.

It had been an arm, right there on the kitchen floor, the thing he had kicked against the kitchen cupboards. It was an arm and James was sure he had just seen it move.

'Shit,' he breathed.

Then he heard it, a shuffling, dragging, creeping sound. The arm was moving. 'Oh shit.'

Tilda was frantic now as she tried to close the back door. A foot jammed it and another one pushed and hopped its way inside while fingers gripped the edge of the white plastic. Giving up on the door, Tilda snapped and snarled at the hands, feet, arms and legs tumbling into the back porch.

James heard Tilda's struggles. 'Tilda,' he called out. 'Tilda, come here!' He still hadn't moved and the backs of his legs were cold from the frigid air escaping the still-open freezer. The quiet but insistent alarm began. Beep, beep, beep, beep, beep…

'James?' Barbara's voice called from the house. He couldn't tell how close she was but she must have been on the stairs at the very least. Barbara's voice spurred James into action.

'Oh shit,' he said not for the last time, and launched himself away from the freezer. 'Barb… ooooohhhh ssshhhiiittt!' He skidded on the tub of ice cream. He went down with a thud, his head cracking on the tiles. A line of ice cream streaked across the kitchen floor as the tub sped away and crashed into the legs of the retreating Tilda. She yelped in surprise and, dropping the leg that she had had fastened in her jaws, began to bark and bark like she would never stop.

James's head rang with the impact and Tilda's barking. Little silver dots swam and burst before his eyes. He could still hear the shuffling of the arm as if it were magnified by the ringing in his ears. It wasn't magnified; it was multiplied by the dozens of limbs now making their inexorable way across the kitchen floor. James could have lay there all night but for one thought: *I don't want a disembodied hand to touch me. I don't want undead fingers on my face.* He forced himself to a sitting position.

'James?' Barbara's voice cut through the gloom and the barking and the shuffling and the pain. But not the undead. *There's an undead arm in my kitchen.*

'James? What's going on?'

There's an undead arm in my kitchen.

'What's wrong with Tilda?'

There's a…

'Barbara!' James clung to the name. 'Don't come in!' he yelled and Tilda rushed to block the doorway.

'What's going on?' Barbara's tone was impatient and demanding now. James was up on his feet and moving unsteadily towards the house. He trod on things that crawled and, as his eyes re-adjusted to the gloom and the spin, slithered. *How can arms slither? Is it the same arm? Am I seeing double, triple, quadruple?* James didn't know the multiple for dozens.

With Tilda barring her way, Barbara couldn't get into the kitchen, and now she was trying to force her back down the hallway. 'Tilda stop it,' she said. 'Stop it, Tilda.'

The perfect date was turning weird.

She'd thought she'd seen movement on the dark floor and she hadn't been able to see James at all even though his shouts had clearly placed him in there. She ducked into the dining room and then darted past a momentarily startled Tilda. She covered the few steps to the kitchen quickly, with Tilda at her heels, but her way was barred again.

'Limbs!' James shouted as he fell through the doorway into the hall, forcing Barbara back again.

'What?' said Barbara. James was on all fours at her feet.

'The door! Shut the door!'

'What?' Even in the darkness Barbara could see the fear etched into James's upturned face.

'Shut the door!'

The urgency in his voice finally propelled Barbara forward to slam the door. Something blocked it.

'Oh shit,' whimpered James.

Tilda growled and snapped at the fingers clutching the door even though the impact had shattered the bones within.

'It won't close!' Barbara could feel her own panic rising to match that of James. James turned and, still on his knees, added his weight to the door. Barbara pushed harder and then something gave, the door closed, James collapsed, Barbara fell on top of him.

The rain battered a thousand canine bodies as Scud threw himself at the implacable door. It was no use. He gestured for others to try. Volunteers from the throng that filled the plaza outside *The Deep* pushed forward.

A flash of a stairwell blurred in passing as a friend of Scud and Dog tried to get Susan. A split second of the back of her head as she swiped her card through a reader next to a steel door. Then Susan slumped through the suddenly open doorway into the rain. Scud looked down at the pain and confusion etched onto the half of her face he could see. Her hair was soon stuck to her face and her cheek pressed against wet concrete.

Her body held the door open.

Scud leapt inside and a thousand baying hounds followed.

'What was that?' Barbara panted into James's heaving chest. 'Are you okay?' she added quickly.

James felt around the back of his head; his fingers came back sticky.

'I don't know,' he answered her. 'I don't know what that was and I don't know if I'm okay.'

They both jumped violently as something slapped against the other side of the door.

'You said something about limbs!' she insisted. 'In fact you said "limbs".'

'I saw,' James began and then paused, still incredulous. 'I saw an arm on the kitchen floor and it was moving, crawling. It was pulling itself along with its fingers!'

Another slap. Barbara looked to James. 'Was that higher?'

'Get the lights on. This is ridiculous. We can't fuck about in the dark when there's limbs on the attack.' James stopped and considered his statement.

'You said limb*s* but you only saw one arm?' she said as she scrabbled to find the light switch. 'Why are the lights all off anyway?'

'I was being green,' James said heavily.

'Always trying to impress,' Barbara shook her head in the dark. 'Did you ever consider that you don't need to try so hard, James? Things were going great and now, because *you* had to try that bit harder we can't see these limbs!' Barbara stopped and considered her statement. 'Are you sure? How hard did you hit your head?'

'Hard. Feel woozy. Don't know if I was…' he stopped, startled by the sudden bright light as Barbara found the switch, then continued, '… seeing double or triple or… there were dozens. What's the multiple for dozens?'

Slap! They both looked to the door. Definitely higher.

'Times twelve.'

'Really?' said James dopily. Barbara gave him a look that said that this wasn't the time.

'Well,' James continued. 'I don't think I was seeing times twelve. I think there were lots of times twelves.'

The handle moved. Tilda growled and Barbara lunged to grab it.

'Find a chair!' she screamed at James who was already rolling to his feet. Crouching for just a moment, he stood and lurched for the dining room. Barbara gripped the handle as if her life depended on it. She glanced through the glass into the kitchen but, with the light on in the hallway, she couldn't see a thing.

Then fingers spread against the glass, clawing and pawing blindly as if they could clutch the glass. Barbara screamed and jumped back. She kept her grip on the handle but she stumbled and fell pulling the handle down with her. Immediately the door started to open.

Tilda barked and barked.

'No!' she screamed as she flung her weight at the door, slamming it shut once more. Twisting, she forced her back against the wooden panel and held the handle up, her arm as rigid as she could manage. 'Where's that chair?' she shouted.

Bang.

She screamed again as something hit the door with such force she was thrown forward. 'Jesus! Jesus! Jesus!' Without giving her fear time to paralyse her, she scrambled back against the door.

'Oh shit!' James appeared at the doorway to the dining room, chair in hands.

Bang.

Barbara screamed again as she was jolted forward. James rushed forward past the barking Tilda.

'Move!' he shouted, and Barbara rolled away just as he shoved the chair under the handle.

Bang.

James and Barbara watched the door bulge with the impact but it held for now.

'What's going on?' Barbara panted through the exertion and the fear and the adrenalin. Tilda stopped barking and started whining. James hung his head and leaned against the wall next to the entrance to the dining room.

'I don't know,' he said, breathing hard.

'Is that gonna hold?' said Barbara.

'It's the old back door from before the extension was built,' James shrugged. 'It might do.'

Bang.

They both jumped but the chair held.

Suddenly two great paws thudded against the glass, the claws scratching and trying to gain purchase. Tilda growled while James and Barbara took an involuntary step toward the stairs

'Is that a dog?' asked Barbara. 'Is it all of a dog or just the paws?' she added. James looked at her trying to ascertain whether or not she was hysterical but he was too hysterical to judge.

'I don't know.' Which was about all he knew for sure. 'Maybe. Probably. All of it, I think.' He touched the back of his head again and his fingers came away covered in fresh blood.

'Let me see.' Barbara got to her feet and came behind James.

Bang.

And more scraping and scratching. It was frantic now like the dog was trying to dig through the door.

He winced as she moved his blood-matted hair aside. 'It looks pretty nasty,' she said. 'But head wounds always bleed a lot, so I'm not sure.'

Crash.

James and Barbara whirled to face the closed door opposite the entrance to the dining room. The noise had come from beyond it.

'What now?' wailed James.

'It's your fucked-up house not mine!' snapped Barbara. 'What's in there, anyway?'

'My granddad's study. I mean my dad's study,' James corrected himself, and then added. 'Well, my study now I suppose.'

'I don't think ownership is important right now, James.'

The three of them backed away from the kitchen door, pregnant with its vile litter, and the study door, hiding its new threat as the handle slowly lowered.

'Oh shit.'

Dog sent the Rottweilers crashing against the door again. Bang. The door held, but only just. He raised himself up to look through the glass, his claws scratching and digging at the transparent sheet. There they were, all three of them, terrified. They looked to be poised between fight and flight. Dog quickly changed his mind. Make that fright and flight. What were they looking at?

Dropping back to all fours, he sent the Rottweilers against the door again. He snarled and drooled as a satisfying crack came from the door and the glass finally shattered.

James and Barbara didn't wait for the study door to open, and by the time the glass shattered, Barbara was already on the bottom step of the stairs.

'No!' shouted James, wrenching open the front door. 'This way!' Tilda howled and barked our protests at his action. In a macabre avalanche limbs fell in through the open doorway. Hands clutched and grabbed, feet shuffled and legs fell over all around James.

Lumps of flesh bumped and dragged and fell across the threshold. James tripped as he span away from the door and made for the stairs. Tilda snarled and snapped at the limbs clinging to James's trousers. Barbara screamed and reached to help him up, her grasping fingers made frantic by the kitchen door as its cracking reached a crescendo.

James's head span, making it difficult to untangle his legs and get back on his feet. The sound of wood landing on the hallway tiles gave him speed and finally he hauled himself to his feet.

Tilda rushed to the top of the stairs and waited there, barking for all she was worth as Barbara helped James to climb the stairs.

'That's it, Tilda,' breathed James. 'That's really helpful.' His head felt like it might explode.

Did any of them hear the study door slam closed? Probably not, but the barks and the howls and the clattering of claws on the tiles were loud enough to drown out every other sound.

Barbara dragged James to the top of the stairs and urged him on to the tower. Tilda ran around and around them pushing them on and barking at their pursuers.

'Come on!' Barbara urged.

'Not capering,' said James. 'Definitely not capering.'

Dog charged across the limbs, pushing them aside with his snout, clawing his way over and through them. He stumbled on the bottom steps, choked as they were by the animated appendages. That stumble saved James's and Barbara's lives. Up again, he rushed at the stairs, his claws leaving deep green gouges in the hard flesh of the limbs and throwing them back to be trampled anew by the Rottweilers and the dogs of Never. Mrs Wimble's poodle, Foffy, led the pack, her needle teeth bared in deathly anticipation.

Onto the landing and follow the scent of fear to the right, to the tower. A dim shaft of light and a blur of movement showed Dog the steps up as his claws hit the steel grill. He stumbled again but kept his balance and pressed on to the steps. He tore up, the Rottweilers right behind.

The trapdoor slammed into his face. He yelped in pain and frustration as he was bowled into the Rottweilers, the three of them tumbling to the floor.

James and Barbara lay side by side on the carpeted floor of the tower's glass loft, their deep breaths covering the noise of the rain. Tilda sniffed at the door to the outside gantry.

'There are limbs and dogs chasing us,' said Barbara though her laboured breathing.

'Yeah,' panted James. 'I know.' He turned his head to face her, wincing at the pain. The thought of blood on the carpet upset him. He'd got the house so tidy; he had tried so hard to impress her. He thought of the clean and tidy bedroom and all his Mum's clothes deposited at the charity shop. *I knew I shouldn't have bothered.*

'You're going to ask me what, why and probably even how,' he said to Barbara. 'But I don't know. I honestly don't know.'

Barbara nodded wearily. She believed him. Why shouldn't she? *Because it's his fucked-up house*, a voice inside her head screamed. She ignored it.

The trapdoor thudded. They both jumped.

'Will that hold?' Barbara asked.

'Yeah,' said James. 'I think.' He looked at her sheepishly. 'I don't know.'

Barbara eyed the steel pole and then turned to Tilda. 'What's wrong?' she said to the dog as she climbed to her feet and walked over. She briefly wondered where she had left her shoes. Tilda scrabbled and sniffed at the door. Barbara looked beyond, out into the night and onto the gantry circling the tower. She could see nothing but rain.

'What is it?' she said to Tilda.

James's granddad had had too many things to work with. That's why the incinerator had been abandoned. And while he had never persuaded an arm or a leg or a hand or a foot onto another body, our erstwhile riverbed compatriots knew a little more about making flesh behave how they wanted.

The man was reluctant. He knew what he needed to do, what he had agreed to do, but he was scared. This was only natural, we assured. He was beginning to realise that there was more to adventure than excitement.

He looked longingly around the neat and tidy bedroom, his eyes resting on the simple but cosy double bed. He drew in a deep breath and let it out in a long sigh as he viewed himself in the full length mirror: solid boots, blue jeans and a plain black t-shirt. His wife had bought him this t-shirt years ago. He'd never worn it.

He left the bedroom without a backward glance.

Foffy ran out of the back door and through the arch, bounding like a bouncing fluffy white ball over limb after limb. She headed for the pile that was forming in the broken driveway, and, using her tiny maw she tried to drag an arm towards it.

Giving up she bounded back through the arch, into the house and up the stairs. She yipped and yapped at a Great Dane and two burley mongrels. The four bounded, ran and loped outside, and under Foffy's direction the three dogs went out into James's shattered lawn and dragged three torsos onto the drive amongst the writhing limbs.

Foffy leapt up onto the chest of one and began to chew and bite at the skin, quickly tearing it open from sternum to navel while the mongrels did the same to the backs of the other two. There was no blood, just a green viscous solution that now dripped from the dogs' jaws. The green solution was already killing them but their possessors kept them moving, beginning what they assumed to be a race against time before they must return to the home recently sealed away from them.

The Great Dane, Charles, dragged one torso on top of the other, the middle and bottom facing down, the one on top facing up. He took the time to tear open the chest of the middle body, filling his mouth with green and beginning his own mortal countdown. The three torsos now had an open fleshy connection.

Foffy began to stumble as she helped an arm begin its joining with the lower torso. The mongrels dragged legs and arms while Charles, his head hanging lower and lower, directed the connections to the upper torso

Bang.

'They don't give up do they,' James pointed out as he watched the trap door rattle.

'Mmm?' Barbara was trying to see out of the door that led to the steel gantry.

'They don't give up.'

'No,' she answered. 'Have you got a phone up here?'

'No,' he said. 'My parents didn't want to be disturbed in here.'

Tilda whined as she sniffed at the edges of the door. We weren't sure what was going on. We have never been able to animate the dead, at least not for long. A fresh corpse could still be made to function, but only for a few hours. These limbs weren't regular dead flesh, however, and so, even though they had been buried for decades, each limb provided a host. We knew that thousands of the others were possessing those atomic limbs and those dogs, but to what purpose? Obviously there was something special about this house. We had known that since the others' attention had been so firmly directed at Tilda. What was the connection between Ivy Arch, the Warren and Eden's Aegis? The others must have found out something through the dog in the cage. In our efforts to keep Tilda and work with the man, we had allowed them more access to the Warren and its secrets.

The questions had to wait; for now we needed to survive. I had jumped into Tilda just that day so there was no rush on that score. It would be five days at least before any problems from long-term joining might arise, and the man would be here soon, so we just needed to get to the driveway.

Foffy coughed and hacked, unable to control the green vomit spewing from her mouth as she watched over the physical joining. Green drool dripped from Charles's mouth and his great legs were bent under the strain of carrying his own body and the construction of another. The mongrels lay down to conserve their strength, sending out a plea for aid.

It was the Rottweilers who heard that call. They told Dog who sent four more dogs to the driveway.

He eyed the steel shaft glimmering in its pale column of light. He padded over to the trap door covering the stairs down to the base of the tower. He stuck his nose into the crack between the two doors straining to hear or smell something of whatever was down there. There had to be something more than just forgotten dust.

He turned back to the Rottweilers who had resumed pounding the door above with their heads. A snarl brought them to a halt; soon the dogs' bodies would be senseless and right now there was no point throwing away good flesh. Dog barked his objection at a Labrador, too keen to flex his muscles and bash his head against the wood. They would wait.

James watched the trap door. He was sitting up now and he thought that his head had finally stopped bleeding. His carefully ironed shirt was matted with blood around the collar, drenched with sweat under the arms and generally no good for a date. He looked at Barbara looking out of the rain-soaked glass, her mobile phone in her hand.

'Maybe they do,' he said aloud.

'Maybe who does what?' she answered, not turning around.

'Give up.'

She turned to look at him questioningly, snapping her phone closed; there was no signal. He nodded to the quiet trap door.

'Oh,' she said. 'We should turn the lights off.'

'Is this really the time, Miss Bean?' he said in mock lasciviousness. Barbara's genuine lassitude meant that lasciviousness, mock or not, was nothing but unwanted arsing about.

'Stop arsing about and get the light off!'

James's eyebrows lowered in genuine embarrassment. He struggled to his feet and moved to the lamp.

'I'm sorry, James.' She moved away from the window, joining him at the table, her smile as dazzling as ever. James looked first at her and then at the remains of their meal.

'Call me Jim,' he said. Barbara nodded and he reached out and turned off the lamp.

The man knocked on the door and waited. He was not calm, not calm at all, but he was ready to put on a show.

A woman answered. She was not yet old but it had been a long time since she was young. White-haired and strong, she made the man nervous. She always had.

'Hi, Mrs Fiss,' he said. She looked him up and down, not unkindly but not friendlily either, as she always did. Some people would never change.

'He's not in,' she said.

'I know. I just need the keys to his truck,' he said, and then, on seeing the suspicion pass across her face, he added, 'Eddie knows about it. I've gotta help Jimmy, James Wynn, with a few things, and with his drive the way it is Eddie didn't want me taking the van down there.' It was so much easier to lie when you were telling the truth. But then people lied all the time, even those who weren't very good at it.

'Bit late.' It wasn't a question.

'It is, it is,' the man agreed. 'But there's no rest for the wicked, Mrs Fiss. No tea-break in the forward momentum of Fiss Fixings!'

She looked him up and down once more and then headed back into the house, not inviting or expecting the man to follow. She reappeared moments later and handed him the keys.

'What are they doing?' James asked.

'Don't know,' Barbara answered. Through the dark and the rain they could see movement, a lot of movement. Eight dogs surrounded a pile of... something.

'What's that pile?'

'Don't know.'

'It's moving.'

'I know.'

The pile was shuddering. It was difficult to make out but it might have been kicking or flailing or both. Tilda was in the middle of the room, looking though the hole in the floor. She couldn't see them but she could smell the dogs down there on the middle tier of the tower.

'Can an arm be a zombie?'

'What?' Barbara turned to James. 'What're you talking about?'

'What,' James cast about for the word, 'constitutes a zombie?'

Barbara started to point out that this wasn't the time, that their lives were probably in danger, were almost certainly in danger, that there were dozens of dogs and God knew how many arms and legs trying to attack them and that this just wasn't the time!

But, she thought, *there almost certainly wouldn't ever be a better time.*

'I suppose it could be,' she reasoned, 'if you take a zombie as being dead flesh animated by other, outside, means.'

'An arm can't groan, though. Zombies should groan.'

'Traditionally, yes, there's a lot of groaning.'

'And shuffling.'

'Well, I think that they've got the shuffling down.'

'Not in a funny-walking kinda way.'

'Shambling gait?'

'No it's just my tea repeating on me,' said James patting his stomach and wafting a hand under his nose. They both burst out laughing.

Through the eyes of a dog, did these people look more or less ridiculous as they laughed so hard they cried while, a trapdoor's width away, thousands of beings wanted to tear their bodies into such tiny pieces the rain would wash them away?

Foffy couldn't yip or yap anymore. Her rain-soaked white fur was stained red and green, and her little legs shook with fatigue. She wouldn't last and neither would Charles or the mongrels. They would've been dead by now if their possessors hadn't prevented it but that prevention was taking its toll on possessor and possessed. It was time to let them go.

As Foffy, Charles and the mongrels sat and then lay down, the other dogs pulled and pushed at the flailing mound of parts stuck turtle-like in the driveway. They rocked and rolled this new body until it could swing itself in a cascade of limbs onto its side and in a reverse avalanche get onto four of its six knees and two of its feet, four of its six elbows and two of its hands. Then it rose to its full naked, headless height, a new breed of insect.

Dog wasn't getting the message from outside. He'd been too long in this body. Years ago, before the host had been taken for granted, before he had been sent out to the yard by a family no longer interested, he had been called Rocky. It had been affectionate, even loving for a time. But it was not for long and a long time ago. Rocky wanted more, and he was coming to get it.

Dog shook his head angrily and snarled at his own weakness. Spittle flew to either side showering the other dogs looking to their leader, their muzzles masks of concern.

Growling, he beckoned the Rottweilers over; he needed them close to communicate. They filled him in on the activity outside. He looked up at the closed trapdoor. *Soon*, he thought. He woofed his orders for the other dogs to be ready.

Barbara wiped the tears from her eyes and then started laughing again when she saw Tilda watching the two of them.

'What is it?' asked James through his own subsiding chuckles.

'Tilda,' she answered. 'She's looking at us with such a look.'

'Looking at us with a look?' said James. 'Now that's clever. I'd swear that there's more than just woofs and wagging tails to that dog.'

'I bet she thinks we're barmy!'

Which was half true. We *knew* they were barmy. Not just these two, all of them. The waste around this whole world. We'd seen it before of course, and at first hand. They were following our well-trod path to self-destruction as surely as a guided missile. As surely and helplessly as driftwood in the Suez Canal itself. The others believed that James and Barbara and billions of others, along with their world, should be ours. Who's to say that they were wrong? But who's to say that we would do any better? After all we've ruined one world. Will we get another chance or are we doomed to be forever searching outside and fighting inside? We can never die in our own space, but we can never live either. And we can never agree. What a way to spend eternity.

We're all barmy.

Tilda woofed unconvincingly.

'Anyway,' said Barbara. 'Of course there's more to her. There's Tilda.'

'Yeah, she's more than just brown.' James laughed and looked to Barbara when he didn't get a response.

'Jim?' she said.

'More than just brown?' he repeated, still trying to impress.

'Jim? There's something at the window.'

Tilda growled, her lips pulled back, her teeth exposed. James looked from Barbara to Tilda and then to the window. He remembered his dad.

Chapter Seventeen

The ladder was difficult at first, but with a shuffling of limbs it was possible to get four feet and four hands on the rungs. The remaining limbs, two arms and two legs, faced backwards, hanging from the front two torsos like a bizarre backpack. Mr Tricks was carried in it.

Halfway up the ladder the left arm of the middle torso tore off under the strain, leaving the fingers gripping the rung. Eventually the fingers let go and the arm fell to the ground and began to crawl to the arch.

The rest of the creature carried on climbing. A consensus was required for the operation of this new body and that left arm had been the most reluctant. The remaining fourteen possessors now pushed on like a well-oiled machine.

The left arm wasn't too upset. She believed in what the others were doing, believed that this world should be ours and she accepted that certain actions, certain distasteful actions, would have to be carried out to achieve this. She believed in the cause, but she was happy not to be its monster.

The man drove the Ford Ranger. He was feeling guilty because he felt like he was stealing. Actually he was borrowing and we tried to tell him this but he knew that Eddie didn't know and because he knew that he didn't know… we stopped listening.

The vehicle was needed and so it was acquired; the man's conscience was of no concern. It was not to be discouraged too sharply, however, as these things can be used. People let their consciences run out of control for many reasons. This time the man was using it to cover his fear, smothering it in a cosy bed of faux remorse. It worked for us.

Turning off the headlights didn't work for us. It was a bad idea justified by the need for stealth. The man, cosseted by his conscience and still very nervous, was not fully in control of himself or the vehicle. He entered the driveway of Ivy Arch too quickly and smashed into the red Mini Cooper parked there.

The thing struggled onto the gantry as James and Barbara watched, mouths agape. They were both rooted to the spot as the last of the monster's limbs swung up from the ladder and onto the gantry right outside the glass door.

'What is that?' Barbara shouted.

'I don't know,' answered James.

Tilda snarled as drool dripped form her fangs and glistened on her blood-red gums.

They both jumped violently at a loud crash from outside. Eddie's Ford Ranger had found Barbara's red Mini.

'What was that?' Barbara shouted.

'I don't know,' answered James.

Bang. Three fists hammered on the door.

James and Barbara screamed and fell back towards the middle of the room, clutching at each other for support.

Bang. The door held firm. James and Barbara stopped, staring.

'It'll never get in like that!' shouted James.

'What are you gonna do, offer it tips?'

'What *are* we gonna do?'

The monster shuffled awkwardly in the cramped space of the gantry and, guided by Mr Tricks, turned one left and two right shoulders towards the door. It flung itself forward. Thud!

'The pole!' exclaimed Barbara.

'What, Ziggy?'

Thud! With the strength of three, the door more than rattled.

'Not Ziggy! The *pole*!' Barbara grabbed James and turned him to face the steel shaft.

'Ah,' said James. 'What about it?'

'Head wounds really don't suit you, you know.' James smiled at Barbara who was losing patience fast. He was just happy that she thought he wasn't really this dim.

Dog looked to the commotion above trying to see, smell and hear through the ceiling. He drooled in anticipation.

'What about Tilda?' said Barbara as the monster thudded against the door.

'No idea. It's your plan.' Tilda continued to snarl at the monster. 'Looks like she wants to stay and fight.'

'For God's sake, Jim, I can't think of everything!'

Thud! James scanned the room desperately. His eyes alighted on the table and sparked into life.

Finally, thought Barbara.

'The table cloth!' he exclaimed.

Maybe not, she added to herself. 'What about it?' she said aloud. 'You gonna make a white flag?'

'No,' said James, a little hurt. 'We make a harness for Tilda and tie it to my belt.'

Thud!

'Oh. Yeah. That's quite a good idea. Sorry, Jim.'

'We're gonna have to stop doing that.'

'What?'

'The things that make us have to apologise to each other.'

Thud!

'Wouldn't that make the world a better place,' she said, not entirely cynically.

James went for the tablecloth and without a pause whipped it off. The remains of their meal spilt and scattered, and smeared and shattered. James smiled, 'And the flowers are *still* standing!'

'A lifetime's ambition fulfilled?' Barbara asked.

Thud! and an audible crack. James hurried to the still-snarling Tilda with the stained white cloth.

'Hurry!' Barbara shouted, unable to take her eyes off the door.

'There's nothing down there, you know,' James shouted over the excitement. 'We'll be trapped.'

'We're trapped up here!'

James hesitated. Tilda's entire body was rigid with suppressed aggression.

'C'mon, Jim!'

He leant forward and wrapped the tablecloth around Tilda's chest and stomach. We did all we could to stop her snapping at James. It was just enough.

Thud! A louder crack.

'C'mon, Jim!'

'There!' he shouted. Barbara rushed over. Tilda was wrapped in what felt like a good makeshift harness.

'Let me help.' And she tied the loose ends to the back of James's belt.

Thud! The door gave and a gap opened at the top.

'Quick!' said Barbara and she scooped up Tilda. James, holding tightly to his belt, stumbled like a drunken cowboy to the hole dragging the two of them behind him.

'You're sure about this?' he said.

'Didn't you ever want to be a fireman?'

'No, not really.' He leant out and grabbed the pole.

Thud! Bang! The double glazing in the door smashed and the monster was slashed in a dozen places, green lines forming as it leaned through the newly created hole.

Barbara, trying to stay calm, lowered Tilda through the hole in the floor. James stepped out and wrapped his legs around the pole. Tilda's weight meant that he began sliding at once. He tried to control his descent as he disappeared into the black hole.

'Shit, shit, shit, shit, shit, shit...'

Barbara spun around to see the monster struggling in the doorway; it couldn't fit through sideways. Mr Tricks was barking insistently. The monster extracted itself from the doorway and began to turn around on the gantry.

Wasting no more time, Barbara reached for the pole.

Dog leapt at the railing when he saw James inching his way down the steel shaft, Tilda swinging below him. He barked his fury at the man and the dog as they passed him by just a few metres away.

Crash! He heard the noise from above. The monster was in but where was the woman? Falling silent he let James pass. As he did so Tilda swung around so that their gazes met. The glowing embers of Dog's eyes held a promise for Tilda. Without flinching, we held that gaze all the way into the dark.

Barbara soon followed, sliding much faster. Dog nodded to the Rottweilers. They took their run and leapt over the railing and out into the space.

Barbara forced herself to stay calm, to ignore the excitement of the escape, the monster, the pole, the speed, but the Rottweilers were too much. The two large dark shapes flew at her and she screamed, letting go of the pole and falling the last few metres. She landed heavily, crying out in pain as she jarred her legs on an old wooden chair that broke her fall by smashing into pieces.

James was already unfastening Tilda's makeshift harness when Barbara and then the Rottweilers landed. One dog fell in a heap with a sickening crack. The other landed on its feet but its own weight snapped its hind legs.

James could only hear all this. The small dim circle in the ceiling two floors up provided no illumination. He and Barbara were trapped in the dark, and something started to shuffle and drag along the concrete floor.

Barbara scanned the room and thought she could make out a James-shaped blur. She dragged her dead legs over.

'Are you alright?' he said as she joined him. Tilda was nearly free and struggling frantically. 'Hold still!' James snapped at her. And so we did.

'Yeah,' Barbara panted. 'Nothing broken. Legs're dead from the fall.'

'Here,' he said. 'Undo Tilda and I'll get the light.' The shuffling was getting closer.

He turned on the light to pandemonium. The harsh electric glare stunned both James and Barbara while the dogs on the steel grating above them all howled their shock and fury.

'Bloody hell!' James exclaimed. Barbara was with Tilda and just a few metres away, the Rottweiler with the broken legs was crawling toward them, dragging its body with its front paws, its useless hind legs trailing behind. 'That's not right. That's really not right!'

Then Barbara had Tilda free and the brown and black Border collie launched against the Rottweiler. Bowling into it, she had it on its back, its throat exposed. She drove her attack home. The scent of blood drove the dogs above into a renewed and deafening frenzy.

James and Barbara stared at Tilda. Blood stained her mouth and chin. It was in the fur on her chest and clogged her paws. That was not something Tilda would have done, it was something we would not have done in any other circumstance, but it was as simple as unhooking the back door.

James went down on one knee and held his hand out to Tilda. 'Good girl, Tilda. Good girl. Come here.' He had to raise his voice to be heard over the din howled by the dogs above them.

'Good girl?' said Barbara.

'She did what she had to.' Tilda put her head in James's hands. He ruffled her fur ignoring the blood.

'Pretty damned efficiently,' Barbara added.

The dogs above pressed their snouts against the grating, their teeth bared. Drool and their snarling grunts dripped through the gaps.

Barbara looked around the room. It was bare save for the steel shaft, the broken chair and a single solid-looking wooden door. She had lost all sense of direction.

'The incinerator,' said James pointing at the door and anticipating the question. He looked up to see fingers curling around the steel grating. The limbs were up the stairs.

'Incinerator? Why've you got an incinerator?'

'Erm...' James didn't know. He had never thought about it because as far as he knew there had always been an incinerator. 'Don't know. Incineration?'

'Ask a stupid question,' said Barbara. 'So how do we get out?'

'There isn't a way out. I told you that upstairs.'

'That's stupid! Why would there be a room that you could only get in to from above?'

James flicked drool from his shoulder with a calmness that belied his fear. 'I think this was the room that Granddad did his experimenting. I guess he needed it this way.' They both looked up at a new sound only just heard above the noise. The trap door to the glass loft was open. The monster filled the gap.

'We can't stay here!'

'There's nowhere to go!'

The man had the tow-rope attached to the red Mini Cooper. He used Eddie's truck to drag it clear of the drive. Once he had it on the road he unhooked the rope. As he headed back to the cab of the Ford Ranger he grabbed at his vibrating pocket.

'Hello?' he said into the phone. 'Yes, I'm here.' He paused, listening to the voice on the other end. 'I *am* hurrying! She's parked at the end of the drive and I've got to get her car out of the way!' Another pause. 'They're at the bottom of the tower and looking for a way out.' Another pause. 'Alright, I'll see you soon.'

He climbed into the truck, his plain black t-shirt plastered to his body by the rain and drove into the red Mini Cooper, pushing it onto the grass verge. The engine roared as the man, in his rush, pushed it over and into the dyke.

'Shit! Sorry Miss Bean,' he said and turned the jeep around and headed onto the broken driveway of Ivy Arch.

With an effort Dog stopped his barking and snarling so as to better study the scene below. James and Barbara didn't seem to know what to do. He glanced at the monster struggling down the steps and smiled a wolfish smile. Pointing his gaze back down he watched as the Rottweilers, unnoticed by the man and woman, once again shuffled toward their prey.

Tilda suddenly joined in with the canine cacophony. James and Barbara whirled to face her, recognising the urgency in her voice. She wasn't looking up at the other dogs; she was looking down at the moving corpses of both Rottweilers.

'Oh shit,' said James

'The incinerator!' Barbara exclaimed.

James shook his head. 'It'll be locked.' The dog with the broken hind legs dragged itself another few centimetres toward them while the other had struggled to its feet, head lolling uselessly on its broken neck as it shambled blindly forward.

'Where's the key?'

'Kitchen. I think.'

'Well it's no use in there is it!'

'Er... no.'

Tilda backed away from the oncoming canine corpses. No point in attacking; the possessor could keep those bodies going no matter how many holes we tore into it. We needed an axe.

'We need an axe,' said Barbara glaring at James, daring him not to have one.

'There's no axe in here,' he said. 'There's nothing!'

Barbara glared at him.

'There's one in the shed,' he shouted.

Barbara glared at him.

James stared frantically around the room. Seeing the wreckage from Barbara's tumble, he grabbed two of the broken chair legs. 'Here you go,' he said as he handed one to Barbara.

She stared at the half-metre tube of broken wood.

Tilda looked up and her barking began anew. James and Barbara followed her stare: the monster was on the steps leading down from the glass loft.

'We can't stay here!' Barbara cried and started for the door to the incinerator. James followed uncertainly. They both stopped and backed away a step when the handle on the door lowered.

'Oh shit.'

Dog watched the Rottweilers drag themselves toward the humans and the barking dog. The Border collie was highly agitated. Dog sneered at the lack of control, and a line of drool ran in a string halfway to the floor below before breaking off and landing squarely on Barbara's neck. She barely flinched as she cast her eyes from the door to the dogs.

He looked to his army of dogs and limbs to find out what was behind that door. The hosts were quieted as he received his answers: no one knew.

James and Barbara looked up at the sudden silence. They saw the dogs looking to the dark brown Pit Bull. Tilda had fallen silent too; we had to try to know what they were saying but they blocked us well. The shuffling of the shambling Rottweilers filled James and Barbara's ears along with loud groaning noises as their great black bodies expelled gases for the final time.

'There's your groaning,' said Barbara. 'Happy now?'

'No.'

The handle finished its journey down. James and Barbara held their chair legs high. Dog pushed his face into the grill. The door burst open and a dark lithe figure leapt out, a metal bar in her hand.

James and Barbara gasped. It was Jane.

She stopped for barely a heartbeat, looking this way and that, and then she launched herself against the Rottweilers. Her booted foot slammed the neck of the first into the floor, the metal bar stabbing down and into its head. James and Barbara flinched at the crunching sound then looked up as Dog and the rest howled their anger, the canine cacophony beginning anew. The monster strode toward the trapdoor, kicking limbs aside, Mr Tricks scampering after it. Jane brought their eyes back down as she pirouetted into the second Rottweiler, kicking its head so hard it whipped around twice on its broken neck. The force of the spin sent it sprawling. Jane was on it and the metal bar in it before it had finished its fall.

'You two!' Jane barked as she span away from the second-time corpse. 'Out!'

James and Barbara dashed for the open door. Dog snarled and headed for the trap door, trying to hurry the monster as it attempted to wrap lifeless fingers around the handle.

The two ran into the small round room that contained the incinerator. James had been a rare visitor to this room and so, while it was familiar, he didn't realise that the incinerator itself had moved.

'What do we do now?' Barbara asked.

'Don't know,' James panted. His didn't know if his head was hurting again or if he was just remembering to feel the pain.

Jane fell into the room. 'That's not right,' she said looking out into the bottom of the tower. 'Those dogs are moving again.'

'Yeah, they do that,' said James.

'What now?' Barbara asked. 'And what are you doing here?'

'I work downstairs,' she replied. 'Let's move.' And she slammed the door shut. James and Barbara both thought that they saw a huge bulk manoeuvring down the steps.

She moved to the incinerator and disappeared down steps that neither of our heroes had noticed. They followed mutely.

The steps spiralled for just a few metres and ended in a short passage. James and Barbara stumbled after the purposeful Jane. They passed a door on their right.

'What's in there?' James asked.

'Trouble,' Jane replied.

They quickly came to the end of the passage and climbed another spiral stair. At the top they moved through an open door into a well-appointed study.

'This is my da... *my* study!' James exclaimed.

'Come on,' Jane stated. 'We're leaving.' She made for the door.

'Couldn't we just hide out here until they go?' James and Barbara both asked.

'They'll be in here once they figure it out, which won't be long.' She pulled the door open and stepped through. James and Barbara hurried after her.

Through the study and into the hall, the four of them ran into the kitchen scattering the few straggling limbs not yet on the stairs. The message was sent. Dog knew where we were.

'Stop!' shouted James. The bleep, bleep, bleep from the freezer rang through the dark kitchen. He remembered the ice cream tub. 'Walk.'

'What? Why?'

'Just do it!'

And they walked across the kitchen floor. The sound of the dogs on the stairs was sudden and loud. James took the lead and his foot nudged against the tub on the floor. He kicked it aside and hurried on as claws hit the tiles of the hallway floor.

Dog bounded across the tiles. They were close; he could smell them.

Then the agent, Jane, was in front of him swinging her metal bar. It connected with his jaw and sent him sliding back into the following pack. Jane turned and ran.

James and Barbara and Tilda burst into the back porch with Jane right behind them. She slammed the kitchen closed just as a thud signalled the arrival of the first dog. Then another and another as they slammed into the door one after the other.

'That won't hold,' said Jane. One of the lower panels cracked to confirm her statement.

'I thought you were off sick? Eddie won't be happy when he finds out,' said James through laboured breaths.

'I've got other responsibilities,' said Jane.

'Eddie doesn't seem the type to take kindly to other responsibilities,' said Barbara.

'Probably not,' said Jane.

'What're we gonna do?' said James.

'Let's go,' said Jane, and she was out of the back door and into the rain. James and Barbara soon followed when a mongrel's snarling snout thrust through the cracked panel. As they fled, James grabbed the key and slammed the door behind them. He lifted the handle and locked it.

They joined Jane who stared at the rain soaked archway.

'This isn't right,' she said. Foffy, green drool hanging from her jaws stood firm in front of a four-legged four-armed monster. They had built another. Charles and the two green-tinged mongrels flanked the beast.

'Hell of a zombie, though,' said James as it lurched forward, the rain immediately pooling in the empty sockets between the two sets of shoulders.

Jane advanced, bar at the ready, Tilda at her side. James turned to Barbara but she was gone. Quickly scanning the yard, he saw her climbing onto the ride-on lawnmower.

Jane swung her bar sending Foffy slamming against the wall of the incinerator. She ducked beneath the swinging arms of the monster and brought the bar back round to smash a kneecap.

Tilda charged Charles, Great Dane and Collie collided in a tangle of fury and fur and gnashing teeth, each seeking the throat of the other.

The two mongrels shambled towards Jane while James watched, stricken. He turned to Barbara; she was desperately trying to get the lawnmower started. Deciding what to do, he ran for the garage, kicking an arm out of his way as he went. As he fumbled with the lock he glanced over his shoulder. Jane was struggling as she held off the mongrels, the monster and Foffy who had rejoined the fray and now bit at her ankles. Jane lashed out with a booted foot, sending the poodle flying once more. That action left her open just long enough for a blindly flailing arm to knock into her shoulder and send her reeling. The mongrels moved in.

James was about to turn and run toward Jane when Tilda barrelled into the mongrels. We had dispatched Charles with ease. Already a slow and awkward dog, death had done nothing for his agility. Jane took advantage of the diversion to climb back to her feet. James turned back to the garage door.

Barbara tried again to start the lawnmower. 'C'mon, c'mon!' She was soaked through but she didn't notice as she desperately stabbed at the starter button and pulled on the choke. Suddenly Foffy was on her, pulling at the hem of her trousers with needle teeth. Barbara kicked at the creature, repulsed by the poodle's dead eyes and the green ichor oozing from its mouth and onto Barbara's trousers and stockinged feet. Kicking Foffy away she tried the mower again and this time it sparked into life. Glancing at the garage she saw that the door was open. She aimed the mower at Foffy who had regained her feet and was shambling towards her.

As the mower neared at slightly more than walking pace, the now slower than walking pace Foffy changed her mind. Too late, she turned to run but the mower was on her, and lumps of red and green and white were fired out at all angles from beneath the mower, scattering on the gravel and splattering on the walls. Barbara turned toward the fight in front of the arch, mowing stray limbs as she went.

Suddenly the courtyard was lit with a dazzling beam vomited from the archway. Barbara turned away to shield her eyes and heard the throaty roar of a powerful engine behind her, in front of her, all around her. James edged his tank out of the garage and into the rain. He stared out of the windscreen and headed directly for the swirling melee. Barbara reversed the lawn mower out of the way. She looked back to the light emanating from the arch and realised why James's engine had sounded so loud: Eddie's Ford Ranger edged its way into the courtyard.

James saw Eddie's truck and, with an insight that was almost telepathic, both he and the man aimed their vehicles at the monster.

Jane batted arms away with the bar and then aimed a kick at another kneecap, forcing the monster to stumble in front of the advancing jeeps. She and Tilda jumped clear.

The two metal monsters slammed into the fleshy construct, crushing it between them. They both reversed and the components slumped to the ground. James saw that the driver was Bub.

'Now!' Jane shouted to Barbara. The mower powered forward and onto the pile of thrashing, broken limbs. The dogs, dead and alive, ran, pieces of their former ally showering them as they went.

Dog watched from the kitchen window as our people were violently expelled from their shattered hosts, too disoriented to try and jump for another host. Dropping to the floor he went back to the Rottweilers. The agent had made sure they would never move again. If their possessors were to survive then Dog must switch off Eden's Aegis in the next hour. An impossible task.

Returning to the house, he entered the study and saw the rug thrown back to reveal a trap door. The monster waited next to it. Dog gestured with a snarl and the monster tried to open it. The glowing keypad next to it told them that it was locked. Dog howled and the monster flailed its fists against the door. Then it lurched to its feet and ransacked the study.

He stopped, remembering something. Axe in the shed, he sent to the others. The monster moved to find a way out of Ivy Arch and into that shed.

Chapter Eighteen

Sirens wailed and blue lights flashed from the ambulances, police cars and fire engines that dotted the streets and roads north and south of the Humber.

Scud had left spies abroad. They ducked between the panicking crowds and ran through the streets and roads sending reports and causing mayhem wherever they could. One ran in front of a police van, meat wagons as the humans referred to them. The dogs wanted the meat on the streets tonight. The driver of the van swerved to avoid the dog. The resultant crash was satisfactory. They attacked fire-fighters, police officers and paramedics. They sowed the seeds of disruption and chaos, and the flowers bloomed in violence.

Bow and Wow, two impressive chocolate Labradors, were beautiful, too beautiful to be on a city's streets at night. No one noticed them, or at least almost no one noticed them. They followed the two men from Never. Eddie and Frankie had split up in search of Ziggy and now they came back together.

'Any sign of him?' said Frankie. He was smirking.

'No,' Eddie sounded worried. 'Try him again.'

'I've tried him ten times! And that's when I could get a signal. Everyone's trying everyone else!'

'Try him again! Try him eleven times! Try him twelve times!' Eddie turned on his brother. 'And stop smirkin'! Nothin' funny here.' Looking around he saw a covered body being loaded into an ambulance. Bow and Wow sent a message about the operational emergency vehicle.

'I'm not smirking,' protested Frankie. 'And I know it's not funny.' The rain had soaked the two men to their skin. It was raining so hard they weren't even drunk anymore. It was raining so hard they wouldn't even be hung over anymore.

'I think we should get home,' said Eddie. Frankie nodded.

The two cars sped away from Ivy Arch toward Never. Barbara sat with Bub in the lead car, Tilda on the seat behind them, her tongue lolling in time to her panting. James and Jane followed in the Mitsubishi. James glanced nervously at his silent passenger.

'What's going on?' he said.

'What's going on?' Barbara demanded of Bub. 'Why are you here?'

'You're on a hotspot,' said Jane to James. 'Your date with Barbara came on the same night as an experiment in the Warren.'

'The Warren?' said James.

Bub looked at Barbara and then returned his gaze to the road ahead. 'The Warren's an underground complex dug out by the government to house Eden's Aegis.'

'Who's Eden and what's her Aegis?' asked Barbara.

Jane looked at James as he turned onto the bypass following the Ford Ranger closely. 'Anthony Eden was PM back in '56 during the Suez Crisis.'

'Never heard of it,' James shrugged. It was a difficult action; his body was so taut he thought it might snap.

'Do you want me to drive?' Jane asked, although it wasn't really a question.

'Was that the one with Israel that lasted six days?' Barbara asked as Bub drew the Ford to a stop, all the time glancing nervously into his mirror.

'No,' he replied. 'That was in '67. Israel were in the Suez Crisis though. We, Britain and France, wanted to take back control of the Suez Canal after the Egypt president, fella called Nasser, nationalised it. So we went in to get the canal and get rid of Nasser.'

'Regime change not a new thing then.'

No. Might have been the first one in the name of oil though,' said Bub, enjoying sharing his little titbits of trivia. 'We went in and did what we had to do but the Americans didn't like it. They told us off so we came out again.'

'And this Aegis?' James asked as he and Jane passed in front of the Mitsubishi.

'A shield,' said Jane. She exuded control as she settled into the driver's seat with a click of the seat belt. She looked pointedly at James and then over his shoulder.

He reached for his own safety belt.

'What kind of a shield?' asked Barbara as Bub pulled away, satisfied that James and Jane were about to follow. The cars moved around the bypass and into Never. Barbara felt like screaming. She wanted pull out her hair and stuff it down Bub's throat for this ridiculous situation.

'The kind that stops a nuclear blast,' said Jane.

James didn't reply.

The cars pulled up outside a semi-detached house on the outskirts of Never. It was only two hundred metres or so from Eddie's central house; you didn't have to go far to get to the outskirts of a place like Never. The five of them climbed out of the vehicles and, led by Bub and Tilda, entered the garage next to the house.

'Everybody be quiet,' said Bub only sort of quietly. Bub was excited. Too excited. This was how the relationship worked with a sentient: they had to want us in, and Bub wanted a certain kind of excitement. He closed the garage door and hurried to join his audience.

Five bodies stood in a rough circle around a bare one hundred watt bulb.

'What nuclear blast?' Barbara renewed the interrogation.

'Any nuclear blast!' said Bub. 'Eden's Aegis was meant to send us, Britain that is, back to the top of the tree. The Suez Crisis was the last nail in the old Imperial coffin. We were fucked before then anyway, but after '56 everyone knew who called the shots: the Yanks. Eden was a flaky fella who ran off to the Bahamas once it all kicked off, sat there on his holidays while everyone else picked up the pieces. Anyway, while he was sunning himself he comes up with the shield.'

'Clever bloke then was he?' said James barely containing a manic cackle. *It'll be okay if I breathe*, he told himself. *Don't look at any more dogs and just breathe.* Tilda stared at him. Or rather I stared at him.

'N…' Jane began.

'Not really,' Bub jumped in over Jane. 'He came up with the idea but it was thirty years nearly before anything was anywhere near ready.'

'So James's house was used as a shield in the eighties?' said Barbara and then turned to James. 'I was just thinking how observant you were.'

James stared at her blankly.

'What?' said Bub, 'James's house?' He wore the patient but excited expression of a Star trek fan explaining Klingons to the uninitiated. 'Ivy Arch had nothing to do with 1990 trial.'

'1990?' said James. 'The Splash?'

'Ye…' Jane started and then glared as Bub leapt in again.

'The Splash! It was caused by Eden's Aegis's first test. Or at least that's what we think.' Tilda woofed quietly and James flinched.

Bub glanced at the Border collie and held his hands apart in a placatory gesture. 'That's what *they* think, I mean,' he added looking pointedly at Tilda.

James and Barbara followed his stare. '*They* who?' they said together, looking blankly at Tilda.

'The aliens!' Bub almost shouted. Jane renewed her glare.

'Calm down, Bub,' she warned.

'Sorry,' he whispered. 'The aliens,' he repeated to the stunned James and Barbara.

'Don't be ridiculous,' said James. Barbara nodded her agreement.

'He's right,' said Jane firmly to stop any further interruptions. 'The Splash was caused by the failed test.'

Silence.

James and Barbara stared at Jane and Bub. Tilda moved her head between the two groups, looking up at each in turn.

'How does a shield cause an accident involving crashing aliens and... and... whatever else?' said Barbara.

'When is a shield not a shield?' asked Bub.

'Alright,' Barbara cut in. 'Time to hear this from someone who doesn't think he's Doctor Spock.'

'Actually it's Mr Sp...'

'Whatever!' Barbara glared at Bub, who fell silent.

'Construction on the Warren began in the late fifties,' Jane began. 'It stretches from Never to Barton on the south bank, and then spreads under the river and some of Hull on the north. It's a maze of tunnels and rooms. It took twenty five years to dig it out, and then another ten to equip it with all the stuff that was needed. It was slow and secret stuff. The government didn't want anyone to know - friends as well as enemies. The only visible part of the project were the shield's projectors.'

Bub was practically dancing on the spot, bursting to tell the next part.

'We can see them?' said James. 'From where?'

'Just about anywhere from round here!' Bub leapt in, ignoring Jane and Barbara's glares. 'It's the bridge! The Humber Bridge!' he repeated in the face of their confused looks.

'The towers of the Bridge,' Jane interjected, 'are the projectors of the shield's energy.'

'Bollocks!' said James and Barbara together.

'But they didn't work!' Bub again. 'Instead of blanketing Humberside with an energy field it beamed,' Bub put particular emphasis on this word, 'the energy into space!'

'And hit some aliens?' asked James. He sat down heavily on a box and held the back of his head.

'Yes!' said Jane and Bub together. Bub was the one who added the exclamation mark. Jane shot him a furious look and he clamped a hand over his mouth in a comedic fashion. No one laughed.

'Their ship was dragged into the Humber by the energy beam,' said Jane. Bub nodded enthusiastically.

'And they've been down there seventeen years!' he added.

'Shut up, Bub,' said Barbara.

'Actually Bub knows this bit much better than me,' Jane sighed.

'Seventeen years in the dark,' he said in hushed whisper. 'You've seen that river. It's a brown river. Not a nice place to be stuck.' He caught Barbara's impatient stare and hurried on.

'Soon after the crash they reached out toward whatever had caused the accident, toward the Bridge. But it didn't work. People were hurt.'

'Hurt?' said James.

'You mean people were killed,' said Barbara.

Bub nodded glumly. 'But they didn't know. They retreated back inside their ship. They didn't dare leave for fifteen years because they couldn't see what was on the surface,' he continued, his voice rising steadily. 'Their sensors,' Bub relished the word, 'had failed and they had to wait for the self-repair systems to kick in, find the problem and fix it.' He paused for breath.

'Not very mechanically minded then?' asked Barbara.

Bub laughed at this and Tilda looked at Barbara. Even Jane smirked.

'What?' Barbara demanded.

'When they got to have a look at us,' Bub continued, ignoring Barbara's frustration, 'they were hopeful of communication; they thought we'd respond positively. You know, be nice.'

'And we weren't?' The question came from James and Barbara. It was asked tentatively as both were nervous at how they were being dragged in to what seemed like a geek's fantasy, which it was from the man's perspective.

'No! But we didn't know. You see, they communicate by telepathy!' The excitement generated by that word was palpable.

'Where they come from any sentient life's telepathic. No one needs to talk, so no one does talk. It's inefficient you see. And insufficient a lot of the time. With telepathy one of these fellas can show you everything you need to know instead of having to take the time to tell you!'

'Show what?'

'Anything! Everything! I've seen a star implode and I've seen six-legged horses that fly and apes that can build a space ship and planets that're so green and so red and so blue and so yellow that just calling them colours makes them seem silly and I've seen a planet die…'

'Slow down, Bub,' Barbara cut in. She turned back to Jane. 'What's all this got to do with us?' she said, indicating herself and James. Bub sagged a little in disappointment but his excitement remained.

'Nothing anymore,' Jane shrugged. 'You were in harm's way and we got you out. That's it. Once the government recover the Warren, they'll be wanting a word with you but that'll be it.' That sounded ominous, thought James, still holding his head.

'Sounds ominous,' said Barbara. 'What do you mean 'a word', and why does this Warren need recovering?'

'Just that they'll want to talk. You've seen things and they'll want to make sure that you won't talk about them,' Jane replied to the first question. Barbara and James both looked up in alarm. 'It'll be okay,' Jane assured them. They didn't feel assured.

'And the Warren'll be overrun with those dogs by now,' Jane continued. 'We've been tracking the same suspicious behaviour on the north bank so there's probably more than just a few dozen there.'

'What'll happen to the dogs?' asked James. Barbara and Bub both looked to the government agent. She shrugged.

'They'll be dealt with.'

'Jesus…' began Barbara.

'But…' James started.

'Your house!' cried Bub anticipating the question from James and covering an awkward topic that threatened to ruin his moment. 'Your house is connected to all this. They didn't know until six months ago, but once they did that's why they held on to Tilda as much as they could.'

'Held on to Tilda? What do you mean?'

'They couldn't talk to us 'cause of the telepathy thing. So,' Bub paused and drew in a breath, 'they tried to jump in. But,' he shrugged apologetically, like he was somehow responsible for something. 'That was even worse.'

'Jump into what?' said Barbara.

'Our minds! That's what they do: make contact, seek permission, jump in!'

'Hang on, hang on! I thought you said that they couldn't make contact?'

'That's where it went wrong,' Bub admitted, glancing at Tilda. 'The first few attempts didn't go well. That's when...' Bub let his voice trail away. Shrugging apologetically, he carried on. 'A mind needs to be open, fully open, for one of them to jump in. They should've known but they didn't understand at first, you see.' Bub spoke directly to James. Jane moved behind him to inspect his head wound.

'The people they tried to jump in to weren't ready, and some,' Bub paused before continuing. 'Some died.'

'My mum?' The garage fell silent as all eyes fell on James. Tilda lowered her head.

'And my dad?'

'Some people the jump hurts or even kills. Others they just seem to bounce off. Or at least they thought they were just bouncing off. Once they found out about Ivy Arch, your mum and dad were priority targets. Your mum was lost straight away but your dad, well, after the first bounced off they just kept on trying. Jumper after jumper. Thousands of them...'

'Thousands?' Barbara interrupted. 'How many of them are down there?'

'A lot,' Bub answered. 'Anyway, all those attempts had an effect on his mind. It drove him...'

'Crazy?' *They really were at the window.*

'Bub,' said Jane. 'Go get me a first aid kit. I want to patch up James's head.' James snorted at this. 'Sorry,' said Jane, 'bad choice of words.'

Words. Words were something we had seen as inefficient and insufficient, but they certainly did help with a story. Bub hesitated; he didn't want to miss any words. He left as Jane's glare became insistent.

Chapter Nineteen

'Bub's excited about all this,' Jane explained to James and Barbara. 'That's why they chose him, I think.'

'*Thinking* seems to be what's lacking,' said Barbara.

'Actually that's about all they can do.'

'All *who* can do?' James suddenly demanded, turning his head to look up at Jane. 'You and Bub with your 'they'. Who?'

'The aliens.'

'You keep telling us about aliens and I keep not believing you. What're we gonna do about that?' said James. Barbara looked at him. She was impressed. And she was confused. And she was angry. It was only the memory of the sound of the metal bar that Jane still carried stabbing into that Rottweiler's head that kept her from grabbing Jane and shaking the answers out of her.

'I don't believe you either,' said Barbara.

'That's your problem,' Jane shrugged. 'They're there, in the river, in the dogs, and in Bub. And in those arms and legs, I suppose.'

Tilda woofed quietly. James and Barbara both looked at her. 'In the dogs?' they both said.

'Yes!' said Bub, returning and handing over the first aid kit with a flourish. Jane took it and began to riffle through the contents.

'They soon discovered that the dogs would be the best alternative. No one bounces off a dog's mind because they're like sponges. They're trusting, open, ready to please; they're our best friends!'

'Nice!' said Barbara.

'Well, that's what it is sometimes. The dogs're taken over and controlled, but not by all of them. Only the others do that, the ones who have Tilda only ride along. They use the dogs' minds as a way of escaping the river for a while. It's pretty dark down there.'

'Yes, Bub, I think they've got the dark thing now,' Jane pointed out as she applied antiseptic cream to James's wound. He flinched. 'Don't be a baby,' she said to him.

Barbara stared at Tilda, stared at me. Her face was a picture of disbelief and wonderment. It made for an attractive combination. 'Others?' she said.

'Yeah,' said Bub. 'Others. There's two factions on the ship. One lot, the others, think that they may as well stay here and have this planet for their own...'

'Oh come on!' said James. 'If you're gonna spin us a story make it a new one.'

'Hey, clichés are clichés because they're true,' said Bub. 'Their planet's knackered and they want a new one. The others think it may as well be this one.'

'And what do your lot think?' said Barbara.

'The friendlier faction,' said Jane to Bub's disappointment, 'are represented by Bub and Tilda. They claim that they just want to leave and carry on their search. They say that our lack of telepathy makes us incompatible hosts and therefore the planet is not suitable for settlement.' She finished wrapping a bandage around James's head as she told them this. He looked terrible. The bruises left by Titz were still clearly visible and were now topped by a bandage even whiter than his face.

'But Bub can't be the only one stupid enough to let one of these things in,' said Barbara. Tilda looked at her, her head cocked. Barbara returned the stare and addressed the dog directly. 'Just check out a Trekkie chatroom, all sorts of pointy-eared-wannabes would queue up to get what he's got. All you've got to do is use these dogs to search for Danger Mouse t-shirts and *jump in*. Hell, they'd be offended if you didn't. What're you waiting for, an invitation? Did Bub invite you in?'

'No,' said Bub. 'They just jumped in. They say that we're *all* lucky it was them that discovered me and not the others.'

'They would wouldn't they. Did they tell you, you were special, Bub? Did they say that you were *chosen*? What do these *voices* sound like? What are they telling you to do?'

'Save your lives for a start.'

Barbara fell silent at that.

'They're here, Barbara. No denying that. The white coats in the Warren could never work it out but they knew it too,' said Jane.

'How come you're mixed up with Bub and aliens if you work for the government?' James asked Jane.

They all turned toward a noise from the house.

'Shit, it's the missus!' said Bub. 'Everyone hide!'

'Where?' said Barbara incredulously. 'This is ridiculous. Your wife doesn't know?'

'She's not gonna believe me, is she!'

The door opened to reveal Bub's wife. 'What's going on?' she said looking at Jane with barely concealed contempt and suspiciously at

Barbara. Then she saw James with his bandaged head. This was not going to go well. 'What the f...?'

Bub ran towards her. 'Now then Isha, this is not what it looks like.'

'I've no idea what it looks like, Bublia! I've never found my husband with his girlfriend and a pair of strangers in my garage before!'

'She's not my...'

'Shut up. Shut up! What is *she* doing here and who are the other two idiots?'

James and Barbara shuffled their feet, looked at their hands, hummed and generally prayed for the hole in the ground which was never going to open. Jane looked embarrassed, a new look for Jane. Barbara gleaned some satisfaction from it.

'This is James and this is Barbara...'

'Hello James, hello Barbara,' said the stick of fury. 'Get out!'

'There's no need to be like that, Isha...'

'Get out, the lot of you!' she rounded on Jane. 'Especially you! Get out!'

Jane, James and Barbara made to leave. Bub followed.

'Where d'you think you're going?' Isha demanded of Bub.

'With them,' he replied.

'You and your secrets. What about our family? What about you and this tramp and these idiots? What about that dog? What about me, Bublia? What about me?'

'I'm going, Isha. I have to. If I don't then...'

'Go on then! But don't come back. You're a waste of space, a six foot stack of shit. I wanted you in the real world, Bublia, but you'll have to find it somewhere else. Get out! Go!'

The five fled the garage, the fury of Bub's wife chasing them all the way. Tilda looked back at the house. Isha had been good to us. We hoped that she would be okay. We like to think that she is okay. And Bub.

The five made their way through the rain down the main street of Never.

'Couldn't we take the cars?' James asked.

'Nowhere to park,' said Jane.

'And I don't want Eddie's mum seeing his car,' said Bub.

'Where are we going?' Barbara asked.

'My house,' Jane replied. They forged on through the weather, passing the Pipe, its dark windows and motley shell closed for the night.

'What time is it?' asked James.

'Midnight,' Barbara replied.

This could have been the moment that Titz re-entered the story. He may have been watching us from across the street or from the shelter of his car or Danny's van. He may have been in his house, watching from the window, or he may have been skulking in shadows ever since we left Ivy Arch.

We don't know but somehow he and his friend picked up our trail and followed us right to the end.

As the rain-soaked group reached a terraced house, only three doors down from the trio of Fiss dwellings, a taxi pulled up.

Eddie opened the front passenger door and shouted to them. 'Bub? Jane? Giz a tenner. This fucker's robbing us blind.' He nodded at the driver. Frankie climbed out of the back seat.

The seven of them squeezed into Jane's small front room.

'Got any booze?' Eddie asked his impromptu host. Four other faces turned to her hopefully.

'Beer?' Jane asked.

'Lovely,' said Eddie, and everyone else nodded. Jane disappeared, returning moments later with six bottles.

'You're back early, Eddie,' Bub pointed out.

'It's all kicking off over there,' said Eddie nodding vaguely northwards. 'Mad as a yard of dogs.' He took a long pull on his bottle, which looked tiny in his hands.

'Why, what's happening?' Jane asked casually. James and Barbara were impressed with the ease with which Jane lied. If they hadn't experienced the events of the last few hours for themselves they wouldn't have believed that anything extraordinary had happened. But, they realised, that had been Jane ever since they had known her, which was a much shorter time than Eddie.

'Dunno. People dropping like flies. We lost Ziggy.'

'What do you mean lost him?' said Jane. 'Where?'

'Dunno. The three of us was in the *Hop and Vine* and then there was two of us. Lasses screaming, lads running, Ziggy nowhere. Ambulances taking them that's collapsed, police chasing about.' He took another pull and put the empty bottle on the coffee table.

James and Barbara swapped looks, so did Bub and Jane. Tilda watched everyone. Eddie and Frankie noticed.

'What you all doing here, anyway? How'd the date go, Jimmy?'

'Erm...' James looked to Barbara. Eddie carried on regardless.

'And what about you?' He looked to Jane and Bub. 'You don't look very poorly. Your missus right about you two?' They both flared red. He looked at Tilda. 'Not letting her out of your sight now she's back, eh?'

Frankie stared at Tilda, at us, at me. 'There was a lot of dogs running about in Hull,' he said thoughtfully.

'What's going on?' Eddie demanded. Bub, James and Barbara immediately looked to Jane. Eddie saw. 'Jane? They're all looking at you. What's my joiner been up to?' Frankie leaned forward so eagerly he looked hungry.

'Well, Eddie,' she said with a smile. 'If I told you I'd have to kill you.'

Bub laughed.

'Tell me or you'll have to.' Eddie's growl contained promise. Jane looked taken aback. Barbara took a little more comfort.

She and Eddie stared at each other. The power struggle was obvious: Jane shouldn't tell this man anything but could he be resisted? Certainly the agent could resist him, but could the joiner? Bub wanted to say; he wanted Eddie's help. He looked to Jane, silently urging her to comply.

'We're in the middle of an alien invasion.' Jane's deadpan statement was delivered like a glass of water: simple, clear and very much here.

Eddie stared at Jane and then to his brother. Frankie smiled a broad smile.

'Shut up, Frankie,' said Eddie.

'Never said a word.'

The monster strode determinedly into James's study, a long-handled axe held in two of its hands. Dog and a few others cleared limbs away as the monster prepared to assault the trapdoor.

Scud brought down another white coat and then ran on through the tunnels. The terrified man was immediately pounced upon by the following pack, swallowed in a pile of fur and fury, his screams quickly cut off.

The walls were clad in white plastic and the lights came on as Scud entered new sections. It was dazzling, disorientating and above all annoying. Where was the control room? Was there a control room? Too many questions, not enough answers. They hadn't been ready to move.

The tunnels echoed to the sounds of desperately searching dogs. Their allies on the south bank had taken casualties and needed to return to the ship. Unless they could find the control room, any control room, then that simply couldn't happen.

Scud could see the travel system that ran alongside the walkways, bullet-shaped cars that would shoot them wherever they wanted to go. The canine snout and claws were not designed to operate these things. He snarled and ran on.

'Shouldn't we ring the police?' said Barbara.

'What's plod gonna do?' said Eddie.

'The government then.'

'Fuck 'em. They've been messin' with us since the Splash. Time to sort it ourselves.' Baron Fiss turned to Jane and Bub. 'So you're double-o-seven, and you're double-o-fuck-all.'

Jane and Bub nodded, smiling.

'You never did answer my question,' said James. 'How does a government agent get mixed up with Bub and his aliens?'

'I was invited.' She smiled at Bub who returned the gesture. The others waited impatiently. 'Bub's been working it from all sides, and so do I now.'

'Now?' said Eddie.

'I was sent into Never to keep an eye out.'

'On us?' said Frankie, lighting a cigarette. Jane handed him an ash tray.

'On everyone and everything. Working for Eddie was ideal: go everywhere, see everyone. They chose me because I was a joiner.'

'Glad to be accommodating,' Eddie grumbled. 'Funny job for a spy, joinery.'

'Got to retire on something,' said Jane.

'And you cut hair as well,' said Barbara, sarcastically.

Jane shrugged, 'I'm not bad with scissors. Although there can be a bit of a mess.' Jane had meant the last comment to be a joke. Barbara just stared. Jane continued, clearing her throat to cover her embarrassment. 'It wasn't till Bub came to me a month or so ago that I found out anything. Anything concrete that is,' she said looking at

Frankie. He was happy. His smile was so big and so odd and so out of place that he looked like the alien.

'I've been working for the government since the Splash,' said Bub. 'When my yard flooded and I lost everything because of the insurance, I tried to put in for some compo.'

'I thought you never bothered,' said Eddie.

'I *said* I never bothered because I couldn't think of an excuse for the refusal. Anyway, I had a problem with the taxman.'

'What was that?' said Barbara.

'We had a communication issue.'

Eddie guffawed. 'You mean you didn't!'

Bub laughed along. 'Yeah. The communication got pretty urgent after the Splash; some bloke, bit of a dick he was, told me I was going away. I spied for them to stay with my family.' Bub stuttered under Eddie's dark glare. 'Spying's a bit of a grand title. I've never been able to tell them anything till a month ago, and then I promised I wouldn't,' he said, and then added cheerfully, 'Cheap tax bill in the end!'

'So what I'm hearing here,' Eddie, the fat boss, leaned back in his chair and accepted the bottle of beer proffered by Jane, 'is that two mates've been spying on me and mine.' His powerful gaze caught Bub and Jane and held them. 'They've been looking for aliens. One's found 'em…'

'Well, they found me, really…'

'… and not told anyone except the other one, who should've told her bosses. She hasn't 'cause the first one asked her not to so's they could save the aliens' lives and let 'em leave.'

'Yes,' said Jane.

'Yep,' said Bub.

'And right now,' Eddie continued, 'there's an alien in the dog.' He pointed a thumb at Tilda who woofed in confirmation. Everyone paused to look at her for a moment. 'And in Bub.' The man nodded proudly. 'Jane's gonna help the aliens even though she's supposed to be working for the government and all her workmates are probably dead. All the dogs of Never, and mebbe all the ones we saw in Hull, are under Jim's house and the river in a place called the Warren, but them dogs're bad guys.'

'Couldn't've expositioned it better meself, boss,' said Bub.

'So the guy in Bub tells us,' said Barbara.

'And that, Miss Bean,' Eddie pointed at Barbara, 'is the problem.'

'What about that it's all bollocks?' said James.

'It's not bollocks,' said Frankie to James, 'and you know it.'

'It sounds like bollocks,' Barbara piped up in support of James.

'No, it doesn't,' said Frankie. 'It sounds like sense.'

'It sounds like sense to *you*, Frankie!' said James.

'What's that supposed to mean?' He couldn't miss the threat in Eddie voice. Frankie's glare suggested that he didn't need to look to his brother for threats.

'C'mon! Aliens? Possessions? Knackered planets? Just a few *regular* people can save the human race and the world to boot? It's bollocks because it must be bollocks! And what about this ship? A space ship crashing into the Humber'd cause a bit more than a splash!'

'The ship's not very big,' said Bub.

'Some of the details are a bit convenient,' Eddie admitted. 'But it explains a lot. This place has been mad for a couple of years now. You mebbe don't know that, Jim, what with you not being around for a few years, but this does make sense. And Frankie's right. You know it does too I reckon, what with your mum and dad.'

'That's going too far,' Barbara warned.

No one else spoke. All eyes were on James.

'So we need to do something. For Never. For everyone,' said James. Barbara looked to James while the rest nodded.

'We can decide in the morning,' said Jane. 'We might know more about what they're doing by then.

'Sounds like a good idea,' said Eddie. 'We'll meet first thing.'

'You two can stay here,' Jane said to James and Barbara.

'Erm...' Bub looked over at Jane.

'I suppose you best had too.'

The next morning James lay wide awake on the living room settee. He was still in Jane's house. He had no suspicions that last night had been a dream, no problems remembering where he was when he woke up. He had struggled to sleep, a novel and unpleasant experience. Tilda licked his face and I watched while she did it. James let her, not taking his eyes off the ceiling.

'Coffee?' asked Jane as she entered the room. She busied herself clearing beer bottles and scooping spilt ash with her hands. James watched her. She was worth watching. Barbara was right.

The view was ruined as he saw her plunging a metal bar into the Rottweiler's head. He turned away.

'Yes, please,' he muttered into the cushion.

'Bloody Frankie and his bloody fags,' she moaned. 'I might have to bring the ban into my house.' And she left carrying some of the exposition's detritus with her.

Guilt. Not a new emotion to James but on this morning he looked at it with a new appreciation. His mum, his dad, the answering machine and the even the postman. He could have done more. He should have done more.

Barbara lay awake in Jane's spare bedroom. She switched between disappointment in the sheets – she had had visions of a satin-clad bed in a room designed for libidinous interrogation – and anger at the previous night's events.

Why was she angry? James's treatment, the lies, the secrecy, the ruining of a bloody good date. Her phone rang.

'Hi,' she said.

'So,' said Diane. 'How was it?'

'Interesting.'

'There seems to be nothing but interesting in Humberside at the moment; you're all over the news. Deaths, dogs and floods. What's going on over there? Are you okay?'

'I'm not exactly sure; it's all very confusing. But I'm fine.'

'Well, where are you? I assume the standby wasn't used; I rang your home phone first. There was no answer...' Diane left the accusation hanging.

'I'm in the spare bedroom of a government spy.'

'Ooo, role-play. Kinky.'

Barbara sighed. 'It was a good night, a great night. He's a really nice guy who made a really nice and genuine effort to impress. And it worked. I was impressed, damned impressed. He cooked the most wonderful meal and served it in the most wonderful setting. He was polite, he was charming, he was funny...'

'Sounds smooth.'

'Damned smooth. He was doing all the right things and without seeming like he was only doing it to...' Barbara paused.

'Get his end away?'

'Yeah.'

'And did he?'

'No.'

'Shame.'

'Yeah.'

'So?'

'*So* what?'

'You're still there I take it? What are you doing talking to me? Jump his bones and then make him breakfast. You'll be moved in and building that new fireplace before you know it.'

'Barbara?' Jane's voice followed a polite knock on the door. 'Are you awake?'

'Yes,' Barbara replied, not believing for a second that the agent wasn't aware of precisely what she was doing.

'Who's that?' said Diane.

'Do you want coffee?'

'Yes, please.' Barbara could feel her best friend straining to hear Jane's voice.

'Will you come down or shall I bring it up?'

'I'll come down.'

'That wasn't the country hunk, was it? Who else is there? Was that a woman's voice? You dark horse. You sly fox. You've been hiding things from me!'

'It's the joiner.'

'Really?'

'Yep. Anyway, I've got to go; things are happening that I can't explain.'

'Are you okay, B? Do you need me to come?'

'No. I'm not sure what to do and you can't help me.'

'You're scaring me. What do you mean? If you need help I can come. I can help.'

'I need to help myself and everyone else. I think I need to be part of this.'

'Part of what?'

'I'll speak to you later.'

'Wait…' Barbara hung up and slipped the phone back into her trouser pocket. She laid her head back on the pillow and ignored the buzzing of her phone as her best friend, she assumed, immediately rang back. How could she speak to anyone again knowing what she knew? What would happen after the government had had a 'word'? What if it really were all true? What could *she* ever do?

In the kitchen Jane, James and Barbara stared at their mugs.

'Aren't you gonna answer that?' James nodded at Barbara's vibrating pocket.

'No.'

Tilda scratched at the back door. Jane got up to let her out. It was still raining.

'How long's it been raining now?' she asked as she returned to her seat.

Barbara and James stared at her.

'What?' she said. 'It's not all exploding wrist watches you know. We can talk about the weather too.'

James couldn't help but smile but he kept it to a slight upturn at the corners of his mouth. Jane noticed. *Of course she noticed*, thought James.

'Have you ever exploded a wrist watch?' asked Barbara casually so as not to let anyone know that she was genuinely interested.

'Can't tell you,' said Jane. 'I'd have to kill you.' And so she confirmed that an interesting job doesn't guarantee a large selection of jokes. Jane cleared the empty mugs from the table to cover her small jocular repertoire. She looked relieved when there was a knock at the back door.

'Hang on a minute,' said Eddie to his brother as Jane opened the door. 'Best let Mork in first.' The two men let Tilda enter the kitchen and then followed.

'Frankie wants to call this *Operation Ejaculate*. Would someone help me out and tell him to grow the fuck up,' Eddie said as he landed in a spare chair. James and Barbara both flinched, expecting it to give way under such pressure.

'Grow the fuck up, Frankie,' said Barbara.

'Triple-o-fuck-all!' Bub announced as he burst into the kitchen, the day's newspaper, covered with stories of rain and predictions of another flood, and a bottle of milk in hand.

'And here's Mindy,' said Eddie. 'Is that you Bub?'

'Yes, Eddie.'

'I'm speaking to Bub?'

'Yes, Eddie.'

'Bub the builder?'

'Yes, Eddie.'

'Okay. What're you talking about?'

'I'm a triple agent. You lot, the aliens and the government.'

'Yes, Bub. You lied to me, and I won't forget that. By the way, I noticed a scratch on your van. Get it sorted. I want Fiss Fixins to make a proper impression.'

'Yes, Eddie.'

'Right, what do we know?'

'The others must be down there to turn off Eden's Aegis,' Bub began. 'It's the only reason that they would risk revealing themselves. They'll turn it off and in that instant get their supporters to jump wherever they can. There could be thousands hurt.'

'I think we can forget the 'hurt' euphemism, Bub,' Barbara cut in.

'Okay, thousands dead,' said Bub.

'Tens of thousands if not hundreds,' said Jane. 'The population of Hull alone is a quarter of a million. Add in Barton, Beverly, all the villages like Never and maybe even places like Grimsby and you're up to half a million. We don't know how far they can get when they jump.'

'Can we get that information?' said Barbara looking from Tilda to Bub.

'They say that they're not sure. This is all pretty new to them too. A couple of miles at the most they reckon. But of course they could piggy back.'

'Piggy back?'

'Jump from host to host. Jup in a dog two miles away, run it for twenty minutes till its exhausted, that'll get you, what four or five miles? Jump another two miles away. Within an hour they could twenty miles.'

'And suddenly it's not a local problem anymore.'

They all sighed.

Eddie leaned forward. 'So what do the fellas in you and Tilda want?'

'The same thing. We want to turn it off. But it's all about timing,' Bub replied. 'In a fraction of a second all of the aliens can be informed of an invasion or a departure. If the others turn off Eden's Aegis first then they can gather the rest up before we could say Ming-the-Merciless.'

Frankie smiled, making everyone look at him again. He pulled his tobacco pouch out of his pocket and returned their stares with a cheery wave.

'No smoking from now on, Frankie,' said Jane. 'You'll have to go outside.'

'Fair enough,' he replied happily. More stares.

Eddie glared at everyone, his best Baron Fiss face locked into place. 'And then what? How do you organise this departure?'

'It all happens at the speed of thought.' Bub shrugged. 'It's instant. The others'll have no choice but to go with the rest as they can't risk losing their ship.'

'This small spaceship at the bottom of the Humber.'

'That's right.'

'How small?' asked James.

'About the size of a suitcase,' Bub replied. The rest, apart from Jane gaped, gaped. 'They don't have bodies. They don't need physical space. Their entire civilisation is a hard drive and an engine.'

'So why can't we just blow the ship up?' said Barbara.

'It's an option,' Jane replied. Tilda woofed. 'It's an option that we've rejected,' Jane quickly added.

'No one wants 4.2 billion deaths on their hands,' said Bub.

Another stunned silence.

'Right,' said Eddie, 'we've slept on it. Who's in?' He stared around the kitchen. Bub nodded wildly. Jane remained stoic - everyone knew that she had no choice. Frankie, through the open kitchen window, nodded determinedly. James looked around the room and nodded as well. Barbara stared at him.

'You're all mad,' she said.

'It's a hell of a fact finding mission,' said James.

Barbara nodded she knew it was crazy but, 'Okay, I'm in. But I still don't know that I trust what these things say.'

'Right,' said Eddie. 'Over to you then, Jane. What do we do?'

'Well, first of all we have to trust them. Whatever happens, they can take us, so we need them to leave.' Barbara started to protest but Jane spoke over her. 'We have to trust them but we don't have to like them. I'm with Bub because I know my employers, and there's no way that they're gonna let these things go.'

'You've all seen *Aliens*,' said Bub. It wasn't a question, just an assumption.

'Erm… yeah, thanks, Bub,' said Jane. James realised that she was a fish out of water. That he and everyone else were looking to her but she was not used to dealing with people like them except as a joiner. And they weren't going out to fit kitchens.

'Shut up, Bub,' said Barbara.

'We need to get down there,' said Eddie. 'How're we gonna do that? Go through Jim's house? Did you say there was a way in next to The Deep? We could use that.'

'There are ways in all over. James's house and The Deep'll be covered by the other faction, so we should take one of the others.'

'Which one?' said Frankie.

'Let me finish and I'll tell you,' Jane's cool was threatening to break. 'And smoking outside is not smoking at the window!'

'Let her finish, Frankie,' said Eddie.

'The Bridge towers!' exclaimed Bub. 'Is there a way there? That'd be a cool way in.'

'Sounds alright,' James said casually. Bub looked to him and nodded.

'Bit of a trek to the towers,' said Jane. 'And Barrow Road's flooded. It'd be quicker to get to them through the Warren.'

'There *is* a way in through the towers!' Frankie's turn to be excited.

'Yes. Look, forget about the towers; we shouldn't need to go there. If I understand Eden's Aegis correctly…' she stopped as she noticed Frankie's and Bub's shared expression of anticipation. She continued warily. 'If I understand it correctly then we don't need to go to the towers. We just need to switch off the shield and then they can go.'

'*Can* go,' said Barbara.

'I think we've covered the trust thing, Miss Bean, time to like it or lump it,' said Eddie.

'You can call me Barbara. We did go to school together.'

'Customers is customers, Miss Bean,' Eddie replied, proud of his professionalism. 'So,' he continued, 'where're we getting in?'

'The closest entrance,' said Jane.

'Do you have shoes?' said Barbara.

Chapter Twenty

'Howard!' Eddie bawled at the top of his voice, ignoring the security guard standing right next to him.

'I could ring him if you like, Eddie,' said the guard.

'You're alright, Steve. Reckon he'll hear me.'

Jane, Eddie, Bub, Frankie, James, Barbara, comfortable but slightly self conscious in a pair of combat boots, and Tilda all stood outside the gated entrance to Splash Land, a shining steel gateway in a large wooden wall of random-looking panels and slats and boards. Various murals depicting comets, sea monsters, tidal waves and aliens and their space ships were daubed on the different sections.

The fence represented all that was salvageable from the timber yard that had once stood on this site. It had been devastated by the Splash but in taking the brunt of the water it had saved Never from serious damage. Had it not been for the yard, the village would probably not have survived.

The owner of the timber yard, Howard Woodman, saw the interest from the media and was the first to react. He made sure that Splash Land was the first and subsequently most famous place to go.

'Howard!'

Eventually a man came jogging toward them. In between an expensive suit and a head of rapidly whitening hair was a face that might best be described as flustered. The flustered Howard Woodman carried an umbrella. An alien's green leering face was splashed across it.

'Now then, Ed,' said Howard from a behind a brick wall smile. 'We don't open for another hour or so, so if you was wanting a go on the *Tsunami*, you'll have to wait.' He laughed as he spoke but he unlocked the gate nevertheless. 'Come in, come in. What can I do you for?'

'A favour, Howard,' said Eddie. 'You alright? You look a bit flustered.'

They all filed in the gate, nodding to Steve the security guard, then set off toward a set of stalls promising all manner of fast, fried and very colourful foods.

'I'm fine, I'm fine,' said Howard quickly. 'This weather,' he continued, as they hurried through the theme park, 'if it carries on we're gonna lose the summer. Bad for business weather like this.'

'Oh I dunno,' said James. 'If it keeps up we could have another Splash.'

'Don't even joke about it!' Howard snapped back. 'All we need's a natural disaster and then that's it, no one's bothered about aliens and sea monsters anymore. If it could happen natural now it could've happened natural then.'

'River didn't look very high last night,' Eddie pointed out.

'Not the river we have to worry about,' said Howard. 'It's all the tributaries; they're gonna go if this keeps up.'

They walked behind the stalls and toward a set of offices hidden from the public's view.

'How is rain bad for business at a water park?' said Barbara.

They all squeezed into Howard's small office. 'People're weird,' Howard answered once they were all inside. 'They don't mind getting wet on the rides but they won't queue in the rain for 'em.' He gave an exasperated shrug. 'Anyway, what's the favour?'

'We need to get in Bub's old yard,' said Eddie.

'What for? Your yard's not there anymore, Bub. It's the *Zoom!!!* now. Marvellous ride that. Have you had a go? Shoots you straight up in the air!' Howard shuddered. 'It's horrible really, but the tourists like it, bless 'em.'

'There's something under where it was. Something we need.'

'Like what?' said Howard, glancing at his watch.

'Listen, Mr Woodman,' Jane began.

'You can call me Howard, Jane, you know that.' He smiled at her. Barbara recoiled from it, but Jane held her ground impassively.

'Howard,' she said. 'We need something. It won't be any bother to you or your park. Couldn't you just let us have it?'

'Of course I could.' He kept his eyes on her when Eddie spoke again.

'Right, so we'll have a quick look, and then get out of your way.'

'Go ahead, fill your boots. Hang around till opening and I'll let you have a free ride.' His eyes remained on Jane. Barbara studied the man from behind the safety of the secret agent.

'Thanks, Howard,' said Jane. 'That's really generous.'

'I'm a generous man, Jane.' He checked his watch again. 'But right now I'm afraid I have to run -' Howard was cut off by a man bursting into his office. The door slammed into Tilda's side sending her sprawling across James who stumbled into Barbara. She put her arms around him to steady herself. James immediately forgot his stumble.

'Howard,' said the new man, who looked like a desperate submariner, bedecked as he was in soaking wet overalls. 'We need to talk.'

'Right you are, Dave,' said Howard, his brick wall smile back in place. He turned to Eddie. 'If you lot can carry on without me, I've got a spot of business to attend to.'

'No problem, Howard,' said Eddie. 'We'll sort ourselves out.'

Dashing through the rain, the group ran past the hot dog stands, the ice cream stalls, the rides and *Tsunami*, eventually reaching *Zoom!!!*.

'That's pretty high,' said James. The metal tower ran to at least sixty metres. A car shaped like an upside down rocket was wrapped around the base, ready to be launched up the tower.

'Well, we don't need to ride a rocket today,' said Jane. James and Barbara noticed the disappointed looks of Frankie and Bub.

'Why's there an entrance to the Warren under Bub's yard?' asked Barbara.

'Not sure,' said Jane. 'I think they must've put it there when Bub started to work for them.'

'But I thought you lost your yard straight after the Splash, Bub?' Barbara asked.

'Not straight after,' Bub shrugged. 'It took a year or so for everything to go right down the pan.'

'Things're looking up now though eh, Bub,' said Eddie. 'So stop moping and get your arse in that door.' He pointed at a small door into the metal tower. They all headed for it.

The control room for the ride was round and not particularly impressive. A single console seemed to control the ride. The only other equipment in the room, a toaster and a kettle, sat on top of an old battered cupboard that stood next to a sink with a draining board. A collection of mugs awaited the Park's staff who would soon come to oversee the ride.

'Hang on a minute,' said Frankie. 'This is bollocks. How could the government build a secret entrance to a secret complex and then not get it noticed when the foundations were dug for that tower for the *Zoom!!!?*'

'Good point, Frankie,' said Eddie and looked to Jane.

'I don't know,' she said. 'I just know that there's an entrance to the Warren at Bub's old yard.'

'Seems a bit fishy,' said Frankie.

'It does,' Eddie agreed.

'Hey,' said Bub, 'you've seen The Matrix, right?'

'Erm…' Jane was beginning to get flustered. 'Look, we act on the information we have, and that information says that we can get into the Warren through here.'

'Neo and Trinity get to go to a room full of guns and get tooled up for the job.' Frankie looked up at this and so did James. 'Is there a room where we can get tooled up, Jane?'

'For fuck's sake!' she exclaimed. 'There's no need for guns. We're gonna go there, flick a switch and come back. This is not a game and it's not an adventure. This is real, and real stuff's not like that. You pay attention and you get the job done, that's it.'

'What about the dogs and the monsters?' asked Barbara and James together.

'Leave them to me,' said Jane.

'There's dozens of them,' said James. 'And you said that they might've been joined by more from Hull. What is the plan for when we get to them? What information can we act on when there's dogs trying to tear our throats out? Or when there's arms and legs and God knows what else swinging for us?'

'I told you, leave that to me.'

'That's not gonna work, Jane,' Eddie joined in. 'We're *all* in this now; it's not just Jim that's lost people. We're all in this to clear the area out, flush it, get it back to normal. We need to be prepared so that we all come out of there and I can start looking for a new joiner.'

'There won't be any trouble. Every section is sealed off. The dogs and monsters won't be able to get to the areas we need to go to. There's more than one control room that I can access Eden's Aegis from. We won't need to go anywhere near any trouble. And if I get caught, or let you lot get me caught, then you won't have to look far for a new joiner.'

'See? There's a silver lining,' said Eddie in a jolly voice, although he eyed the agent suspiciously. 'If it all goes tits up then you can carry on working for me. I know the darts team'll miss you if you go back spying. And the cricket team; we've never had a seam bowler so good!'

'Hey, I've just realised,' said Bub. 'You're Jane Bond!'

'Or Jane Bourne,' said James.

They all laughed, apart from Jane.

'Could do with that Matrix room,' Bub said to James wistfully, and out of the agent's hearing.

'Yeah,' he replied. 'Terrible sequels though,' he added.

'Oh yeah, terrible sequels,' Bub agreed.

'We're gonna need some equipment before we go down there,' said Eddie. Everyone but Jane nodded in agreement.

'I'll keep you all out of harm's way,' she said.

Eddie shook his head. 'Better safe than sorry. I'll get the van, some handy things on there, and I'll give Gal and Baz a knock as well. You lot carry on looking for a likely way down.'

'May as well put the kettle on,' said Frankie when Eddie had gone. He lit up a cigarette, smiling at the brand new No Smoking sign that someone had taped a biro-written sign to: *Not til Sunday wnkr!!!*

'When the Baron's away,' said Barbara.

'What was that?' said Frankie.

'Nothing,' Barbara replied. She saw James smirking out of the corner of her eye.

'Who wants what?' said Bub. The collection of mugs on the draining board looked to be rejects from the Park's gift shop: blue aliens, green aliens, red serpents, pink asteroids and green tidal waves adorned the ceramic surfaces. Bub made a grab for the green alien.

'Tea,' said Frankie.

Bub looked to the others questioningly.

'Erm… coffee?' said James. 'White, one sugar?'

'Same for me please,' said Barbara.

Jane glared at Bub.

'What?'

'Are you lot taking any of this seriously?'

'Of course we are,' said Frankie. 'But there's no point doing it thirsty.'

Bub made the drinks. Jane relented and had a coffee, but when Bub found some bread, she drew a line at toast. No one else did.

Barbara found an old tub in the cupboard and filled it with water for Tilda. She was very grateful, and cast a glance at James.

'Thanks,' he said to Barbara. They stood apart from the others. Bub and Frankie were exploring the console while Jane, monster mug in hand, explored the room for a way down.

'Wasn't there a *Zoom* ice lolly?' Bub asked Frankie.

James laughed quietly at the question and left them to their discussion as he returned his attention to Barbara.

'That's okay,' she said to him, nodding at the drinking Tilda. 'It's the little things that get forgotten at times like this. Not that I know what times like this are supposed to be like.' She sipped her coffee and nibbled at her toast. Her mug had a picture of a yellow

Humber Bridge with a purple space ship flying between the towers. James's had a sea serpent, also yellow, wrapped around the mug like the slide on a helter-skelter. The head of the serpent was missing, as was the handle.

'Looks like Jane doesn't think that times like this should be like *this*.'

'No,' Barbara agreed.

'Bet you wish you had your notebook. This is one hell of a fact-finding mission!'

Barbara smiled. She looked up into his eyes and then took in the rest of his still-bruised face. Something had changed: it was ready, much more so than since she'd known him, which, she had to remind herself, was not quite a week. Alright, five years and a week, but the years didn't count. It was a good face, and that small chin just meant that he wasn't too handsome.

They stared at each other for a long moment.

'It was a good night, last night,' said Barbara.

'Yeah, it was.'

'Before all the dogs and limbs and maybe-zombies, I mean.'

'It was. Mind you, you were pretty good after then as well.'

'So were you. In fact you were amazing; I don't know which I enjoyed most, the curry or seeing you and Tilda slide down that pole.'

'I know which I enjoyed the most!'

''Scuse me, Romeo.' Jane bustled between them, searching around the cupboard that held the kettle and toaster.

'No, that was the *Fab*, and that had hundreds and thousands on it,' Frankie was saying.

'You sure?' said Bub.

'Help me with this,' Jane said to James. They shifted the cupboard away from the wall. There was nothing there.

The door opened and Howard stepped in, shaking the rain from his umbrella.

'Found what you were lookin' for?' he said.

They all stood and stared at him, mugs and half-eaten toast in hands. The monitor on the console was active and Frankie was using his body to shield it from the Park owner's view.

'No luck then?' Howard quickly scanned the rest before his eyes settled on Jane. He looked no less flustered than before.

'A cellar!' Bub exclaimed. 'I had a cellar! And I think I left some gear in it.'

'What, fifteen years ago?'

'Yes.'

'And you've only just remembered?'

'Erm... yes. It was good gear.'

'Right,' said Howard slowly, finally taking his eyes off Jane. Bub shifted awkwardly as Howard's gaze rested on him. 'Bit late now, I reckon. There was a cellar, or something like it. Can't really remember properly. Either way the tower for the Zoom'll have filled it in.'

'Shit,' said Frankie.

Howard looked around the room at the disappointed faces. 'What was so important? Your gear can't have been that good if you left it for fifteen years. What's going on?'

'Nothing,' said Jane. 'We'll just have to look elsewhere.' She put her mug back on the draining board and turned to leave. The others followed suit.

'Come back anytime,' Howard called after their retreating backs, while opening his umbrella ready to follow them out. 'We never see enough locals in the Park.'

They milled about the base of *Zoom!!!*. Howard watched them from underneath his alien-faced umbrella.

'It doesn't look very big,' said James staring up at the shining silver tower. The others glanced up and nodded their agreement.

'I've seen bigger, Howard,' said Jane.

The Park owner stared at them all in disbelief. 'Don't you lot know about the *Zoom!!!*?' He looked hurt and shocked.

'What about it?' said Barbara.

'That's the biggest one of its kind in Europe!'

'Yeah, you said. I just didn't think it looked very big for being the biggest,' said James. 'I mean, don't get me wrong; it's big, it's *very* big. Just, you know, not *that* big.'

'Yeah, Howard,' said Jane. 'I thought you'd be bigger.' Barbara looked at the spy with a renewed respect.

'Haven't you seen the adverts?'

'For what?'

'For the Park!' Howard was upset. 'The *Zoom!!!*'s the biggest one in Europe because half of it's underground!'

'Really?' said Jane. The rest stared, mouths open.

'Yes! It's been all over the TV and radio for the past two years. Plannin' permission was a bitch; I had to get the government involved.'

'I bet you did,' said Barbara looking to Jane.

'I kicked up such a fuss, and all for the sake of Nether on Humber. The government finally let us have it but only if they chose who built it. But that doesn't matter because it's up and running now and if it wasn't for this weather it'd be coining it in for all of us. I've been expecting a visit from Eddie for the last year or more about it; what with the government builders, I haven't been able to give him much work in the close season.'

'We've been busy,' said Frankie.

Howard looked at him in surprise. 'Well, that's good. Local economy's doing well; people can afford to have their houses and wotnot done up.'

'That's probably down to local entrepreneurs bringing all this business to the area,' said Barbara.

'Yeah,' said James realising the target of Barbara's flattery. 'If it wasn't for the *Zoom!!!!* and the *Tsunami* and the rest of it, Never'd be buggered by now.'

'Well, I've only done what any public-spirited citizen would've done,' said Howard, turning a deep shade of pleased-as-punch red.

'No, Howard,' Jane joined in, 'you're too modest. You should take some credit for all this.'

'Well,' said Howard, his chest swelling, 'I did personally oversee the installation of the water tank. You know, the one the car splashes into?'

'Then that'll be the best bit, Howard,' said Jane from behind a dazzling smile.

'My kids're always on about this place and I reckon they can't wait to ride the *Zoom!!!*,' Bub chipped in.

Howard was lost for words.

'You come to the visitors' centre don't you, Bub?' said Frankie. 'Who was it a couple of weeks ago?'

'Yeah, you had Chekov here a couple of weeks ago,' said Bub to Howard.

'Who?' said Howard.

'From Star Trek,' Bub reminded him.

'Oh yeah, Mr Koenig, Walter Koenig,' said Howard. 'He was in *Babylon Zoo* as well,' he added proudly.

'Erm... that's *Babylon Five*,' said Bub.

'Could we get down to the bottom of the *Zoom!!!*'s shaft, do you think?' said Jane.

'Don't see why not,' he said to her. 'I've always said that the Park's open to locals.' He glanced over Jane's shoulder. The submariner, Dave, was heading urgently over. 'Wait five minutes and I'll take you meself.'

'Couldn't we go alone?'

Howard's eyes very nearly popped out of his head. 'Of course we can!'

'No, I meant me and this lot.' She waved a hand at the rest of us a little too desperately, Barbara thought. It was nice to see the cool slip a little. It made Jane seem like a joiner again.

'Well...'

'We won't be long. Quick in and out job. You won't even see us leave I bet.'

'Oh I'll always notice you, Jane,' he said with a smile. 'Why not? What're you gonna do, blow the place up?' He chuckled at his little joke. 'Go ahead, fill your boots. You can get in through the service hatch.' He held up a hand to stall Dave before indicating a small hut just a few metres from the car wrapped around the wide metal shaft. 'In there.'

'Can I borrow a broom?' Jane asked.

Chapter Twenty One

'Shouldn't we have waited for Eddie?' asked Bub as the group descended a metal spiral staircase. Electric lights glowed at regular intervals on the vertiginous path.

'We need to get moving,' Jane replied. She carried a long wooden stick, the handle of the broom leant to her by Howard. 'You know that, Bub. This is your mission after all.'

'I know, I know. Just, you know safety in numbers and all that.'

'We're going to be safe. We're entering a government installation. Any threat can be easily avoided down there.'

'Define 'easily',' said Barbara suspiciously.

'Keep behind me and do as I say. Doesn't get any easier than that.'

'How far do these steps go down?' asked James.

"Howard reckoned that the *Zoom!!!* runs sixty metres underground and this access shaft goes under it, so just over sixty metres for a guess,' Frankie answered him.

'That's quite deep really, isn't it? I mean it's maybe not cavernously deep, but it's a long way down.' James couldn't take his eyes of the metal grills passing beneath his feet. 'I mean, if you tripped over and fell, there's nothing to stop you.'

'Wooh!' Barbara gave him a nudge from behind.

'Jesus!' James exclaimed, stumbling only slightly. 'What are you doing!'

'Sorry, Jim, just an accident.'

'I could've fallen! It's a bloody long way down!'

'Stop messing about, you two,' Jane warned. 'Accidents'll kill more people than dogs.'

'Bloody hell,' said Frankie. 'Health and safety in the secret service.'

'It's an important issue in any service, Frankie,' said Bub. Frankie tutted and rolled his eyes.

'Has anyone told these aliens about health and safety?' said Barbara. 'I mean they jump at or into people and if they don't fit the people die. Where's the risk assessment, Bub?'

'Some of the others have been trying to get into people on and off for years but they're reluctant to try too often. Very tiring for them apparently.'

'And they're killing people,' Barbara reminded him.

'Oh yeah, that too,' Bub said with a smile. 'Although, they're not all so bothered about that,' he admitted.

'What's to stop them from jumping at our minds?' James asked. 'They could take us all out just like that.'

'No one's getting taken out,' Jane reminded them.

'The fellas in me and Tilda are running some kind of block. And the others would have to be pretty desperate to try it at the moment, what with all the importance of timing,' said Bub. 'And they need living bodies for after. Jumping at minds is like turkeys voting for Christmas for most of these fellas.'

Frankie had listened to this avidly. Jane noticed. 'Don't get too excited, Frankie.'

He shrugged. 'What about the unpredictable dangers?' said Frankie. 'What about when we take it in turns dying?'

'What're you on about?' asked Barbara.

'Group like this always dies one by one,' said Frankie.

'Don't be ridiculous!'

'No he's right, Miss Bean,' said Bub. 'Doesn't matter if it's a crack team of commandoes or a bunch of frightened teenagers, they always get picked off one at a time.'

'Yes, well, we're not that kind of group.'

'Yeah we are,' said James getting over his shock as they reached the bottom of the staircase. The space at the bottom was small but promised greater things as the large banks of hydraulic machinery blocked one end. 'I just hope we're not in an 18.' Frankie and Bub laughed and nodded their agreement.

'Eh?' said Barbara.

'The deaths get really gory and painful in an 18,' said Frankie.

'Yeah,' said Bub. 'You want to be dying in a 15, or even a 12!'

'What're we looking for, Jane?' Frankie called out to the spy who had disappeared amongst the machinery.

'So, who's gonna go first?' said Bub.

'Mmm,' James was mulling it over.

Barbara shook her head then sighed. 'For maximum drama it'd have to be Jane,' she said.

'True, true,' Bub nodded.

'Thanks a lot,' Jane called over.

'Bub's gotta go,' said Frankie. 'He's the one that's got us into all this. He's Obi Wan.'

'Yeah,' said Bub, and then stopped in his tracks. 'Hang on.'

'You're not getting out of this,' James said to Frankie. 'You're the one no one believed but it turned out that you were right all along. You've had it. Your cards're marked. And you might get the worst death as well. Then we'll all feel extra sorry for you when we realise that you're dead and we were horrible to you for all those years.'

'Might get the hero's death,' mumbled Frankie.

'No chance,' Barbara joined in. 'James is right; you need the sympathy.'

'So that's a fighting death for Jane, heroic death for me and painful death for Frankie,' said Bub. 'What about you Jim?'

'He's the fifth wheel,' said Barbara.

'Thanks!'

'The unknown quantity in any narrative,' she continued. 'He could be the hero or the villain, vital or trivial. He might even get the girl.' She glanced at him and winked at his hopeful face.

'And what about the girl?' said James, happily receiving the wink.

'Oh she'll survive,' said Bub. 'One of the girls has gotta survive, and it's usually the sceptical one.'

'You might have to get your tits out though,' added Frankie. 'Especially if it's an 18.'

'Excuse me!'

'Or a 15 these days,' said Bub.

'Not a 12 though,' said Frankie.

'Oh no, not a 12,' agreed Bub.

'Here's hoping for 15 then,' said Frankie.

'You can all piss off!'

'Censorship is a terrible thing, Miss Bean,' said Bub.

'Unless it's your cock,' said Jane the joiner, returning from the maze of hydraulics. 'Right, let's go,' she added as the others all laughed at Bub.

'What've you found?' said Frankie.

'Secret entrance.'

'Cool!' said Frankie and Bub together. Jane rolled her eyes.

'Remember,' said Jane as we rode the lift down into the earth, 'we're not fitting kitchens.'

'We remember,' said Frankie and Bub. They both looked giddy.

James and Barbara stood at the back of the brightly lit cube. They were steeling themselves for the ordeal ahead. Jane's assurances that they would not get into any trouble were no help as they didn't answer the fundamental question: if they were in no danger, then why were they needed?

They could hear Bub mumbling to himself. 'There is no spoon. There is no spoon,' he said over and over again.

'If we're in no danger then why are we needed?' asked Barbara.

'Human shields,' said Frankie quickly.

'Shut up Frankie,' said Jane. 'Would you have wanted to stay behind?' she asked Barbara. 'Either of you? I assumed not, so here you are. Plus I need to keep an eye on you so that my bosses can have that word.

'Joke,' she added when she saw their shocked expressions. 'I also don't know what Tilda's gonna be like when all this over. She'll need her owner. Or Bub for that matter, I may need help carrying his body.'

'Nice!' said Bub.

A good answer, I thought. The real reason was that we'd asked Bub to tell her to bring them.

Barbara wasn't satisfied with the answer but her objections were swallowed as the lift came to a halt with a stomach churning suddenness.

The doors opened.

No one moved as we all peered out. The first lights of the white corridor had flickered on as the doors opened. The rest of it stretched away into the darkness. It was a horizontal pit.

'Puts the fore into boding, doesn't it,' said Barbara.

'Let's go,' said Jane as she left the lift. Tilda trotted out after her. The rest paused, suddenly unwilling to leave the confines of the lift.

Frankie and Bub went first, cautiously stepping out, then James and Barbara. The corridors were stark white rectangular holes, the very green but very white lighting made the darkness beyond its reach seem all the more black. Walking down these tunnels was like holding a light bulb swallowed by a giraffe.

We weren't sure how long we walked or how far we travelled; it was hard to tell such was the monotony of the surroundings. Around corners, down straights, steps and stairs, and not a sound as we crept along, huddled together. The way was not complicated: no junctions or forks in the road, no choices to make. The only thing that changed was the smell. Finally the silence was broken.

'It fucking stinks!' said Bub.

'It really does,' James agreed.

'Dog,' Frankie stated flatly. And that summed it up. The stench of dog trapped underground for twelve hours was so strong that I ignored Tilda's nose.

'What d'you reckon, Barbara?' asked James. 'How does a writer sum up a stink like this?'

Barbara thought for a moment, still smarting a little over the boob jibe. She sighed. *No point smarting,* she said to herself. 'Mephitic,' she said aloud.

'What's that then?'

'A bad stink,' said Frankie.

'Ask a silly question,' James muttered to himself.

Tilda's ears cocked just as Jane raised a hand to demand silence. Funny thing about being in a giraffe's neck: people comply. We all stood as still as statues as we strained to listen. Tilda had heard it, a low growl somewhere up ahead. Jane gripped her broom handle.

Suddenly there was a light up ahead and it was moving closer. Whatever was there was sprinting toward us, the light looming like an express train, but instead of steam and a whistle it was an animal growl that accompanied the headlamp.

'Back,' ordered Jane. 'Everybody back!' The tunnel was filled with furious and determined fur as one rage on many legs poured forward. The only thing slowing them was their own bodies as each sought to be first to repel the intruders.

'Oh shit, not again,' shouted James as he turned and ran.

'Save it for the sequel, Jimmy, and run!' Bub called over his shoulder.

We ran and ran, the dogs a broiling mass behind us. James and Barbara concentrated on running, on breathing, on keeping their legs and arms pumping.

'Keep running,' Jane shouted. 'Just follow the tunnel, you can't go wrong. Get out and go home!'

This gave Bub pause. He looked back over his shoulder. Jane had come to a halt so quickly that the rest of us were already leaving her far behind. He slowed so as to carry on watching. Jane had brought the broom handle round in a wide corridor-filling arc, taking out several dogs in the front row and tripping those behind allowing her precious seconds to assume a combat stance. It didn't look anything like a scene from The Matrix.

Bub's passenger urged him on but he couldn't run. He slowed to a stop and turned to watch. Jane swung and danced around the beasts as she knocked first one, then two out and then turned her stick to the others. Bub began to edge forward, creeping closer to the melee. Jane whirled and crouched and sprang. Each flick of the leg and whip of the arm sent another dog sprawling.

It was awesome.

Bub was transfixed at the small figure of Jane that seemed to fill the corridor, barring the dogs' way. A hand on his shoulder brought him round.

'C'mon, Bub, what the hell are you doing!' Frankie's voice was urgent. The spell was broken and Bub could see that there were just too many for her; they were creeping around her flanks, surrounding her. She would swipe one dog's legs away and another would jump over. She would bat away another and two more would take its place.

'C'mon, Bub!' James had joined Frankie in urging the builder away.

'We've got to help her,' he whispered.

'We can't! C'mon!' The two men grabbed an arm each and hauled him away.

Bub watched as the lights between them and the agent went out leaving two bright puddles of activity. Jane skewered a dog with the broom handle and hurled it into its fellows. The action left her open and a German shepherd leapt at her exposed side. They turned a corner and she was gone, lights and all. There was no sound but the snarling of victorious dogs.

'For fuck's sake, Bub, run!' Frankie snarled. And finally the man's legs remembered how to work and he ran and he ran.

But we weren't fast enough. People are only as fast as their slowest member, who was James, and the sprint was beginning to tell on them all. Tilda could run forever, could run like the wind. She had to be kept safe. So she did. As the sound of the pursuing enemy grew louder and louder she ran and ran, leaving the rest behind. I had to force her to do this; she knew that there was danger in these tunnels and she didn't want to run away.

Bub ran. His passenger, now his driver, forced him on.

Bub pounded down the tunnel, unable to breathe, his limbs burning. Tilda stayed with him, glancing back, seeing the others still running freely, not yet overtaken. Not yet. Head down and run. Tilda pulled away from Bub.

There was light ahead. The doors to the lift yawned, a huge figure stood waiting. On seeing us it lumbered into a run. Cricket pads were strapped to its arms and legs, and tied to its flanks. It wore thick cricketing gloves and a batsman's helmet. It carried a cricket bat in each hand. One of them looked brand new.

By the time we realised it was Eddie, he had already thundered past. He ran in his builder's boots, big and tan steel toe-capped boots. He roared as he ploughed through James, Barbara and Frankie and into the sea of muzzles and claws swinging his bats and his booted feet, sending whimpering, howling canines flying in every direction. Including toward us.

Frankie was first to react, kicking one clean on the jaw and pressing home his advantage as the mutt was stunned. Tilda leapt into the fray, snapping and snarling at Eddie's cast offs. James and Barbara watched in mute horror as dogs were bludgeoned with bats and boots.

Bub collapsed against a wall.

James and Barbara watched the dogs leap at Eddie time and again. He swung and battered at them, even as they hung from his padded arms and legs. One had even tangled its jaws and teeth into the face grill of his helmet.

James stepped forward cautiously and kicked at a cur that had come around behind Frankie. It turned its attentions onto him.

'Oh shit.'

'Nice one, Jim, you've found us a friend!' said Barbara. The dog leapt.

Barbara kicked.

Not just a wild lash borne of fearful desperation, this was a well-aimed well-executed side sweep of a combat-booted foot into the side of the dog's head. It was sent flying into the walls of the tunnel, sliding onto the floor, to be trampled by the stamping Frankie.

'That was,' James silently mouthed superlatives until he found the right one, 'ace.'

They joined the fray.

We fought well. We fought like lions. But it wasn't enough. Every dog needed several smacks from a bat, several bites from Tilda, and several kicks when they were down to stay down. We retreated along the tunnel, Eddie's charge was long since spent and now the tide turned against us. The big man was bleeding in several places where the dogs had found ways through his defences, but still he kept them at bay meaning that the rest of us had only to mop up those that bounced off him. As we reached the prone, desperate form of Bub, struggling for breath, we knew we could go no further or risk losing him forever.

From out of the lift came Baz and Gal running to help. A rucksack bounced across Gal's back. They grabbed Bub and began to haul him toward the lift. The rest of us continued the steady retreat. Every metre was carefully trod as Eddie did his best to keep the tide at bay whilst the rest of us threw and kicked the dogs back behind him.

Finally we reached the end, the lift. Baz, Gal and Bub were already inside. Barbara and James soon followed while Tilda followed her master. Frankie stayed with Eddie.

'Into the lift!' the big man roared at his brother.

'We go together!' he shouted back, kicking a spotted Dalmatian in the chest and sending it stumbling back.

'Get in there, Frankie. Do as you're told for a change!'

The brothers fought side by side and dogs flew in all directions. James held the doors open. 'C'mon!' he shouted into the melee. But it was no use, only one could come. If both entered the lift, who would keep the dogs at bay while the doors closed?

Gal and Baz lowered Bub into a corner. He fought for breath as panic shone in his eyes. His heart raced: thump, thump, thump each beat a hammer blow against the inside of his chest.

'Try to calm,' said Baz in broken English, as he laid a gentle hand across Bub's chest.

'Jesus Christ!' shouted Gal. 'What the fuck's goin' on? What're we doin'!' he looked scared and hung over.

James and Barbara watched the scene outside the lift. The dogs were no longer throwing themselves at the brothers in reckless leaps and dashes. They were trying to get around them with feints and lunges, distracting one and nipping the other. A terrible intelligence now firmly guided the deadly violence. Both brothers flinched from attacks, both bled, neither seriously yet. They lashed out with bats and feet, Eddie still roaring at his younger brother to get into the lift, Frankie still refusing. They were on the verge of being outmanoeuvred, and when they were it would be over.

'We're going back out there,' said James in answer to Gal's question. His arm was raised, holding the lift doors open.

'What? We've gotta get out of here! Get them two idiots and let's go!' shouted Gal. He glanced down at Bub. 'We need to get him to a hospital.'

'Still. Be still,' Baz urged Bub.

James looked to Barbara. She nodded. They both sprang forward.

Chapter Twenty Two

Dog circled the control room. The monster had hacked open the trapdoor in James's study and now they were in The Warren. He growled and snarled at any who came close frustrated at the inactivity around him. Dogs and a few limbs milled around control panels and consoles. The equipment was not beyond the possessors, but the possessed could not hope to operate it. Small switches and buttons, touch screens and finger print identifications. All beyond the dogs.

In an attempt to overcome the dextrous limitations of the canine form they had jumped into the fresh corpses of the Warren's workers. White-coated zombies had clawed and pawed ineffectually at controls. It hadn't worked and pretty soon the unfettered dogs became more than a nuisance. Now those bodies lay discarded and crumpled before consoles and control panels and monitors.

He snapped at a newly-arrived arm whose blind fingers were reaching for a console under the direction of a Yorkshire terrier named Yaffle. This terrier had been trying Dog's patience. She seemed to think she knew a thing or two but Dog couldn't understand her. He barked aggressively at Yaffle, and the terrier backed away, cowed, the arm dropping from the console.

Dog looked to the monster and cocked his head as if listening. He was trying; everything was trying. The monster, axe in two of its hands, was trying to tell him something. The fourteen possessors were trying to pass on information about our little break-in but Dog couldn't hear them. He was Rocky now, Rocky with a mission maybe, but still Rocky.

Scud knew this. He stood in the open circular doorway, a four-legged hobbit in his ill-gotten hole. The large door was held open by a small mound of white-coated bodies. No external trauma had caused their death and so they were bloodless, brain dead corpses. The only gore was from a pool of congealed blood which had long since spilled from a hand chopped from one of those white-coated corpses and was now discarded.

Scud's possessor's identity was safely sealed away from the Doberman. But looking at Rocky, he knew that they couldn't fail, that they had to find a way.

The fingers of the arms and the monster had been in the ground too long and they couldn't operate any of the controls. The dogs had had some success with snouts on the touch screens, but the problem was keeping it clean and keeping a fresh hand to foil the system's regular security checks. The dogs weren't fast enough and the spectacle of watching one disembodied limb trying to use another was not at all funny.

Soon they could use their prisoner. Scud glanced at the cage. Dick Jones was crammed in, covered in vomit, his own, and urine, some of it his own. Errol, his legs wobbling due to a damaged brain, kept watch on the scientist, and had relieved himself on his former home. Dick sobbed as he rocked on his heels.

'I don't know what you want,' he said. He kept saying it. 'I'll do anything. Get you anything you need.' He kept saying that as well. For now the rest of the dogs ignored him; they hadn't found a way to answer him yet.

Scud was beginning to worry. There were well over one thousand dogs in the Warren and there was no food and no walkies. These bodies needed sustaining. Energy must be consumed, waste ejected. The smells now permeating the entire complex were interesting to the Doberman and every other dog down there. Scud's possessor ignored it. He went to those gathered around the touch screens to see if he could inspire them to greater efforts.

'Frankie!' Eddie yelled. 'Get in the lift!' He swung a bat and sent a shiatsu flying.

'No.' Frankie kicked a mongrel square on the jaw, its head snapped around and the cur slunk away.

'Get in there and see Gal!' He swung the other bat, missing a Bulldog. It lurched forward under the bat only to run into Barbara's foot. It banked away allowing the next dog, a Staffordshire terrier, to begin its attack run.

'Why?' A Pekingese slipped past Frankie's defences and bit into his ankle. Frankie howled, kicking the little dog against the wall.

'Just do it! Gal's got your stuff,' Eddie yelled. 'From under the stairs, behind the spare Hoover bags.'

Frankie fell back toward the lift. The excitement in his eyes was unmistakeable. James filled the space. He kicked and slapped at the approaching dogs, upping their attacks as they quickly realised that he was not a fighter of Frankie's calibre. And, sure enough, try as he might, he began to fall back. The line held by Eddie and Frankie began to waver.

'Go help him,' Eddie shouted to Barbara. 'I'll be okay.'

Barbara had already been turning toward James. She moved across, and kicked an Afghan hound, sending it barrelling into its smaller colleagues.

Tilda watched Frankie as he went to Gal. The brown paper package he handed him was small. Frankie handled it carefully, reverently. He unwrapped it. It was a gun, a handgun.

Frankie unrolled a slim black cartridge and slammed it into the handle of the weapon. Gal stared at him, his eyes and mouth wide in horror and hope. Frankie left the confines of the lift and advanced to his brother's back. A Schnauzer had sunk its teeth into his shoulder and Eddie roared in pain and anger. Frankie raised the weapon, aimed, fired. The Schnauzer's head disappeared in a bloody red mist and haze even as the shot rang out loud over and over again.

Everything stopped. Frankie stared down the sight of his gun at the dogs. They all looked his way, and in every canine eye the fear could be seen, felt. James and Barbara stared open-mouthed at Frankie. Eddie staggered back against the wall, his shoulder, face and helmet drenched in blood. Tilda stuck her head out of the lift, barely hearing Bub's laboured breathing and Baz's imploring through the ringing in her ears, ignoring the stunned gaze of Gal who obviously hadn't known what was in the package.

I could see the fear and the doubt in the others. Whoever had been in that Schnauzer's mind was now splashed to the same winds as its head. Frankie pointed the gun at the Afghan. It cowered, slinking back from the weapon. Everyone looked between Frankie and his target. He leant forward. James watched his finger as it started to squeeze. The only sound was Bub's breathing echoing out of the lift and down the tunnel. The Afghan backed away slowly, head down staring into the gun's barrel.

Tilda barked, everyone jumped, the shot rang out, the bullet struck the wall and the dogs ran. The echoes of their flight lasted a minute or more before Bub's breathing was the only sound once more.

'You've got a gun?' said James.

Frankie turned to him. 'I told you I had a gun.'

'You said you had a couple of shot guns.'

'I have.'

'Well what's that then?'

'A Luger CZ 85 B 9mm.'

'I brought the shot guns too,' said Eddie shrugging his way up the wall.

'You've got a *hand* gun!' said James.

Barbara was doing her best to help Eddie stand; it was like watching a twig trying to prop up a breeze block. 'Isn't that illegal?' she said.

'It's a replica.' Frankie shrugged unconvincingly. The word febrile jumped into Barbara's mind.

'It looks pretty fuckin' real to me!' said Gal. 'What about Bub? We've gotta get him to hospital.'

'Where's Jane?' said Eddie going to Bub. He looked down on his friend. He was worried.

'Jane's gone,' said James.

Eddie looked at him. He didn't need to ask to where.

'The dogs came at us. Jane held them up so that we could escape. Bub didn't want to leave, I don't think. Something made him run.' Barbara poured this out quickly, breathlessly.

Eddie kept up with every word.

He span round, turning on Tilda. 'Listen up, brain boy or whatever you are. My people're not coming out of this with a profit.' Tilda tried to back away but Eddie grabbed her by the scruff of her neck and held her still, the batsman's gloves making his huge hands look even bigger. 'Now, tell me why I should carry on. Seems to me that we're making the sacrifices and you're getting the benefit. Bub and Jane believed in this, and I believed them. Now they're neither in a state to talk, so it's time to step up and tell me how we're gonna do this, 'cause I'm three seconds away from getting in that lift and having a day out in fucking Splash Land instead.' The human and the dog, their faces inches apart, glared at each other. Blood ran down Eddie's shoulder and flanks, dog spit dripped from his face guard and his hard and heavy breathing filled the tunnel.

We'd tried Eddie in the past. He was one of those that we would bounce off. We had never tried Frankie. And he seemed a likely candidate. Bub was useless now, or as good as.

James and Barbara watched. We had never tried them either. James hadn't been in the area when we had our first random efforts, and Barbara would have just been lucky. These people had grown accustomed to sudden deaths and illnesses over the past two years and they were ready for it to end. More than ready, they were eager, they wanted us out. But first we would have to jump in. My friend in Bub tried.

He bounced off. Frankie's brain wouldn't take him. We were surprised; he seemed ideal. We had thought that he was like Bub, but of course he wasn't. For Bub the idea of aliens and space travel was romantic, exciting, the ultimate experience. For Frankie it was a source of derision and paranoia.

Frankie looked to Tilda but her eyes were still firmly on his brother.

'One.' Eddie's flat tone suggested that he wasn't bluffing.

James saw Frankie look to Bub. His breathing subsided a little and the immediate danger seemed to have passed.

Frankie knew. No one had ever known before. James's dad had been driven mad by our constant attempts to jump in but he never *knew*.

'Two.'

James or Barbara, which one? We had always assumed it would come down to this. That we would have to jump from hosts. James and Barbara had seemed as good a choice as any. Both so lonely, so unconnected. Both of their lives suspended. We had decided on James as Barbara's cynicism so often seemed to outstrip her curiosity. We had argued about it. My friend was convinced that Barbara was the one, but we had agreed on James. The time was now; my friend in Bub would have to jump to James before all this was for nothing. This was why we wanted them along: one or both of them would be needed, and we had no idea if we could even use them. All we could do was hope that they would accept us.

James. *Go. Now!*

My friend jumped and at the last second ignored me. He jumped to Barbara.

'Three.'

'Wait!' Barbara shouted to Eddie. She held her hands up to stop him; they were covered in blood, a mixture of hers and the dogs'. James, who had never moved more than two metres from her side since descending into this place, knew that something was different.

'Barbara?' he said.

'Why would I wait, Miss Bean?' said Eddie.

'No reason at all,' said Gal. 'C'mon, we're off.' He had not left the lift.

'We have to go on. It's the only way this ends.'

'Barbara?' James repeated.

'I'm here, Jim. I'm not going anywhere.'

My friend chose well, maybe too well. Barbara's mind was hungry - he would do well not to be swallowed.

'Let's go.' The blooded giant rose and headed down the tunnel, pads flapping and bats resting on his shoulders. 'Your kit's in the lift, Frankie.'

'What about Bub?' said Gal.

'Leave him. He should be safer here,' said Eddie's retreating back.

Bub would be distraught to miss out, but he was in no condition to move. Tilda padded after Eddie, and Frankie shouldered two shotguns.

'Want one?' he said to James.

'Erm...' he hesitated too long.

'Give it here.' Gal took one of the guns and strode off after Eddie. Frankie smiled at James.

'Never mind,' he said. 'Maybe you can pick up Jane's broom handle.'

'Jesus, Frankie,' said Barbara and James together.

'She's not even cold yet,' James finished off. Frankie sauntered down the tunnel, shot gun on his shoulder, hand gun in the small of his back protruding from the waist of his jeans. His black and white, blood-stained top was rucked up around the black handle.

The two turned to Baz and Bub, the latter still lying in the corner, still breathing uncontrollably. Had it really only been a couple of minutes since Eddie came charging down the tunnel? Baz looked to James and Barbara. 'I stay with him?'

'Up to you, Baz,' said Barbara, 'but I'm sure we could use you. Bub'll be alright here. He can rest.' Bub looked on the verge of tears; he had lost so much. But that sledge hammer of a heart beat was still booming. Barbara could hear it now. She marvelled at her enhanced senses. *Can I take you on a fact finding mission?* she said to the guest in her mind. *I could see so much!*

Baz rose to his feet and, with one last look at Bub, he joined the two standing in the lift doorway. Bub raised an exhausted hand toward them imploringly. They turned and left. Seconds later the door closed and Bub was taken away.

'What is going on?' Baz asked. Barbara donned Bub's exposition hat and, as our party set off cautiously, launched into the Suez Crisis, Anthony Eden, the crashed space ship and possessed dogs. She spoke slowly and clearly so that the Pole would understand. Baz listened to it all in amazement.

Jumping into Barbara was refreshing. She was original not copied. Bub wanted us there to confirm things he thought that he knew but Barbara wanted us there to show her what she didn't know. She looked into the tunnel and beyond the pool of light that followed them. She could feel the rain pounding on the earth so far above them, feel it seeping through and down. She could feel the layout of the tunnels and could sense how far they stretched away. She saw our loneliness, the isolation of billions upon billions of miles in a futile search. Our own lives in suspension. Her heart ached for us. I could have loved her just for that.

We looked into Barbara's mind and saw her throughout her life. She almost resisted. If she had my friend would've been finished but she saw it as a fair trade in the end. We watched her date with James and saw him in a new light. We watched Tilda and now we saw more than just a dog, more than just a vessel. Barbara viewed life and the world in the most simplistic but beautiful ways. She studied, she analysed but she didn't judge. And that was beautiful because it wasn't pre-meditated, it was just the way she was. The phone in her pocket vibrated. She ignored it as she continued her conversation with Baz.

She had planned to find out James's opinions on talking in the cinema. She had wanted to know if they shared any values. She had planned to make a judgement. But without thinking about it, without ever deciding, she hadn't. I could have loved her just for that as well.

We were almost to the point where we had lost Jane. Barbara was just finishing her conversation with Baz. The Pole nodded his comprehension and was just about to ask a question when Barbara hushed him. Frankie mumbled something to Eddie. The corner was just ahead, the lights not yet on around the bend. Blackness waited. The big man steeled himself, hefting his bats. Frankie and Gal cocked the shot guns. Tilda stayed between the two groups as James, Barbara and Baz brought up the rear.

The leaders rounded the corner and for a few seconds disappeared from view. We slowed our approach, suddenly aware of how big the complex was and how alone we could be.

Around the corner, carnage. A circle of canine corpses surrounded a clear space of floor, empty save for a broom handle. Frankie picked it up.

'Here you go,' he called to James, and threw the wooden pole to him. James caught it. It was wet with saliva and blood. He felt the gouges torn into the haft by dogs' teeth, and each end was jagged from the assault. He held it grimly.

'Move!' Barbara suddenly urged.

The others looked around. 'What?' said Eddie. 'Why?'

She looked to James and he nodded in understanding. 'Let's go,' he concurred. 'Gonna get nasty round here.'

As he spoke one of the dogs, a Jack Russell terrier, was struggling to its feet. Its head was caved in on one side, its white fur streaked with fresh blood.

'Shambling!' shouted James. 'There's shambling!'

'What the fuck?' said Frankie.

'That ain't right,' said Eddie. He stepped forward and swung the bat in his right hand. It was the new one, already ruined with teeth marks and dents. The blow launched a small dog ten metres down the tunnel. 'Let's go,' he said. The rest began to pick their way through the corpses.

'Aaaarrgghh!' Frankie yelled as a mongrel's dead teeth sank into his ankle. He swung his gun and pointed it at the floor. The mongrel, its legs broken and unable to walk clung on, unfazed by the weapon that he knew Frankie wouldn't dare to fire so close to his leg.

Suddenly the whole group was under attack. Barbara kicked out and ran. James stabbed down with his wooden staff skewering the neck of a Spaniel, slowing it but not stopping it as he pulled the staff free. Blood squirted up his trousers, under the hem and onto his legs. He felt the still-warm trickle of the dog's formerly vital fluid. He ran. Eddie swung his bats, clearing a way through the shambling shoal of beached fish. Baz and Tilda ran behind James and Barbara, avoiding the zombie dogs and their clumsy lurches. Gal went to Frankie's aid, levelling his shot gun at the beast and blowing its body away down the tunnel.

'Oh shit!' Frankie cried when the mongrel's head and more importantly its jaws remained attached to his ankle. He kicked and flailed but the head hung on, the teeth sinking deeper into his ankle. He kicked against the wall smashing the head against the white cladding time after time, its wet, bloody neck leaving splashes and trails along a blank canvas. Gal tried to help. At first he pointed the shot gun at the head but Frankie's long and desperate 'Noooooooo!' changed his mind. Then he made a grab for the head, pulling it and Frankie's leg up in a wrenching arc. Frankie screamed.

Then Eddie was there, and Baz, James and Barbara had come back too. The latter three kicked and cleared the zombie dogs away while Eddie knocked his brother down, knelt on his leg and grabbed the dead mongrel's jaws. With all his strength, he prised the teeth apart and when Frankie's leg was finally free he kept on pulling until he ripped the lower jaw away from the head in a shower of blood and saliva. He threw both parts back up the tunnel and turned to his brother.

'Shit, shit, shit, shit, shit, shit...' Frankie rolled on the ground clutching at his ankle. Blood flowed freely from the deep wounds.

'Bandage!' shouted Eddie. No one moved. Eddie leant forward and ripped his brother's black and white shirt in two. He wrapped the two pieces of material around and around the wounded ankle, finally tying it off in a secure knot.

He picked his brother up and shouted to the others. 'Grab the bats and let's go!'

'Don't bother wasting shells on these,' yelled Barbara. 'They'll only get up again.' She and Baz picked up a cricket bat each and led the way. They knocked dead dog after dead dog aside with wide sweeps. James and Gal, one using the broom handle the other the butt of the shot gun, cleared their wake so that Eddie and Tilda had a clear run down the tunnel.

They moved as quickly as they could, those shambling dogs always at their backs. Death had slowed them but they still kept pace with the two-legged, wounded humans.

Finally they reached a large metal door with a wheel in the middle and a circular glass window above it. James couldn't help but think of a submarine and all the pressure and isolation that went with it. Gal ran forward to turn the wheel while Baz, Barbara and James turned to keep the dogs at bay.

'Here they come!' Barbara yelled. The dogs fell on them and were slapped, smacked and stabbed back. But they just kept coming.

'Use the bats on their legs if you can,' shouted James. 'They can't walk on broken legs!'

'Can't even shamble!' Barbara shouted back.

'Door, Gal! Be quick!' Baz yelled. His bat slapped into the shoulder of a Setter, sending it stumbling into the dog the next to it and away from James who had spun too far and left his side exposed. Barbara swept the dogs' legs from under them with her feet, sending them stumbling and then brought the bat crashing down onto any exposed legs.

Eddie watched desperately, still carrying Frankie.

'I can't open it!' yelled Gal. 'It won't turn! Eddie, help me!'

The big man looked down on his brother cradled in his arms.

James thrust his shaft into the throat of a mongrel and finding purchase pushed forward, ramming it deeper and deeper into the dog. He followed his weapon further into the dogs' midst.

'No!' shouted Barbara. Too late James found himself surrounded by dogs. Barbara surged forward, bat gripped with both hands and swinging wildly, clubbing the dogs out of the way. James was bitten by one then two then three dogs. He beat at their unfeeling bodies, crying in pain as their teeth sank into him. Barbara joined him and added her bat to his haft as they bludgeoned the dogs. It was no use, they would never submit, never let go.

'Eddie!' shouted Gal. 'Help me!'

Eddie put his brother down and went to help Gal. Baz dashed to Frankie and took the handgun.

'Be still hold!' Baz was with James. He flinched when he saw the gun and the bullet ripped into the dog's chest instead of its head.

'Be still!' Baz shouted again.

'It'll be okay, Jim. Just be still for him!' shouted Barbara as she swung her bat time and again.

Baz pointed the gun at the dog's jaw and fired, twisting the gun to an angle so that the bullet would pass through the brain. The head, its top blown away, span away and off James. Baz quickly did the same with the other two, leaving James with three deep but otherwise not serious wounds. The three retreated toward the door. There were fewer mobile dogs now.

Eddie and Gal had got the door open and the former had retrieved his brother. We all passed through, slamming the door after us.

No one thought to consider how the door had been closed in the first place.

Chapter Twenty Three

A room. Circular with a steel shaft in the middle running from floor to ceiling, and the walls covered with control panels and consoles. The only sound was the hum of energy and the scrapings of dead dogs on a big thick metal door.

'Where are we?' asked James.

With one sweep of his padded arm, Eddie cleared a desktop. A mountain of paperwork and a computer and monitor crashed to the floor. Carefully, he laid Frankie down.

'I'm alright, Eddie,' Frankie insisted, the pain clear on his face. 'I'm alright.'

Eddie took off his helmet and looked down on his brother, his big red face scoured with concern.

'I would say that we're under your house, Jim,' said Barbara.

No one looked surprised, but everyone was disappointed to find themselves little more than a mile from the lift after so much effort and loss.

Gal took a packet of cigarettes from his pockets. He took one for himself then handed the pack round. Eddie took one, James waved it away.

Barbara reached out her hand, her fingers danced over the open packet. 'No thanks,' she said, and reluctantly withdrew.

'Actually, Gal,' said James, 'changed me mind. Why not, eh?' He reached out and took a cigarette. Gal lit it for him.

Barbara watched jealously as James inhaled deeply and then blew out a long stream of sweet-smelling smoke.

Baz had moved to the centre of the room and was looking up at the steel shaft. 'Ziggy tell me your house is fucked up,' he said.

'Yeah,' James replied. 'It's the subsidence.' His head spun with the smoke. He smiled and smiled.

Barbara laughed. The sound echoed around the room making everyone look at her. 'I'm sorry,' she said, trying to control her mirth. She failed and burst out laughing.

James joined in and then Baz took it up followed by Gal. The wheezy old man soon began to splutter and cough clutching at his suddenly heaving chest as ash fell from his cigarette.

'Cut it out,' said Eddie. 'We've lost enough without giving Gal a heart attack.'

Now Frankie began to laugh as well. He laughed and cried as he sat up and clutched at his ankle. James clutched at his thigh,

Barbara her side and Baz his arm. Everyone bled. Everyone hurt. Eddie started to chuckle. Everyone laughed.

They laughed for a long time, healing just enough to continue.

'What about these computers,' said Eddie, eventually. 'Can we use 'em?'

'No idea,' said Gal looking mystified as he scanned the banks of impressive-looking equipment.

'All looks a bit sci-fi,' James agreed.

'C'mon, Gal,' said Eddie. 'I brought you along for your skills.'

Gal shuffled warily to the nearest console. He stood and stared for long moments before reaching out and tentatively flicked a switch. A light came on and something bleeped, he jumped back in surprise.

'Fuck's sake,' Eddie rumbled. 'You're an electrician.'

'That's right, Eddie' said Gal. 'I'm a 'lectrician, not a fuckin' rocket scientist!'

'You must know summuts!'

'Why must I? It dunt look much like re-wiring a house, does it?'

'Jim,' said Barbara. 'You have a look.'

James moved toward a console.

'Jimmy,' said Eddie. 'You've told us your skills and they're about as much use as my winnets. What about you, Frankie? You're always on the computer at home.'

'Surfing for porn doesn't count as an IT skill,' James called out. He buried himself in the console while the others argued.

'Any luck?' Barbara asked him minutes later. She had extracted herself from the argument raging around Gal. Frankie had hobbled over to join in, and they were all jabbing at buttons and flicking switches.

'Should they be doing that?' asked James.

'All they're getting is error messages and demands for passwords. What about you?'

'I'm okay,' he said with a smile as he looked at her. Her hair had come loose from its band in many places and was now sticking out wildly. She looked like a drier version of the Barbara he had first met. 'Nothing a few jabs at the doctor's won't sort out. And I'm better for seeing you.'

'I meant with the computers,' she said. She kept my friend's impatience out of her voice. 'But I'm better for seeing you too.' They leaned forward, their faces and their passions just centimetres apart. It was thrilling to experience such desire. In that moment my friend forgot all about the mission, our people, everything.

'No time for shagging, you two,' said Eddie as he barrelled up to them. 'C'mon then, Jimmy. What've you got?'

They parted again and James turned to Eddie. 'It's just Windows for the simple stuff about running the place. I can access the doors and the cameras and a map. I don't know where to start with the science stuff though.' He shrugged his shoulders in apology.

'Good man, Jimmy. That's a lot more than the fuckwits over there.'

'Cameras?' said Barbara. 'Let's have a look then.'

We looked through tunnel after tunnel, room after room. The Warren was filled with dogs, hundreds, even thousands of them.

'We're not gettin' through that lot,' said Gal as he hefted the shot gun. 'Not even wi' these.'

'How many shells have we got left?' said Barbara.

'Plenty,' said Gal, indicating the rucksack. 'But we can only fire 'em so fast.'

'And the handgun?' She looked to Frankie.

'There's still eleven in the mag, and one spare. Twenty six shots in all.'

Barbara held out her hand to Baz. 'May I?'

He handed the gun over, looking pleased to be rid of a burden. He quickly showed her how to eject the magazine, reload and remove the safety catch. 'Then, point, shoot,' he said

'You can get fifteen bullets in a handgun?' said James. No one answered.

'Where do we need to be going?' said Eddie.

'There was a room just like this one but with a cage. It was always busy, always something going on. That's where they operated Eden's Aegis from last night.'

'Everyone look for a room with a cage,' Eddie ordered as the images continued to flash past.

Frankie rolled a cigarette. 'We'll never get in there even if you find it,' he said. He had returned to his makeshift bed. He was pale, very pale. Tilda stood between him and the rest of the group. They ignored him as they flicked through the images on the screens. Tunnel, tunnel and more tunnel along with room after room. The only thing to let the viewer know that the different cameras pointed along different sections of tunnel was the series of numbers displayed across each image. The rooms were different. There were small rooms, big rooms, round rooms and square rooms. There were store rooms, control rooms, rooms filled with machinery and living rooms: recreational areas and dormitories, kitchens and laundry rooms. And everywhere there were bodies and dogs.

'What are they?' said Eddie as the screens showed different kinds of tunnels: round with the bare rock and earth still showing.

'Don't know,' said Barbara, 'but they look just the right size for one of those.' She pointed to another view screen which showed a hanger of sorts containing four large white torpedoes.

'Are they missiles?' said James.

'Can you zoom in?' said Barbara. James fiddled with the controls and eventually a close up revealed the torpedoes to be cars or shuttles of some type.

'Useful looking things,' said Eddie. Barbara nodded and James continued scrolling through the images.

He gave a yell and stopped flicking through the cameras. There on screen was the ground floor of his tower.

'The spying bastards!' he exclaimed.

'Spin on,' said Gal. He wheezed as he puffed on a cigarette. 'Let's get this done quick as. You can write your MP after.'

The next image was of the incinerator, then the tunnel beneath Ivy Arch's driveway, then James's study. The whole room had been devastated and the trapdoor in the floor looked to have been battered open. He fumed quietly and flicked past and back into the Warren.

'I said,' Frankie said in between licking the glue on his cigarette paper, 'we'll never get in even if you do find it.'

'Why's that, Frankie?' said Barbara wearily.

Sparking his cigarette to life, he inhaled noisily and deeply. A stream of smoke beamed into the room, mingling and spreading amongst the cloud already there. Before he could begin speaking, Barbara stopped him.

'You know what?' she said. 'It doesn't matter. Fuck you, Frankie. Fuck you and your dramatics. Fuck you and your paranoia. Fuck you and your misery. Fuck you, you victim. Just smoke your fags and shut up, 'cause you aren't helping. Take a part in this life and live it, or fuck off somewhere and evolve; it's up to you.' She turned her back on him and returned her attention to the screen.

James looked to her and smiled. She nodded grimly.

Frankie stared at her back, his suddenly limp cigarette dangling from his stupefied mouth. He turned to Eddie. His bloodless lips regained control of the cigarette. The older, bigger brother shrugged and turned to the screen.

'Fuck you all,' Frankie mumbled and lay back down. The white in the black and white material wrapped around his ankle had turned a dark red.

'There!' Barbara shouted. White-coated bodies littered the control room, and dogs, dozens of dogs, pressed their snouts into the equipment. Barbara and James immediately recognised Dog. He dashed about the room, snapping and snarling at the other dogs before coming to a halt in front of a Doberman and the monster. It held an axe in one of its five hands.

'What is *that*?' asked Eddie.

'I think it was buried in my front garden,' said James.

'Gonna take a big hole to fit that bugger,' said Gal.

'Well, I think it was in bits when it was in the ground,' said Barbara. 'But the aliens managed to get them to link.'

'Bit like them?' said Gal, pointing to the bottom of the screen. Several arms were crawling their way across the floor. He pointed out other limbs near the consoles.

'Yeah, they're the ones.'

'Told you I saw something in your garden,' said Eddie.

'I'll never doubt your eyes again,' said James.

'No reason you should,' said Eddie.

James quickly looked to the screen. 'Where is that?' he said. 'How far away I mean.'

'Don't know,' said Barbara.

'This was the bit we needed Jane for,' said Eddie bitterly.

'Looks like they didn't even get chance to run,' said Gal, indicating the white coats. 'They're all still at their work stations.'

'I can pull up a plan of the place. Maybe we can use those numbers to find out where it is,' said James.

'Sounds good,' said Eddie. 'Show us the way, Jimmy boy!'

'So,' said Baz as James bent to his task. 'You go in Middle East country 1956. Your pretend is to remove a man from top?'

'That's right,' Barbara nodded. 'Abdul Nasser.'

'Yes,' Baz's turn to nod. 'You go to Egypt to do Nasser, but really you go to free Suez Canal for oil supplies?'

'That's right.'

'And the Americans didn't help you?'

'Nope.'

'They try to actual stop you?'

'Yep.'

'The Americans?'

'Yep.'

'Funny how things turn out, eh Baz,' said Eddie. 'How we doing, Jimmy?'

'I've only been doing it a minute!'

'Thought computers was fast,' sniffed Eddie taking one last drag of his cigarette before grinding it out with his heel. He glanced at Frankie who lay on his back, smoking and staring at the ceiling.

'Right,' said James. 'Here's the map.' The screen showed a layout of the Warren.

'Not so big when it's on there, is it,' said Gal. He was smoking a fresh cigarette.

'Where're we, then?' said Eddie towering over James's shoulder.

'Here,' said Barbara, leaning in and pointing at the screen. She indicated a circular room amongst the labyrinth of glowing lines. 'There's only two other rooms like this one. Here and here.' She pointed north and then west on the layout.

'Which one is it?' asked Gal. Barbara shrugged.

'Is there a way you can you match the numbers from the security camera?' asked Eddie.

'Hang on, I'm trying,' James replied.

Barbara stared closely at the screen, narrowing her eyes and tilting her head this way and that. 'There's a man in the cage,' she said.

'Really?' said Gal peering over her shoulder. 'Dunt look big enough for a man.'

'He's squashed in but he's in there. Can you give us a close up, Jim?'

'Erm...'

'Get the numbers first, Jimmy,' said Eddie.

'Let's see exactly what's in there first,' said Barbara.

'We know what's in there,' said Eddie impatiently. 'Dogs, arms, legs and a funny looking summuts with an axe. A bloke in a cage doesn't make much difference.'

'If there's another human being in there, surely you'll want to get him out!'

'He's nothing to do with me. What about you, Gal, anything to do with you?' Gal shook his head. 'Jimmy?' Another shake, although this time reluctantly. 'And I bet he's nothing to do with you either,' he finished, looking down at Barbara.

'We need to know,' said Barbara firmly. 'Get the close up, Jim.'

'Erm...' James's hands danced awkwardly, hovering between two sets controls.

'Just find out where it is and let's get going,' wheezed Gal. His last words were drowned out by a bought of coughing that James and Barbara thought was impressive for both delivery and content. Gal took another drag of his cigarette.

'Think Frankie need hospital,' Baz called over. Eddie left the argument and went to his brother's side. Barbara nudged James and he started on her close up.

'What d'you reckon, Frankie, you gonna make it?' said Eddie as he loomed over the prostrate man. He glanced worriedly at the ankle.

Frankie blew a stream of smoke at the ceiling. 'Fuck me remember, Eddie. Fuck me.' He never took his eyes off the ceiling.

'Baz is right,' said Eddie. 'We gotta get you out of here.' He turned to Barbara. 'You reckon we're under Jimmy's house, yeah?'

Barbara nodded. 'According to the plans there're some steps just outside this room. There should be a door opposite the one we came in.' She nodded to a set of consoles and Baz went to investigate.

'You were right,' James said to her, nodding at the screen.

'I know him!' she said.

'You do?'

'Well, no, not *me*. My guest,' she indicated her temple, 'has seen him before in that same room.'

'A door!' Baz shouted from behind the console. 'It is open.'

'That's how Jane got up to the house, I suppose,' said James.

'No shit, Sherlock,' said Eddie, then turned back to his brother. 'Can you climb those steps?'

'No chance,' said Frankie rolling another cigarette. Flat on his back on a desk seemed to be no hindrance to his art.

'Baz,' Eddie called out. 'Go with him. Help him.'

'*We* could use the help,' Barbara pointed out. Eddie ignored her and turned to the screen. A close up of a man in a cage greeted him.

'Fuck's sake,' he breathed. 'Is this the room or not? North or West, Jimmy? If your missus'll let us know that much.'

'West,' said James. 'You were right, Eddie. Every section's got the same kind of number that showed up on the cameras. That room's number,' he indicated the screen, 'matches the security camera.'

'Right under the north tower,' said Gal. 'No wonder they didn't put it in the river like the south tower.'

'Yeah,' agreed Eddie. 'Proper sneaky bastards, alright. Prob'ly how they got most of this place dug out: used the Bridge as cover.'

'That man could help us,' said Barbara nodding at the screen.

'Who?' said Eddie.

'The man in the cage!'

'Fuck the man in the cage! Let's just get this shield thing turned off and that'll be that.'

'But he could help us do that. He was quite high up, one of the head scientists maybe.'

'Christ, we only want to turn it off!'

'The dogs haven't managed it yet,' James pointed out.

'Well,' said Gal. 'They're just dogs ain't they.'

'No,' said Barbara. 'They're not.'

'We've been through this, Gal' said Eddie.

'I'm going then, Eddie,' said Frankie. He had one arm around Baz's shoulders, a cigarette dangled from his free hand. The white in his bandage was totally consumed by blood which looked to have drained directly from his face.

'Frankie?' Barbara called out. He looked to her, his eyes wide. 'Have you got the spare magazine for the handgun?'

Frankie reached into his back pocket and, taking out the magazine, he threw it to Barbara.

'Take care,' said Eddie. 'I'll see you soon. He smiled. It looked forced. Frankie limped behind the console and was gone.

'So what's the plan?' said Gal as the remaining four and Tilda stared at the screen. Dog prowled the floor space seemingly unaware of the camera.

'That's the one who led the attack last night,' said James. It was still difficult for him to think of a dog coordinating anything.

'We get in there and smash it up,' said Eddie.

'No,' said Barbara. 'That's not gonna work. Don't you think they would've done that by now if it would?'

'Whatever they've been trying, they've been trying it too hard,' said James.

'What d'you mean?' said Gal.

'I think the system's locked out.'

'Eh? I thought you were in,' said Eddie indicating the security monitors and the map.

'No, that's just universal stuff. You know, stuff that anyone could access. I could've probably got at this from outside if I'd known it was here. Take a bit of doing but the security's crap on it. It's all a bit slack really for a big government secret. But the other stuff, the stuff for operating this place, that's locked down. I'm locked out'

'That's a lot of *stuff*,' said Barbara.

'How d'you mean?' said Eddie.

'You know, like at a cash machine and you get your PIN number wrong three times and it eats your card. Or if you get your password wrong on internet banking it...'

'Locks you out,' said Eddie.

'And you can't do anything until you get in touch with the bank,' Barbara finished off.

'Exactly,' said James looking at the caged man. 'And he's the bank.'

Eddie sighed. 'Looks like we'll be helping your mate after all, then.'

This could have been the point where Titz entered the Warren. The location I mean, not the point in time. He was either already in or soon to come in. This seemed the most likely point of entry. Ivy Arch was open and empty, the secret entrances and passageways yawned for any who might wander in, no matter their reasons for being there.

The car sped through the round tunnel. The white cladding was conspicuous in its absence as the bare and seemingly barely supported earth and rock closed in around them.

James shrank from the sides trying to pull his body further to the middle of the car's cabin. No lights came on as they arrowed through the tunnel but the car was lit from within illuminating the walls.

The five of us sat in grim silence in the smoke-filled cabin; Gal and Eddie were both smoking themselves calm. Gal and James gripped the double-barrelled shot guns; Barbara had the hand gun and Eddie his bats. He was silent under his helmet, his great red podgy head and face glowing from behind the grill.

'Not much of a plan,' said Barbara for the third time. The other three glowered at her. James quickly turned his frown upside down.

'Nice to be away from the smell at least,' he said. Actually it was still pretty smelly, but right now they needed to cling to something other than the mephitic.

'D'you think they know we're comin'?' said Gal, also for the third time. He blew more smoke into the already choking cabin. Barbara coughed pointedly. To do so she took long deep breaths of the tobacco cloud. She held her jangling leg still.

'I told you, Gal, those ones we fought in the tunnels sent signals back loud and clear.'

'If you can hear them, then can't they hear you?' said Eddie.

'No,' said Barbara. 'I think it works like normal conversation. They talk to whoever they like and make them hear as they like. So they can shout or they can whisper. I think that when mine and Tilda's are talking they're whispering.'

'Can you hear them?' said James.

'No,' she said. 'But I keep thinking I can sense something. Like catching a glimpse of something out of the corner of your eye but when you look at it it's gone.'

'But *how* do they know?' whined Gal. He wasn't getting the telepathic alien-possessed dog thing.

'Don't worry about it, Gal,' said Eddie. 'So what if they're waiting, we've got to take them on some time. May as well be now. What are they gonna do, anyway? Build up a line of dogs' logs to keep us out? We'll be alright.'

Barbara stared at Gal's cigarette. He took a deep nervous pull, the end glowing an impossibly bright red. It reflected on the front windscreen of the cabin, a red light in our path, and then it was gone.

'Want one?' Eddie said to her.

'No!' she snapped. Eddie and Gal smirked. 'It's not much of a plan,' she said for the fourth time.'

'Guns, guns, guns,' said James.

Scud waited. They had guns. This would be a problem, he knew. They had more than enough dogs to swamp them, to tear them limb from limb and make these tunnels slick with their blood. But dozens would go with them. And none of them were soldiers. He looked over to Dog. Rocky couldn't hear him. Scud wondered how he would do in the coming fight. It was a shame; he had been a great leader once.

He turned to Dick Jones. The man tried to shrink further into his cage but it was impossible. His mind was a barrier, a sheer, impassable cliff, much like the man who had owned Ivy Arch. Scud momentarily regretted not trying to jump into his son. The risks had seemed too great just twenty four hours ago. What he wouldn't give for just a few more hours now. The government would come soon and reclaim its tunnels. They had set up a continual procession of jump-attempts into Dick's mind. It seemed to be having an effect. He rocked in his confines, or at least he shifted his weight a few millimetres back and forth, his faecal aberration squelching and squeezing against the wire grill of his cage. He smelled of fear and confusion and maybe madness. This man was probably already of little use to them.

Much like these systems. Scud glared at the consoles and the crumpled white coats before them. They were locked out. He was sure of that now.

He warned a pack of mongrels away from the body of the agent. The rest of the bodies were useless now, no more suitable for possession than a packet of mince on a supermarket shelf.

He left the control room and went to the shuttle tunnel's terminus.

Within seconds the car arrived and four humans and one dog jumped out, guns blazing.

James and Gal leapt out first and emptied four barrels into the advancing dogs, blowing some apart and most of them back in a blizzard of gore. They cleared enough space around the car for Eddie and Barbara to get out. Then they dropped back to reload, and Barbara dashed forward to keep the dogs at bay. With just a little help from her friends, she fired the handgun with pinpoint accuracy. Three dropped down dead with shots between the eyes.

Eddie, suddenly and temporarily redundant, stood his ground and roared at the dogs, waving his bats in the air like some deranged and deadly scarecrow.

The car zipped away, leaving an empty space behind us, a sudden void that the dogs would try to push us into. The doorway to the control room was only metres away, ten metres according the plans. We could see that it was open.

'Ready!' shouted Gal.

James was so excited he nearly fumbled the cartridges but eventually he slotted them home just as Gal had shown him.

'Ready!' he shouted.

Barbara and Eddie dropped back. James and Gal advanced and emptied their barrels into the dogs again, again driving them back.

This time James and Gal stayed put as the other two drove forward. Eddie roared even louder as he swung his bats, connecting with thwack after thwack on dog after dog. Barbara joined him, holding fire with the handgun to preserve ammunition. Her swift booted feet added to the bats' assault.

And so we advanced, slowly and four barrels at a time.

The numbers of wounded and dead dogs, along with their bodies, quickly mounted and the splatter on the white walls marked our progress. We didn't have time to push the bodies back and we were soon surrounded. We had known that this would happen and that the push for the control room would be slow. We just had to hope that it would be fast enough and that we could make it before we were overwhelmed. Once inside we could shut the door and use the man in the cage to turn off Eden's Aegis.

Tilda's jaws joined Eddie's bats and Barbara's feet as we kept dogs, alive, dead and wounded at bay so that James and Gal could reload.

At first we made good progress, four metres covered in the first minute. But we weren't advancing quickly enough and all too soon it was taking all our effort to simply to keep a space around us. The big push had stopped only half way to our goal.

Another double boom resounded around the tunnel. It was not aimed well, the lethal shower of pellets raining into those already dead and wounded, including a dazed and confused Errol who had struggled over to join in. James and Gal had shot at the nearest foe rather than the most threatening. Three very much alive and very agile dogs, a German Shepherd and two mongrels, leapt at James and Gal. Both froze in the act of breaking open their guns, their fearfully wide eyes glowing targets for the dogs' jaws. Out of nowhere Eddie, bloodied and roaring and down to one bat, crashed into the airborne dogs and sent them flying.

'Shoot the fast ones!' he yelled. Then he weighed into the dead and wounded dogs threatening to overwhelm Barbara and Tilda.

Barbara had turned to the handgun once more and fired quickly and desperately into the shambling dogs. Her pinpoint accuracy was gone but she was still hitting and wounding with every shot as she blasted away at the seething mass. Eddie returned to her side as James and Gal snapped their guns shut in unison.

Another double boom and this time the live targets were selected. But Eddie's assault had spread them out and the German Shepherd, called Misha by her owner, made it through and was baring down on James. He held up the butt of his rifle in a desperate attempt at some defence. The dog clamped down on the wooden stock, and its momentum, weight and aggression sent them both tumbling. Man and dog sprawled on the floor, crashing into the wall of the tunnel. James banged his head yet again and silver stars danced in his eyes, blurring Misha. She let go of the gun and went for James's face and throat. Just in time and relying on instinct alone he raised the gun's stock in front of his face, using it for a shield.

'Jim!' Barbara screamed. She was desperate to go to him but she couldn't. They were all backed against the wall now and on the verge of being overrun. Gal had ducked behind her and Eddie to reload. She would have to do the same herself soon, her handgun was empty and she didn't have time to reach to the spare magazine in her back pocket. Eddie swung his bat; the jaws of half an animated corpse were embedded in the wood. The body, just jaws to rib cage, added extra weight to his swing.

But then another dog, this one a live Jack Russell named Patch, leapt from nowhere onto his arm, its teeth sinking into the cricket pads. Eddie swung the dog against the wall, battering once, twice and then a third time, all the while still swinging the bat. But the weight was too much. He poked and prodded impotently at the advancing dogs, and by the time he had finally shaken and battered Patch from his other arm they were on him, swarming onto his legs snapping at his thighs and his breakfast-bun-belly. He roared in pain and frustration. It was amazing he was even still on his feet as dog after dog leapt, clawed and shambled up onto him.

Then Gal was there, both barrels blowing a hole in the back of the pack. He hadn't dared to fire too close to Eddie, and so the big man still stumbled and roared under the weight of the dogs. Gal grabbed his rifle by the barrels and swung the butt in wide arcs, clubbing dogs with each desperate sweep, trying in vain to keep them at bay.

Barbara kicked with her feet and lashed out with the handgun, swiping and clubbing as best she could. A dog, she never saw it, bit her hand. She yelled in pain and the gun flew from reddening fingers. She stumbled backwards, her back soon pressed against the wall. The dogs came on.

It wasn't much of a plan.

Rocky had run at the first bang of the guns. Things were beginning to end.

Scud remained in the doorway to the control room. He watched as the dogs gradually overwhelmed the humans and the one dog that they had been after for so long. She was useless now and she wouldn't be spared. He glanced into the control room. The monster was ready and there was still one thing left to try. Scud sent it on its way.

Dick Jones was frantic in his cage. It was cruel really; the sound of the fighting had given him hope. Scud had no way of telling him that the battle was won, that he had no hope, or even that, for them, it was a hollow victory. Scud knew that soon the human government of this island would come to reclaim this place.

A noise brought his attention back to the tunnel: the car pulled up at the terminus.

'Yippee-kay-ay, mother fucker!'

Barbara looked up at the shout and she cried out in relief. Bub was running into the dogs, Jane's broom handle in his hands. He swept into the rear of the pack, beating them back and away. Quickly he was on Misha, the German shepherd still trying to break down James's defence. He rammed the pole into her side, sending her sprawling, and then leapt after her, stabbing repeatedly into her head.

James was on his feet in seconds and rushing to Barbara, copying Gal's broad sweeps of his rifle. There was no finesse as he dizzily clubbed the dogs out of his and then Barbara's way. Gal and Tilda went to Eddie and between them they scraped the dogs off the big man, leaving great gouges in his stomach and legs.

'Bub!' shouted Barbara. 'To me!' Bub withdrew from Misha and formed a line with Barbara.

'Behind us!' she shouted to James and Gal. 'Reload!'

The two men stepped out of the dogs' attacks and reloaded. Eddie covered the rear, both hands gripped firmly to his bat, the half-corpse still adding weight to his swings.

Another double boom and the plan was back on. We advanced to the door, with Eddie behind keeping the ever-slower, ever-deader dogs at bay. As we forced our way through, Barbara shrieked for everyone to hold. She stooped and retrieved the handgun. Before long we were at the doorway to the control room.

No one noticed that Misha never got back up.

Before we even got to the doorway, the dogs ran. They fled our wrath and our determination. Those whose hosts were shattered slunk and skulked out of our way. Then the Doberman in the doorway moved aside. We were in.

'Shut that door!' Gal barked. Eddie wearily began to move the white-coated bodies holding the door open. James rushed to help him, shuddering at the macabre task. Gal snapped his gun closed and covered the empty doorway. Barbara and Bub went to the cage.

'Quick!' said Gal.

James hauled a body out of the way. His head swam and he wanted to be sick. Eddie calmly moved the gruesome blockage. Blood oozed from his wounds.

'Are you alright?' said James.

'Reckon I'll have to be,' Eddie said in return. 'Help me with this.' He was tugging on the last body firmly jammed into the teeth of the circular door. The two of them heaved and tugged as Gal sweated and wheezed.

The tunnel outside went dark. Gal raised his gun, expecting attack.

'Don't worry, Gal,' Barbara called over. 'That means there's no movement.'

He strained to see into the gloom as he moved forward one step then two.

'Hang on, Gal,' grunted Eddie. He and James yanked the last of the white coats free, and the door, stuttering at first, began to roll closed.

Suddenly the lights came on in the tunnel and the leaping forms of two dogs, a mongrel and Mr Tricks appeared in the shrinking doorway. Gal fired at point-blank range, blowing them out of the air. The door caught their hurled bodies, grinding them into the grooves as it rolled home. The dogs burst in a slop of blood.

Gal dropped to the floor quite still, his shot gun clattering beside him.

'Gal!' shouted Eddie, rushing to the prone form of his dead friend.

Chapter Twenty Four

'I can't help you!' Dick Jones repeated. He shivered on the floor. Barbara had released him from the cage and was beginning to wonder if he'd soiled himself. Her nose had thankfully become at least partially accustomed to the stench of faeces.

'Why not?' said Bub.

'The system's locked down. Those dogs saw to that.'

'We know. And we've come a long way to get you out. Time for you to thank us proper,' said Eddie. The mongrel's jaws were still clamped around his bat; its dead eyes stared up at the big man. His helmet was off and he was covered in bandages taken from the first aid box which still lay open on top of the cage.

'It needs two to restart the system! I can't do it alone!'

'Who else is needed?' said Barbara, her hand wrapped in a bandage and dipping into a plastic carrier bag that she had found. 'We've got a lot of finger prints in here.' She looked pointedly at the bodies slumped before their work stations.

'You'd need a retina scan as well and that wouldn't work,' he added glancing nervously at the bodies. 'They've been dead too long.'

Barbara pulled a packet of cigarettes, a lighter and an opened box of pain killers from the bag.

'Fuck's sake!' roared Eddie. Everyone turned to look at him. 'How hard can it be to turn this thing off? It's not rocket science!'

'And you're not rocket scientists,' sneered Dick. Eddie moved to the floored scientist quickly and purposefully. Dick shrank back from the advance. Barbara moved to intercept him, the carrier bag swinging from one arm. She struggled to hold him back but Eddie did stop.

'Thanks,' she said sarcastically to James and Bub. Neither had made any move to help her.

'There must something we can do,' she said, taking out a cigarette. 'Jim, check the plans again. See if there's anything we missed.' James turned to a console and brought up the plan of the Warren. Eddie moved to look over his shoulder.

'C'mon, Dick,' she said, lighting the cigarette. 'How can we turn off the shield without accessing the system? There must be a way. *You* must know a way.'

'Can't be done,' he said a little less confidently as he eyed Eddie's back.

Bub suddenly moved over and kicked him in the head. 'C'mon, you wanker. Tell us or I'll beat it out of you!' He kicked him again, and again. Dick recoiled from the blows, his head and body flopping like a rag doll under the attack.

'Stop it, Bub! Stop it!' Barbara yelled. The assault continued. 'Bub! Stop it!'

Then Eddie was on him, grabbing him by the shoulders. 'Christ, Bub, calm down. You'll finish him off if you're not careful.'

Bub stared at his boss and friend. For a moment it looked as though he didn't recognise him. He blinked away the confusion and after a further pause he said, 'Everything ends, Eddie. The last Potter's out next month.'

'Well, we'd best be getting out of here if you want to read it,' said Barbara, shaking her head at Bub's outburst. She looked at him, wondering if it was all getting too much for the builder, and wondering also if she would come through the occupancy in her own head unscathed.

No use worrying about that right now, she told herself and drew deeply on the cigarette; it was wonderful. Her head danced around the room and she smiled and smiled. 'Let's get that shield turned off.' She turned to Dick. The man's bloody face looked up at hers. The fight had gone from his eyes. The dogs had taken most of it and now Bub the rest.

'The towers,' he gasped. Eddie had to grab hold of Bub again as he went to kick him some more. Dick shied away and continued desperately, 'The shield's emitters are on top of the towers. Destroy them and the bubble will collapse!'

'Find us a route to the towers, Jim,' Barbara called over.

'Aren't we under the north tower now?' said Eddie.

'Of course we are!' Barbara slapped her forehead. 'I forgot. Where's the nearest way up, Jim?'

'The map's not responding like before. I think that the system may be degrading,' he said.

'That's all we need,' Barbara sighed, and then cheered herself up with another drag. She grabbed a wheeled chair and pulled it over to Dick.

Eddie returned to looking over James's shoulder.

Sitting down, Barbara spoke to Dick. 'How do we get up to the towers?'

'I don't know.'

'You must!' She flicked ash at him.

'Why must I? I'm a scientist. I don't climb things. I think that they're reached by stairs from an access tunnel but I don't know where it is.'

'Liar!'

'I don't know!'

Barbara changed tack. 'How do we destroy the emitters, Dick? Is there anything down here we can use?'

Bub hovered, ready to reapply his own brand of pressure. Barbara held her hand up to the builder. He was red-faced and panting. He looked desperate to be at Dick Jones.

'There are emergency generators,' said Dick. 'Not far from here. They're petrol powered. There should be spare cans of petrol. Douse the emitters and set them on fire.'

'And that'll be enough to destroy them?'

'It'll be enough to damage them.'

'How many are there?'

'Four.'

'Do we have to destroy them all?'

Dick shook his head, 'Just one. That will be enough to disrupt the beam.'

'Any luck yet?' she called over to James.

'I can't get into the map properly.'

'It's there on the screen,' said Eddie.

'Yes, but I can't navigate.'

Eddie looked at him dubiously. 'C'mon, Jim, get in the game,' he said.

'I'm trying, I'm trying!'

'Where's this petrol?' Barbara demanded of Dick.

'Out there,' he indicated the closed door. 'To the right and three doors down. There's a staircase at the bottom. The generator, it should be in there. You'll need this.' He handed over a swipe card which bore his face.

'I'm going for the petrol,' Barbara called over to James and Eddie. She stood still for a moment, waiting for the room to stop spinning.

'On your own?' said Eddie. 'Take Bub with you.' He threw Gal's shot gun to Bub. Barbara took one last drag, ground the cigarette under her heel and opened the door. The two of them left.

Tilda stayed with James and Eddie.

Barbara padded along the white clad tunnel while Bub clumped alongside her. The lights kept pace with them.

'Try to be quiet, Bub,' Barbara hissed.

Bub remained silent but quieted his steps.

'What's wrong with you?' she said. 'First door,' she added as they passed a door on their right.

'Nothing,' answered Bub. The barrel of the shot gun led the way. He held it causally but eagerly, like a regular client of a mobile homeopath.

She let it go. We were all nervous and this wasn't turning out to be the adventure that Bub had thought it would be.

'Second door,' he said.

They continued along the tunnel in their bubble of light, darkness before them and darkness behind.

'Third door,' said Barbara. Taking a deep breath, she swiped the card and they went in.

'What about switching it off and on?' said Eddie.

'It's not a telly!' snapped James.

'It's not far off!' Eddie snapped back. 'It's just a monitor showing a signal. Now is it the monitor or the signal?'

'Erm…' James was flustered.

'Well?'

'Erm…'

'Give us a look.' Eddie shouldered James aside and grabbed at the controls. 'What's wrong with this then, Jimmy? It works fine. There's a way up just outside this room. Looks like the same sort of thing that took Frankie up to your house -'   Eddie's speech was cut short as the cricket bat slammed into the back of his head. The big man slumped forward, crashing into the console.

Tilda backed off, looking at James. He turned to the dog, cricket bat in hand. He lurched for the Border collie. We turned and ran, the swipe of the bat just catching our tail. Dick Jones's stunned face watched us go.

He didn't like his new body. It was very difficult to control. James's mind was trusting and open, ideal for possession, but it was strong and independent too. It fought for control, and lifting that cricket bat was the hardest thing he had ever had to do. He was tired from the effort and knew well that James could use this fatigue to take back control. He had to let Tilda go.

Dick Jones watched as James slowly lowered the cricket bat.

'What are you!' he demanded.

'More than you'll ever be,' James answered. He shouldered the bat, grabbed the shot gun and stepped out of the room.

'I'll let you go first,' said Barbara to Bub. They stood at the top of a stairwell that descended into the dark.

'Ladies first, Miss Bean,' he said. Barbara suddenly knew that something was wrong.

The shot gun lowered until it was pointed at her chest.

Bub had stood too close. Without waiting, Barbara grabbed the end of the double barrel and pointed it at the ceiling. The boom echoed around the room and dust fell from the ceiling. Using the gun as a lever she pulled herself toward Bub and brought her knee up and into his groin. She kept hold of the gun as he doubled over and clutched at his injured parts. He crumpled to the floor, his groaning interrupted by vomiting.

Barbara looked down on him with pity. 'I'm sorry, Bub,' she said, and then fled down the stairs.

Tilda burst into the room. We knew what had happened. Once Bub had been disabled, the mental block that he and James had been broadcasting was disrupted.

Bub was just beginning to get back to his feet, his possessor bypassing the pain and making him stand. Tilda growled a warning that he stay where he was, and dashed down the stairs to Barbara.

She was just on her way back up, jerry can in hand. 'C'mon,' she said, 'time to get to the top of that tower. Have Jim and Eddie found a way up yet?'

There was no need for her to speak aloud, and no one answered her question as she already knew the answer; Eddie had said there was a way up in front of Tilda, but she seemed satisfied nonetheless.

We edged past Bub, the shot gun levelled at him, one barrel still loaded as he well knew. Then we were out of the room and running back down the tunnel.

Ahead a pool of light, coming closer.

'Jim?' she called ahead. 'Oh no, Jim. No!' she cried down the tunnel. She stopped, but she knew it was useless, she knew we had to keep moving. 'We're coming, Jim. Don't shoot.'

'You'd best stop where you are, or I might have to,' he called back in a faltering voice. They heard their own voices as if from a distance. Like living speech bubbles, the words hung in the air, detached from their mouths.

'You stop too,' said Barbara slowing down and reluctantly stopping.

The two pools of light stood twenty metres or so apart. The inhabitants' shouts easily heard down the confines of the tunnel.

'So what happens now? We just stand here and wait till it's too late?' she shouted.

'I won't let this world go,' James replied.

'It's not yours to let go of! We can't take this world. We must carry on searching. We must leave!'

'Never!'

Behind James another pool of light approached and merged with his.

'Sounds like a plan for you, you wanker!' This from a new voice, a voice with a London accent. 'Get him, Danny!'

James turned to see two men running at him from around a corner. The younger of the two was in the lead, and had he continued his charge would have bowled James over. Instead he came to an abrupt halt. James and the young man's eyes locked. The field, the lonely tree, the trousers around the ankles and the smoking gun. Danny froze with embarrassment. James glared at him, daring him to look him in the eye. Danny failed.

'What you waiting for? Get him!' Titz ran up behind the young man frozen in the headlight of James's stare.

Barbara and Tilda hadn't waited for the new situation to resolve itself. Taking advantage of the diversion, they had sprinted forward. She smashed the rifle's stock into a surprised Titz's face, knocking him over and taking out his nose and a few teeth with it. Tilda bowled James over and Barbara and Tilda carried on running.

'Eddie's in the round room this way,' she called over her shoulder to Danny. 'Get him and the rest of them out of here!'

Danny stood stunned as he watched James climb to his feet and take off after the woman and the dog.

We burst into the control room, a precious few seconds ahead of James. Eddie was slumped on the floor, with Dick Jones standing worriedly over him.

'How is he?' Barbara called out as she began to trot around the edge of the room. She grabbed the abandoned broom handle.

'I'm not sure,' said Dick.

'Well help him, you idiot!' she shouted at him.

There, opposite the door, was what she was looking for. A bank of control panels stood away from the wall and behind them a door. She put down the jerry can and started to fumble with the handle.

'Does this door lock?'

'I don't know.'

James ran into the room. 'Wait, Barbara!' he called.

And Barbara almost did. There was something in his voice.

Then she was through the door and…

'Oh shit!' she shouted and dashed back for the forgotten jerry can. James was coming closer. As she reached out her mobile phone fell from her pocket and the shot gun slipped from her grasp. Ignoring both and grabbing the jerry can, she slammed the door closed just in time and jammed the battered length of wood under the door handle. James hit the door with a thump and immediately began rattling at the handle.

His laughing, taunting shouts followed her up the first few flights of steps. 'You'd best hurry, Barbara! Time's running after you! And ahead!'

Outside the rain continued. There was talk of a flood. Bow and Wow had decided not to keep their heads low as some news broadcasters picked up on the missing dogs. Hull was awash with bodies and chaos but the dogs were missing. All the dogs. All except two Labradors.

This was fast becoming the lead story and Bow and Wow were its stars. Death tolls were ever-more meaningless, even though the toll on Humberside was certainly high. But the twenty four hour news outlets needed other angles lest they show the same figures and images again and again. They were very excited about this. The numbers, 367 dead people in Hull, 155 on the south bank, all emergency vehicles damaged, the 999 switchboard was down, police officers, fire fighters and paramedics all on foot and doing what they could. The news reporters reported that it simply wasn't enough. There were fires. Looting was predicted. News reporters, looking more like their Middle East counterparts in flak jackets and helmets, shouted and squirmed and jerked in front of cameras as they told their tales with flaming, chaotic backdrops or bathed in the intermittent glow of the now impotent blue lights of overturned police cars, ambulances and fire engines. If it wasn't for the rain, they opined, the streets might be even busier with people running, pointing, helping, taking.

Humberside had long been a source of morbid entertainment for the world, and now this. Bow and Wow were convinced that the only way the news men and women could get any more excited would be if the Humber broke its banks, which they increasingly speculated might happen.

But people liked dogs and so the canine mystery, were they concealed or gone, was threaded throughout the coverage. Bow and Wow sat in a large, screen-filled van, sheltered from the rain. Satellite dishes and long, waving antennas spiked the vehicle, broadcasting and receiving images and information to the whole world.

On one screen Howard Woodman was explaining to the world that Splash Land was still open for business even though its chief attraction, *Tsunami* was temporarily closed. Apparently high water levels meant that it couldn't operate safely. Howard Woodman recommended *Zoom!!!* for the thrill seekers who weren't put off by a 'bit of rain.' He had added that he was sure that such strange weather had absolutely nothing to do with aliens. He had winked into the camera as he said it. This quote was picked up by every network, and the world's eyes were fixed on Humberside.

The consensus was that there would be a flood. The sheer volume of water that had fallen and kept falling had to go somewhere. Once the tributaries were full, where else but the fields, roads and streets of Humberside?

There was an argument outside the van.

'But they're our dogs!' said a near-hysterical female voice.

'We just need them for a few hours,' said the pretty face of the broadcaster from beneath the clear plastic of a raised visor of a riot helmet.

'We can certainly come to some agreement of compensation,' said someone else. And that was that. Bow and Wow settled down to watch the end of the world.

Barbara and Tilda ran up the cold, echoing stairs. Carrying the carrier bag and jerry can, Barbara quickly tired. We kept going.

James returned, smiling to the room. Dick Jones recoiled from him. Eddie stirred, groaning.

'What the fucking hell's going on?' Titz demanded through the hand holding his nose as entered the room. His mouth and chin was slick with blood. Danny and Bub were right behind him. The former avoided James's glare.

'What you looking at?' Titz demanded of the staring James.

'Not much,' he replied. Titz's eyes blazed a new with anger. He flew at James, wrestling him to the floor. James looked up into his face, blood dripped from his shattered nose, drool spilt from his excited mouth. He pummelled James's body as they fell, punching and grabbing at him at the same time. By the time they had rolled over he already had James beaten.

Eddie raised himself unsteadily to his knees.

He relaxed, allowing his body to be abused yet again, allowing something else to take the strain of fighting Titz. He watched from an impossible distance as he took a beating at the hands of Titz. The man's rage was palpable and petty and pathetic.

Bub ran over to Titz and started hauling him off. James had to act now: he pushed against the intrusion in his mind just as it was fully intent upon Titz. It was like it was standing on the edge of the precipice, it only took a nudge. The alien presence fell and fell and fell. He bounced off Eddie, jumped onto Danny, and the young man slumped to the floor. Next was Titz, but our adversary bounced off and fled to the only place left.

Eddie stumbled over to the fight, grabbing Titz just as Bub let go. Bub fell back away from the fight as two of the others turned his mind into a battlefield as they fought for possession.

James watched Bub as he struggled to a sitting position. There was nothing on his face, just a blank stare as his body slumped against a console just a few metres from Dick. Eddie contained the struggling, shouting Titz.

'Get off me, you fat fag! What the fuck's going on? Get off me!'

'Shut up, Titz, you prick!' Eddie commanded. James got to his feet and went to Danny. The young man was still alive. Looking to Bub he stood helpless. What could he do? He went to Titz.

'Time to stop being a dick,' he growled into his bloody face. 'There's more here than you, more than all of us. Help or stay here, it's up to you.'

Titz's struggles subsided. 'We ain't fucking finished,' he hissed at James.

'Yes you are,' said Eddie.

'Grab Bub and him,' James indicated the young man, 'and let's go. We've gotta help Barbara; I don't think that she knows what she's running into.'

Eddie let Titz go and the two men grabbed their friends. Dick Jones looked from face to face in amazement.

'Who are you people?' he said.

'We're from Fiss Fixings,' said James. 'After this is over we'll come fit you a new kitchen if you like.'

'Special rates for you,' said Eddie. 'Twice the price seeing as you've been so co-op'rative.' He slung Bub over his shoulder, and staggered at the weight.

'You alright?' said James, concerned at any sign of fatigue in the big man.

'If you're gonna go for a piss in a storm,' he replied, 'aim it high…'

'And do it downwind,' Titz finished off.

Barbara had lit another cigarette. She puffed and wheezed on it as she and Tilda climbed flight after flight of steel-grilled steps.

'It's nice,' she said to the dog. 'It helps me.' She smiled a desperate smile.

'For a top secret, top of the range, top banana government installation, there's a definite lack of lifts.' She took another drag and continued her self-motivational grumbling through a haze of blue smoke. 'I mean, there must be a lift to the towers. If you're gonna have these projectors on this important, nay vital, piece of equipment then surely you might want to get to it in a hurry. There could be emergencies or some kind of damage, like a… blockage, or… a loose wire!'

A terrible breaking noise echoed from below. Tilda glanced at her. They climbed.

James and the rest looked up at the unending stair. The door lay broken behind them.

'You're taking the piss,' said Titz.

'And you're not helping,' said James.

'C'mon, Dick,' said Eddie rounding on the quivering scientist, Bub's head lolling with the movement. 'Where's the lift?'

'What lift?' Nonchalance was a hard thing to achieve when Eddie Fiss was looking down at you and Dick Jones wasn't the first to fail. But everyone noticed the attempt.

'I told the woman!' he babbled. 'I'm a scientist! I don't go up to the towers!'

'Sure you don't,' sneered Titz. 'I tell my woman all sorts. It's nice to tell women things: keeps them happy and keeps us free. Now where's the fucking lift, brainiac?" Titz's bloody face was just inches from Dick's. Dick finally gave way.

'Next door.' The words were a release. Dick sagged with renewed shame.

'What was wrong with telling us earlier?' Eddie demanded.

'This is a top secret government installation!' Dick wailed.

'You never tell the builder where your kettle is,' said James. 'Certain builders that is,' he added when Eddie and Titz turned glowering eyes on him. 'Present company excluded of course.'

They left the stairwell and re-entered the control room. James stooped to pick up Barbara's phone and tucked it into his pocket. It vibrated immediately.

'What's wrong?' said Eddie.

'I think the phone's ringing,' James replied.

'Best leave it for now, I reckon.'

They all left the room and headed next door.

The cigarette was cast aside. Barbara had meant to count the flights of steps. She'd forgotten within twenty as she realised that it was all up. Numbers meant little when it was all up.

'I wonder how deep the towers are?' she mused. 'They must go right into the ground. Especially the south tower with it being in water. Or maybe that means it needs less. No that's silly.' She huffed some more, her head in a cloud. 'If we're level with the bottom of the towers in the ground then how far to the bottom of the towers *on* the ground? Are we in the river yet?'

Scud liked his view. When the old man had shot the Doberman he had flown to this bolt hole. There were dregs, some mental debris of the former owner's mind. If only he had been able to jump in when it was alive! It was wonderfully intricate, and filled with such useful skills, and so ready and willing to be moulded further. Too late now, it would be nothing but dust in a matter of hours.

The rain beat against the monster's multiplicity of limbs. Up here the wind was strong and three of its five arms were required to keep its balance; the other two gripped the axe. Scud guided the monster now, no more need for a guide dog or blind fumbling. He could see to the end of the world.

The monster stood atop the north tower of the Humber Bridge amid the wind and the rain, the dark heavy blanket of cloud close enough to touch.

'There's nothing to worry about,' said Howard Woodman's reassuring face on the screen. Bow and Wow were following the story about water levels in Splash Land. The proprietor had been accused of opening the park when it was unsafe to do so. Both *Zoom!!* and *Tsunami* relied on huge underground water tanks. One of the original designers, a man named Robert Full, had spotted an opportunity to get himself on television. According to Full, Howard Woodman had cut corners on the costs of the rides, and those underground tanks were not properly anchored. A summer of torrential rain put the entire park at risk, Bob told the cameras, smiling for all he was worth.

Despite the Media's attempts, fears of the Humber breaking its banks had subsided. As those levels of fear fell, the broadcasters desperately speculated to get it back up again.

Bow and Wow ignored all the fanciful hypothesising of the original Splash, the ridiculous theories as to what might make the Humber splash once more, and concentrated on a small but very real report on the Humber's many tributaries; they were going to break their banks.

There is an ominous anonymity to creaking. James had only just noticed it, and wasn't sure when it started or if it had always been there and he was only now noticing it.

'Can you hear that?' he said to Eddie as they waited for the lift.

'Sounds like creaking,' he replied.

'Creaking's no good,' said Titz. 'Not under a river.'

'Press the button again,' said Eddie.

'I've pressed it three times,' said James.

'Well press it again!' Titz added. One of Danny's arms was draped around his shoulders, the other around Dick's. They were standing in front of a yellow cage, the exposed cables of the lift dangling in the space within.

'What was that?' said James whirling round. He looked through the open doorway and out into the tunnel.

'I didn't hear nothing,' said Titz.

'Didn't hear *any*thing,' said Dick, and then looked fearfully at Titz, immediately regretting his correction. Titz smiled a humourless smile at the man just a body's width away.

'Quiet!' said Eddie. 'Jimmy's right. I heard something too.'

'Jesus, this is a slow lift! I didn't know you could get lifts this slow!' said Titz.

'The installation was never really finished,' said Dick. 'There are many areas that are still basic at best.'

'I can hear it coming,' said James. 'Sounds a bit rattly.'

'Rattly's better than stairs.'

'I can still hear something else,' said James. He moved to the open doorway. Looking out into the tunnel, he identified the source of the noise. 'Oh shit!'

'What is it?' Eddie called over.

'Dogs!' He glared down the tunnel, wishing that the pool of light wasn't rapidly approaching. In the doorway he could hear their canine noises echoing in the tunnel, could hear their claws on the floor. Frantic. The word popped into his mind. He wished that it hadn't. The phone in his pocket vibrated again.

'Wishes and fishes,' he said as he ran back to the others waiting for the lift.

'What?' Titz demanded.

'Neither'd be any use,' said James.

The sound of the charging dogs was clear now. James raised the shot gun.

'Phone's ringing again,' said James.

'Popular ain't she,' said Eddie. 'Here you go, Titz,' he added proffering the other gun. The Londoner left Danny with Dick and took the weapon. As he stood with James he grinned.

'Nice day for it,' he said.

They could see the light approaching now. It was a dim glow seeping around the edge of the doorway, gradually then rapidly growing brighter. The lift rattled above them, dropping all too slowly, like a tangled Tarzan in a suit of armour.

'C'mon!' said Eddie.

'Ripley!' shouted Bub feverishly. The two alien presences in his mind fought on, each trying to gain ground. Neither was winning and the only loser was Bub. Parts of his mind were trampled, squashed and barged. His memory was degrading and his ability to quote the entirety of the first series of Danger Mouse was already lost. He desperately clung to Aliens and Star Wars as the parts of his mind that he could call his own yodelled like a Wookie to save what he could.

'They're coming!' shouted James.

'Course they're coming,' said Titz. 'We know they're coming!'

'I was just saying!'

'Well don't!'

The sound of the lift very nearly drowned out the sound of the dogs. The light at the edge of the doorway was bright now, very bright.

'It's here!' Eddie yelled. He stepped forward and with one hand slid aside the cage door and then opened the concertina door of the lift. 'Inside!'

'Crumbs!' Bub yelled.

James turned and dived for the lift. He landed inside just as Dick struggled in with Danny. Titz backed up toward the open cage, the shotgun levelled at the opposite doorway. The light was full and suddenly the dogs charged past. Some noticed them inside and skidded to a halt causing a furry pile up in the tunnel. A couple got through and bounded forward.

'Inside!' Eddie repeated, and Titz turned and dove for the lift's caged interior. James turned and levelled his shot gun at the approaching hounds. Eddie leaned forward and slid the cage door shut, slamming it home. The dogs crashed into the metal mesh with a rattling thud. Many more poured into the room and quickly surrounded the cage, beating at it with paws, claws and heads.

'Close the door! Close the door!' Dick screamed.

'I am! I am!' Eddie yelled back.

'It won't go if you don't close the door!' Dick screamed again.

'I know! I know!' Eddie pulled the lift door across. 'Shut the fuck up!' he added. And Dick didn't. Even scientists weren't clever enough to know what was good for them.

'Press the button! Press the button!'

'Shut. The. Fuck. Up,' growled Eddie.

James dropped his gun and reached for the control panel. Titz turned and pointed the double barrels out through the door of the lift and fired. A red mist showered the dogs in front of the cage. The rest pressed on. Titz reloaded.

The lift shuddered and started to climb. Titz snapped his gun shut and fired again into the dogs, this time damaging the concertina doors as he had to pull the barrels inside.

'For fuck's sake, Titz!' said Eddie. 'There's no fucking need!'

'Couple less to follow isn't there?' he sneered.

'I've got a bad feeling about this!' sang Bub, a delirious smile on his face.

Barbara panted and wheezed. She stood stock still before a door. Her legs were lead from the climb and her arms were numb from carrying the jerry can and the carrier bag. There was still more up, but there was a door. The door was tempting: go through it and no more up. But she was trying to get to the top. She had to take the up; up was the only way to get to the end, and she really wanted to get to the end. Just a peek, she thought.

It was locked.

'Of course it's locked. Why wouldn't it be locked?'

There was a card reader on the side. Tilda nudged the carrier bag.

'No more fags,' she said breathlessly. 'At least not yet. Maybe when we've done all the up. You can have one too!' she said slightly manically.

Tilda nudged the bag again. Barbara dipped inside. There was the card. Dick Jones's face stared at her blankly. She swiped the card, the door unlocked.

She opened it to rain and wind and grey. Stepping outside she relished the freshness, was immediately soaked. After the dead calm of the stairwell the strength of the wind made her stumble. The view was not so welcome. She was standing on the deck of the Humber Bridge. Cars thundered past on the raised road atop a painted metal slanted bank right next to her. A green metal railing, surprisingly short given the drop on the other side, marked the edge of the path as it skirted around the tower. She looked up and up and up at a never ending slab of dark concrete, a hollow cliff. 'Lots more up,' she said to herself and went back inside. She left the door open, glad of the draught.

Clunk!

Such a safe word, almost dull; surely nothing menacing could clunk? It could. It was the sound of an axe crashing into a shield emitter when the wind takes most of the noise away.

Clunk!

The monster stumbled. There was little room and a lot of wind. Its extra arms gripped firmly to the railing. Scud was not happy with the progress. There was clearly damage to the emitter but there had yet to be any satisfying sparks or pops. Not even a whiz. He didn't dare bring the monster's complete strength to bear for fear of falling. Steadying himself, he readied the monster again.

Clunk!

Howard Woodman spoke to the camera. He told of his duty to the public, and his genuine concerns over their safety. He told how he was closing the park for the day and that he would be giving all his valued customers a voucher for a half-price ticket. His generosity was beamed around the world. He sweated as a journalist pressed him on why he wouldn't allow cameras into the park. He laughed as he told them that the aliens in the basement had a no media clause in their contracts. He assured everyone that his park was safe and that rain couldn't hurt a water park, then coughed and made his excuses as Bob Full confronted him live on the ten o'clock bulletin.

The tributaries had burst their banks. The news crews had quickly sent out vans to film the wet misery. One sequence showed a country lane. It was particularly impressive because the dyke on one side of the road was trying to expel a red Mini Cooper. Water had flooded the road and was pouring and gushing along a broken driveway toward an arch that split an unusual house.

The rattling was joined by a rumbling and a shaking, and all three danced and jigged in the echoing.

'Get ready for a surprise!' Bub screamed happily. He lolled in a corner.

'Can someone shut him up?' said James.

'Don't be a tosser,' said Eddie; 'he's been through a lot, and he's still going through it, I reckon.'

'He'll be going through a lot more if he don't shut it!' snapped Titz.

Dick was hyperventilating. His bout of shouting had left him with lungs that just couldn't get enough. His chest heaved, his brow sweated and his smell became obvious as his panic exuded from every pore and orifice.

'I think he's shit hisself,' said Eddie nodding at Dick, and drawing the attention away from Bub.

'Dirty bastard!' Titz spat.

'C'mon,' said James, 'he's been through a lot.'

Dick had pressed himself into a corner and now slid down into a foetal position. He whimpered between those heavy breaths.

James's pocket vibrated. He fished the phone out. The smooth chocolate tablet looked impenetrable. 'How do I answer it?' he asked the lift.

'What are you, a baby?' said Eddie taking the phone and sliding it open. He handed it to James who held it the right way round.

'Hello?'

'Who's that?' said the voice of Barbara's best friend.

'James. Jim,' said James, hurriedly correcting himself.

'Hello, James-Jim! I've heard all about you. Don't worry, nothing good. I'm Diane.'

James was sure that the voice was somehow winking down the phone. 'Erm...'

'Is Barbara there?' said the voice, cutting into his embarrassment.

'Not right now, no.'

'Can you get her? Or is she too busy changing your fireplace?'

'Eh?'

'Just a little joke.' Diane paused. James waited. Eddie, Titz and Dick looked at him expectantly. James shook his head, pointing at the phone. 'You know,' the voice continued, 'she really likes you.'

'I...'

'Really like her?'

'Yes.'

'She knows. Where is she?'

'I should catch up with her soon. Can I take a message?'

'No, it's okay. I'll ring her back. Don't do anything I wouldn't do.'

'Okay. Erm, she is very busy. You might want to leave a message. Just to, you know, say something.'

Eddie glared at James and gesticulated angrily at him, mouthing the words 'What the fuck are you doing?'

'I don't understand. Where is Barbara?' James looked down at the phone. He looked to Eddie.

'Just close it,' said the big man with a sigh. James did so.

'What are you trying to do, scare people to death?'

'She said that Barbara likes me.' A stupid smile was barely contained.

'Whooped-de-fucking-do!' Titz interjected.

'Time to re-focus, Jimmy.' Eddie laid a huge hand on James's shoulder. He smiled and then squeezed a squeeze that would have floored Mr Spock.

'Ow!' James cried, bruises, new and old, flaring. He hit the metal-grilled floor of the lift.

'Get up, nancy boy,' said Titz.

James clung to the floor a moment. Just as he was about to push himself up, he heard a noise. 'Can you hear that?' he said.

'That's enough of that, Jimmy,' said Eddie. 'You've heard enough for a life time I reckon.'

James peered through the steel-grated floor into the darkness below. 'Sounds like a toilet,' he said.

'Well, save it for Dick,' said Titz.

James could hear water. It was running and crashing and filling. Flushing described it well enough.

'Water! Water! Water!' Bub yelled dreamily. His hand lifted in a feeble point at nothing.

'Shh!' James hissed and pressed his ear to the floor. The noise was growing louder. 'Can this thing go any faster?' said James, wishes and fishes pouring from his pockets.

'She'll do the Kessel run in less than five parsecs!'

This time everyone stared at Bub, just for a moment.

'What's he talking about?' demanded the demented Dick. The rest ignored him.

'We'll be there soon enough,' said Eddie.

'I'm not so sure.' James could clearly hear the water now; it was louder than the rattling, clattering lift. It sloshed and sped ever more rapidly. Something splashed against his ear. He pulled back as if he'd been bitten, bowling into Titz.

'Fuck's sake, you prick!'

'Oh shit!'

They all looked down and it could clearly be seen. The light from the lift was reflecting and glinting on water that was only a few metres from the lift and rising fast.

'You're taking the piss!' Eddie shouted uselessly at the floor.

Dick unfolded himself and stood up. His breathing intensified and his whimpers turned to squeals.

'Shut up, Dick!' Titz shouted. He prowled what little space he could. The lift was not small but with prone bodies and three grown men, pacing space was at a premium.

Barbara and Tilda emerged at the top of the tower. The wind blew the door out of her hands and at first she didn't notice the monster because she turned to check that Tilda was okay. She thought that she might have heard a clunk, but she dismissed such an innocuous noise.

Scud turned to the door. Leaving the railing, he strode over and, lifting the axe high above his head, swung down. The wind and the rain punished such a reckless assault and the blow was wide of the mark.

Barbara whirled around as the axe blade bit hard into the doorframe. She screamed as the monster stumbled away, flailing like an ungainly but deadly octopus. It turned back to her and came again, axe raised.

Barbara dropped the jerry can and ducked and rolled out onto the top of the north tower as the axe whipped over her. Tilda barked at the monster and jumped at its exposed side as it completed its swing. A spare arm knocked her aside and sent her tumbling against the railing.

It was a long way down.

Barbara leapt to her feet, adrenaline pumping life into her dead legs, and turned to face the monster properly.

And then she stumbled back, horrified. The three torsos, five arms and six legs were now topped by a head. Jane stared back at Barbara.

'No!' she screamed.

A ghoulish smile played at the corners of Jane's mouth, and inside, Scud laughed and laughed and laughed. He suddenly missed being a dog as the urge to howl filled him.

Jane's mouth gaped uselessly.

The towers of a smaller Humber Bridge collapsed into the ground, water splashing and crashing from unseen reserves.

The image was grainy and wobbled as the ride fell, and was quickly followed by more amateur footage. The tall shaft of *Zoom!!!* fell straight through as if the ground beneath it had suddenly been whipped away. As it disappeared a plume of water flew into the sky. There was no mistaking the two most famous rides in Splash Land. The excited voice of the commentator told Bow and Wow that two tourists had taken the footage just before Howard Woodman had finished clearing his theme park. The tourists' whoops of delight could clearly be heard. It was believed, so said the commentator, that there were no casualties, although Mr Woodman himself is not commenting on the disaster and has in fact locked himself in his office.

254

The dogs had run from the lift, through the control room and up the stairs. Their long desperate journey upward had begun when Bow and Wow had told them the probable cause of all that anonymous creaking. Anonymous wasn't good, but knowing wasn't any better.

The news of the collapsing rides had come just before all of the lights had flickered to florid life and the Warren had suddenly turned red. Something was wrong. We can only imagine what must have happened. The unsecured tanks of *Zoom!!!* and *Tsunami* collapsed into the tunnels beneath Never filling them with water and then compromising the control room beneath Ivy Arch. From there the water spread along the tunnels. Those bare-rocked shuttle passages were probably the first to collapse, letting water from the Humber itself into the Warren. Certainly Bow and Wow monitored an unexplained and very sudden drop in the Humber's high water level. This was surely as miles and miles of tunnels suddenly filled with brown water and thick sludgy sediment. Ivy Arch, so carefully and hopefully cleaned by James, was in for a muddy shock.

Some limbs, friends in need, were carried by the dogs, but most were gone, the water and the mud claiming them for its own. They had no way to run.

On the stairwell the back markers, mostly the smaller dogs who had been trampled by the rushing bigger dogs, were beginning to be swallowed whole by the implacable water. Those in the lead just kept running and climbing.

They were knee deep in water and it was still rising. Danny was draped between James and Titz, and Eddie held Bub upright.

'We're gonna need a bigger boat!' shouted Bub.

The lift continued up.

'We'll have to go for a drink when all this is done, I reckon,' said Eddie.

'Just for a change you mean?' said James.

'We don't have to invite you, you know,' said Eddie. 'Len's got his 'Smoke-Up!' night tonight. Should be a laugh.'

'Yeah, but that's not a special just-risked-our-lives night out, is it,' said Titz. 'We'll do it Sunday.'

'Can't,' said Eddie, 'got cricket over in Goxhill.'

'Monday?' said James.

'Pre-season for the football,' said Titz.

'Bit early isn't it?' said James.

'Can't be too prepared,' said Eddie. 'Anyway it's more of a signing up followed by piss-up sorta thing.'

'Combine the two?' asked James. Eddie and Titz looked at him like he was a child.

'How about Tuesday?' Eddie continued.

'Darts,' said Titz humourlessly.

'Oh. Yeah,' said Eddie looking between the two men who were steadfastly ignoring each other.

'Wednesday?' said James. Titz nodded at the suggestion.

'Yeah,' said Eddie carefully. 'Hang on. Is that the first Wednesday of the month?'

The other two thought for a moment and then nodded. 'It's the fourth of July!' said James, affecting an American accent.

'Can't be Wednesday, then,' Eddie continued. 'Frankie has his mobile homeopath come round on the first Wednesday.'

James gagged. The others looked at him as if he was having a fit.

'You could use a good kiss!' yelled Bub.

'What's wrong?' said Eddie.

'Nothing!' James only just managed the reply. Controlling himself, he turned to Dick. 'How much further?' he demanded. The water was rising, the lift too slow to get them away.

'How should I know? I ride the damn things not build them!'

'Hang on, Jimmy,' said Eddie calmly. 'We'll make it.'

'Well, why don't you outrun them? I thought you said this thing was fast,' said Bub.

Titz began throwing water into Danny's face. 'Wake up! C'mon, wake up! I'm not carrying you all the way!'

'Watch your mouth, kid, or you're gonna find yourself floating home!' Bub quoted as if his life depended on it.

'Shut up, Titz. You'll carry him if you have to,' said Eddie. He looked worriedly at Bub.

The water was at their waists. It was cold.

'Keep your legs moving!' Eddie shouted over the rattling and the sloshing. 'Be ready to jump out when we get there!'

Danny began to stir. 'C'mon, wakey, wakey!' Titz yelled into his ear.

The lift surged just ahead of the rising tide, but the water had reached their chests.

Barbara jumped away and immediately regretted it. As soon as her feet were off the ground the wind swept her away. She landed awkwardly, sprawling on the rain soaked floor at the tower's edge. She looked down the vast cable as it curved away and down and then up again to the top of the south tower. The traffic moved along the deck of the bridge and she thought she could see movement on the pavement beside the road. The rain and the cloud made everything a disorienting grey.

Barbara lay there for several seconds. The dizzying height along with the torturous climb made her consider not bothering to stand up at all.

She forced herself to move. Rolling onto her back she was just in time to see the axe hurtling toward her. She ducked her head one way and then rolled and scrambled back to the middle of the platform. Standing, she prepared to dodge the monster again.

Tilda circled around behind. We needed to get on the front foot; there was no point being the mouse. But this cat was so strong, and Tilda remembered all too clearly what had happened to Foffy and Charles when they had bitten these limbs.

Barbara ducked and tried a kick at a knee cap. She was good but she wasn't Jane; her booted foot missed completely, sending her off balance once again. The monster caught her shoulder with a flailing arm. It saved her life, batting her out of the way before the axe whistled overhead.

'Wish I had a lawn mower,' she panted into the wind.

Scud settled the arguments amongst the arms quickly. No time for blame, only retribution.

The dogs ran and ran. Some of those who had carried limbs had dropped them in the need for speed, but others had dead fingers wrapped in collars or clinging to tails.

Those in the lead could smell the open air not far ahead, and soon the darkness was pierced by a grey gloom.

Another flight of steps, another, one more and there it was, the open doorway left by Barbara. They poured out onto the eastern walkway of the Humber Bridge. The leaders kept ahead of the tide as it surged from the doorway, pushing dogs along the pathway, crushing them against the railings, tearing their passengers from collars and tails and sweeping them over the side.

Then the aliens started to jump. Drivers slumped at their wheels, passengers collapsed. Cars and a double-decker bus swerved, crashed and fell.

The toll was rising.

They all held their heads up, their mouths gaping and gasping desperately. Eddie's extra few centimetres meant that he could just about keep Bub's face out of the water. Danny had regained consciousness just enough to hold onto the sides of the cage and float. James and Titz helped him where they could but had to concentrate on keeping their own heads above water. Dick floundered, Dick panicked, Dick thrashed.

'Jesus Christ, just stay still!' Eddie shouted at him.

Then the water dropped or rather it stopped rising so quickly and the lift got a little further ahead. The water dropped to their waists. They looked around. They had entered a slightly wider space. The water flowed out of the lift, pressing them against caged door.

The lift, its rattling deathly, stopped.

'That's not right,' said Eddie.

'One knackered lift,' Titz agreed.

'Get the door open! Get the door open!' Dick spluttered.

'Open the blast doors!' shouted Bub.

James and Titz took Bub as Eddie yanked at the concertina door.

'Come on! Come on!' Dick gurgled.

James wanted him to shut up so much he almost pushed his head under the water. He glanced at Titz who glared at Dick with murderous eyes.

Eddie pulled the lift door aside and grabbed at the cage door, sliding it away. They had to climb out of the lift, adding precious seconds as they hauled the dead weights of Bub and Danny. They waded across the room, Eddie supporting Bub, and Titz and James dragging Danny. They came face to face with another door. The water continued to rise, faster now that they were they still. Much faster.

'Open the door! Open the door!' shouted Dick.

'Shut up!' James shouted back as he reached out for the handle, the water flooding over it. He stumbled as Danny's weight shifted as the young man gained a little more consciousness. Dick dashed in front of them, shoving James aside, and hauled on the handle.

Bursting out, they all fell as the water rushed away and over the side of the top of the tower. They grabbed desperately for the railing as the water pushed and battered at them trying to take them with it all the way back to the river below.

'Close the blast doors!' Bub yelled.

'Shhhhiiiittt!' was the chorus from the others as arms and legs dangled over the precipice. Eddie, James and Titz grabbed at Bub and Danny, trying to keep them from falling.

'Help me!' Dick's cry split the air. The three men looked to him without menace or joy in their eyes as they saw that he wasn't going to make it. His rush to be out had taken him away from the rest and now his grip on the railing was battered by the wind and rain as the escaping water pushed him little by little over the side.

'Help me!' he cried again. And then he was gone, his scream clear for less than a second before the wind took it and him away.

'In my experience there's no such thing as luck,' said Bub.

'And if you're just joining us, we are witnessing incredible scenes on top of the north tower of the Humber Bridge. Some *thing* is attacking a woman...'

Bow and Wow watched Barbara pushed back against the railing from two different angles: the jumpy grainy footage on the screens and through Jane's dead but not yet finished eyes. They saw Tilda jumping ineffectually around the monster's legs. They saw the axe whirl and Barbara dodge from front and back as it struck the hand rail with a muted clunk. Barbara was on her backside and running out of time.

'We understand that the police are on their way but their resources are already stretched to breaking; it's difficult to imagine that there's anything they can do. We can't even get an interview with...'

The camera swept forward trying to get Barbara's final moments in fine detail.

'Oh my God!'

On the tower the wind and the noise grew as the helicopter came closer. The monster windmilled its arms at the intruder. Scud struggled to regain control. Barbara got to her knees. And then water, brown water, surged through the open doorway, knocking the monster off balance. Scud watched helplessly as a leg was torn off and disappeared over the side, its possessor, too shocked to jump, swept along with it. Barbara was pushed back against the hand rail but she managed to stay on her knees, the water up around her chest and splashing into her face. She reached out and grabbed the jerry can, jamming it against a railing bar so that she could keep hold of it in the pouring torrent. Then with her other arm she clutched at a desperate Tilda. My friend and I guided her into Barbara's embrace. Barbara held onto rail and brown Border collie for life.

Soft fuzzy lumps battered against all three of us. At first we didn't know what they were, and then a few were caught against the railing: dogs, all stained brown by the mud of the river. Some were still alive and yelped and struggled but they were soon washed over the side as easily as those already dead.

Barbara struggled against the flow, the volume of water keeping her pinned in place. But Tilda and the jerry can weighed her down so that she couldn't move anyway. The carrier bag along with the cigarettes had gone. She could have screamed.

And then she heard a scream. She tried to look around; there was the monster tangled in the railing, flailing against water and gravity. Had that been the source? In the grey and the gloom everything looked the same. Maybe the scream had come from her, and the wind had taken it from her mouth and given it to her imagination.

Slowly the force of the water lessened and Barbara was able to push against it. She dragged her body and the jerry can to a standing position, keeping a firm hold of the hand rail as the water, down to her knees now, continued to rush past. She still couldn't move as Tilda braced herself against Barbara's legs, the water up to her neck.

Scud barked at the limbs. He could feel the water's pressure lessening, and they had to be ready. As it finally slowed to little more than a stream, the limbs began to untangle. Five legs and five arms extracted themselves from the railing, and the monster rose. Scud laughed once more, the slight smile back on Jane's lips. He glared at the advancing Barbara, momentarily abashed at her purposeful strides. He laughed again, what could she do? The laughter stopped when he saw the gun.

She couldn't believe that she'd forgotten about it. There it was sticking out of the back of her trousers all the time, an uncomfortable lump. The flickering smile on Jane's lips died as she pointed the gun at her face. With no satisfaction Barbara pulled the trigger.

Click.

'Where is she? Where's Barbara?' said James looking about the top of the tower. The water had gone, the Warren's flush complete, and a fine film of brown mud now covered every surface.

He could hear the whup-whup-whup of a helicopter and he saw it hovering close to the deck of the Bridge.

'Careful,' said Eddie. 'It's slippery.'

They all grabbed the hand rail and held on tightly. James looked away from the helicopter below them. He could feel the height. It was like standing on a pin.

'Get away from her, you bitch!' shouted Bub. He stared across at the other side of the tower.

'Shut up, Bub,' said James absently.

'Let's get out of here,' said Titz. 'Your bird's gone. Mebbe she never even made it up here. There was a ladder down in there,' he pointed to the doorway. 'We could prob'ly get down to the path.'

'You're all clear, kid!' shouted Bub.

'She must have made it,' said James. 'She must have.'

'Now let's blow this thing and go home!'

'Bub's right,' said Eddie, earning a pair of dirty looks from Titz and James. 'We gotta get rid of the emitter.'

They all turned and looked at the complicated machinery humming quietly.

'Well, we can't burn it,' said James.

'We could shoot it,' said Titz.

'Seems a bit too easy,' said Eddie scratching his chin.

'Worth a go though,' said James.

'Yeah,' said Eddie thoughtfully.

James and Titz raised their guns.

Click, click, click!

Shit! The monster came forward. Scud howled inwardly for all the world to hear.

Barbara frantically scrabbled at her back pocket; there was the spare magazine. She fumbled around the grip looking for the catch that would release the spent magazine. Tilda barked furiously, impotently.

The double boom made Barbara spin to face the other side of the tower. What was going on over there? Then we sensed it, the tumult in another's mind; it must be Bub or James. And there was a fight for control.

The monster came on, taking its time, realising that the mud would punish reckless haste. Then Tilda rushed at the monster, jumping at its chest. It raised the axe using the long wooden haft as a shield against the dog's jaws. Tilda clamped down on the haft and the monster swung her around aiming to send her flying out over the edge.

It was time to leave.

'She's across there!' shouted James, lowering his shot gun and whirling to face the other side of the tower.

'How d'you know?' shouted Eddie. The wind was getting stronger, noisier. It whistled and howled as it flew between the towers and the cables making them thrum with a wild energy.

'I've got Tilda in me!'

The other two looked at him nonplussed.

'Tilda's alien! They're over there and they're still alive, but that monster's over there too!'

'What monster?' said Titz.

'You don't wanna know,' said Eddie.

'That rabbit's got a mean streak a mile wide!' shouted Bub.

'We've gotta get over there!' James shouted.

'One more shot into this,' shouted Eddie, 'and we'll go!'

'It's got big pointy teeth!' shouted Bub.

'We've got Bub and Danny to look after and an emitter to break,' said Eddie. 'We haven't got time to be running after your missus!'

'I'm going now!' James shouted back.

'Ooo, he's got an arm off!' shouted Bub.

But we were gone before he'd finished, dashing through the doorway and onto a ladder in a recess next to the broken lift. We began scrambling down, our progress hampered by the shot gun.

A boom above told us that Titz had fired into the emitter once again. For us it was time to run to Barbara.

Down, down, down, hand over hand, foot over foot. It was dark in there, the only light a square of ever decreasing grey. James moved with a purpose and with no need for help from me as he ran down that muddy ladder as quickly as he could towards his goal.

Another boom, Barbara now knew that it was Titz alone firing into the opposite emitter. It wasn't enough; Eden's Aegis was still operational. Dick had lied, or at least he had left out the truth. They would have to damage both emitters.

Finally the spent magazine slid from the handle of the gun. Barbara grabbed the spare from her pocket and slid it home just as the monster bore down on her. Raising the gun she fired. The slug slammed into its chest, green ichor spewing forth as the monster stalled. She backed off and fired: another hole, another little river of green and another step back.

How much more down? In the darkness it was impossible to tell. Just keep going, keep the hands and feet moving. Down, down, down.

Barbara calmed herself and stepped forward. Bang. Bang. Bang. Five holes now in the creature's chest and it was falling back.
    Barbara stepped forward: Bang. Bang.
    It was against the railing once more, and flailing under the onslaught, the chest now one big open wound, green dripping freely, ribs and redundant lungs exposed.

At the bottom at last, James took a precious few seconds to steady his legs before grabbing the door handle. It was unlocked, the card reader on the wall dark and powerless. We burst out onto the western walkway, the dull grey blinding. He staggered for a moment and let the wind and the rain batter him till he could let his hand drop from his eyes. The traffic above us was still and we leapt at the paved bank that would lead us to the road.

Scud panicked, the alien in the front torso was gone, splashed to the wind. Those in the front arms, holding the axe couldn't keep the grip on the mangled torso and keep the weapon. It clattered to the floor as they desperately tried to hold on.

We dashed across the four lanes of traffic chaos: crashed cars, slumped drivers and passengers, dazed survivors, a double-decker bus slumped on the concrete embankment and hanging over the side of the bridge. It teetered. The helicopter hovered near, its clamorous noise and draft dominating. James carried on through the shouts and the screams, and the honking of the traffic, angry geese faced with no room on the pond. He dodged dog after dog as they ran amongst the traffic. We stopped; ahead of us was a Pit Bull. Our eyes met. We moved forward and Rocky watched us go with barely a flicker of recognition, then he was off running with the other dogs.

Barbara stepped forward to within touching distance of the monster and lowered the gun. Bang. Bang. Two shots into the kneecaps of the front legs. They buckled, the creature falling forward. The front hands shot out to steady the creature and slid from the sockets of the destroyed torso to flop uselessly on the floor of the platform.

We ran up, up, up the flights of steps. It was easier than a ladder but James could barely move, the shot gun growing heavier and heavier. He threw it down. I helped him through it, helped him to run to Barbara and the emitter.

Barbara took a step backward and raised the gun. She pointed it at Jane's face and pulled the trigger.

Scud leapt for her mind but my friend, my friends, were ready. He bounced off and fell and fell and fell.

She emptied the magazine into the creature's remaining legs and left it a forlorn and useless pile of parts.

Turning to the emitter, she took up the jerry can. It was light in her jellied arms as my friend helped her with this last stage. As she unscrewed the cap she pondered for a moment on how small the emitter was, no more than half a metre square, just a tiny profusion of electronic gadgetry. She emptied the jerry can, careful not to spill it too far, trying to use her body to shield the flow from the wind. She ran a trail to the railing and then went down on her knees. Retrieving the pink disposable lighter from her pocket she lit the liquid fuse.

Bow and Wow had watched it all. The helicopter, bouncing and swinging with indecision, hadn't known whether to concentrate on the fight at the top of the tower or the canine and car chaos on the deck. It had withdrawn to try to show it all with brief close ups of both.

'And there's a… a fire on top of the north tower!'

The image swept up and there, beneath a halo of flame, two people embraced. A short woman, her face indistinguishable, her long blonde hair blowing in the gale, hugged a man, taller than her and just as anonymous, as if she would never let go. A brown and black Border collie danced around them.

Eden's Aegis collapsed and we were gone. There was no time for goodbye.

Acknowledgements

There are so many people I have to thank for making 'Suspended' possible. I got by on snippets of compliments and slices of criticism but just the thought that it could be read and was read kept me going. I need to thank my dad who saw just about every draft and he provided the photograph for the cover. Thank you to my friends who want to write, and sometimes even do, Anj and Peter, particularly Anj for believing long before I did. When a local journalist once asked if a sci-fi rom-com with a hint of horror (or a horror rom-com with a hint of sci-fi) could even work, Anj was the one that told him it did - and quite forcefully too. Thanks for that. My friends who listen to me moan and tell me what's bad and even manage the odd bit of good, Tina and Nicola. Thank you, guys for helping me bring it back out of the drawer. Lucy was the one that told me to just put it out there. Keith, Arnie and Natalie were among the first to finish it and Duncan told me he liked my similes, while Vicky assured me it was funny. Snippets that have kept me going. And Emma read it, listened to me moan, told me it wasn't good enough, listened to me moan, read it again and said it was okay. Without all of you, I would eat fewer crisps, drink a bit less and not obsess about whether or not readers would like the dogs or the people the most, but most of all this book would not have happened. Thank you.